© Jerry Bauer

Constantine Pleshakov is the author of several works of history, including *Stalin's Folly*, *The Tsar's Last Armada*, *The Flight of the Romanovs,* and *Inside the Kremlin's Cold War*. He teaches at Mount Holyoke College and lives in Amherst, Massachusetts.

Also by Constantine Pleshakov

Stalin's Folly: The Tragic First Ten Days of World War II on the Eastern Front

The Tsar's Last Armada: The Epic Voyage to the Battle of Tsushima

The Flight of the Romanovs: A Family Saga (with John Curtis Perry)

Inside the Kremlin's Cold War: From Stalin to Khrushchev
   (with Vladislav Zubok)

There Is No Freedom Without Bread!

There Is No Freedom Without Bread!

1989 and the Civil War That Brought Down Communism

Constantine Pleshakov

Picador

Farrar, Straus and Giroux / New York

www.picadorusa.com

Picador® is a U.S. registered trademark and is used by Farrar, Straus and Giroux under license from Pan Books Limited.

For information on Picador Reading Group Guides, please contact Picador.
E-mail: readinggroupguides@picadorusa.com

Designed by Abby Kagan

The Library of Congress has cataloged the Farrar, Straus and Giroux edition as follows:

Pleshakov, Constantine.
    There is no freedom without bread! : 1989 and the civil war that brought down communism / Constantine Pleshakov.—1st ed.
        p. cm.
    Includes bibliographical references and index.
    ISBN 978-0-374-28902-7
    1. Europe, Eastern—Politics and government—1945–1989. 2. Soviet Union—Politics and government—1945–1991. 3. Poland—Politics and government—1945–1980. 4. Poland—Politics and government—1980–1989. 5. Berlin Wall, Berlin, Germany, 1961–1989. 6. Communism—Europe, Eastern—History. 7. Communism—Soviet Union—History. 8. Anti-communist movements—Europe, Eastern—History. 9. Anti-communist movements—Soviet Union—History. 10. Anti-communist movements—Poland—History. I. Title.

DJK50.P59   2009
947.0009'048—dc22

                                                                        2009010185

Picador ISBN 978-0-312-65533-4

First published by Farrar, Straus and Giroux

First Picador Edition: October 2010

10 9 8 7 6 5 4 3 2 1

To the memory of Sasha Sumerkin (1943–2006), who often said: "If there is one single good thing about emigration, it is that sooner or later you suddenly realize that all the awful things we blamed on communism or the unfortunate peculiarities of our fatherland are, in fact, just human nature"

Contents

There Is No Freedom Without Bread!

Introduction

In June 2007, Reuters reported from Warsaw: "A 65-year-old rail-wayman who fell into a coma following an accident in communist Poland regained consciousness 19 years later to find democracy and a market economy, Polish media reported on Saturday . . . 'When I went into a coma there was only tea and vinegar in the shops, meat was rationed and huge petrol queues were everywhere . . . Now I see people on the streets with cell phones and there are so many goods in the shops it makes my head spin.'" The incapacitating accident happened in 1988, a year before communism fell in Eastern Europe and three years before it would collapse in the Soviet Union.

We've all read and heard much about the fall of communism, and some of us have actually lived it. The conventional wisdom tells us that 1989 was about a unified Eastern bloc that rose up, in the name of free-dom and the free market, to throw off the yoke of Moscow, an occupy-ing power that had exported communism at the point of a gun. That is not exactly what happened.

The origins of communism in Eastern Europe are much more com-plex than the at-the-point-of-a-gun interpretation, and if we want to understand the upheavals of the 1980s, we must go far back. Just one example to illustrate the point: twenty-five years before Stalin's troops occupied Eastern Europe—in the process of liberating it from the Nazis, it must be noted—a Communist revolution wracked Hungary. The 1919 revolutionaries, completely indigenous, proclaimed the Hungarian Soviet Republic and attempted an egalitarian transformation of their country—the endeavor cut short only when a foreign power, Romania, wary of the possible further spread of the Communist bug, sent its troops into Hungary. By the time Romania struck, the Hungarian experiment had already inspired a Communist state three hundred miles to the west—the Bavarian Soviet Republic in the south of Germany. The freak regime lasted for just five weeks, but it proved popular enough to cause at least one thousand rebels to die in the streets of Munich fighting the central government's troops sent to crush it. The crackdown didn't extinguish the egalitarian impulse in Germany, and the Communist Party grew into the major opponent of an extremist movement coming from the opposite end of the political spectrum—the Nazis. This is how the historian Frederick Taylor describes the confrontation: "Berlin streets were in constant uproar. Knives, knuckle-dusters, firearms, and even explosives were used in battles that really did resemble engagements between armies in a vicious little civil war." After Hitler came to power, the German Communists became the first victims of the Nazi terror.

World War II, which started six years later, helped the Communist cause. The swift German victories discredited the prewar European governments, and the devastating effects of the German occupation undermined every social structure on the continent. In this vacuum, communism appeared to be a promising alternative again, particularly since the Communists fought bravely in the resistance movement. In the first postwar elections in both France and Italy, the Communists got over 25 percent of the popular vote. In Greece, the Communists and the Royalists clashed in a civil war that claimed at least fifty thousand lives.

In 1944–48, the whole Old World experienced a pandemic of the red bug, yet only Eastern Europe became Communist. The common wisdom says that Europe was divided along a very simple fault line: the westernmost advance position of the Red Army in the final days of

World War II. That is not true. The Red Army also occupied Finland and eastern Austria, but later withdrew without imposing communism on either nation.

If Joseph Stalin had ever been a revolutionary, after 1945 he was just a calculating empire-builder. He wanted a buffer zone between the USSR and a potential adversary—the American troops stationed in Western Europe. He thought World War III would arrive soon, possibly in his lifetime, and needed his army properly entrenched before it came. The surest way to secure the territories required for that was to encourage ideologically fraternal regimes that would be dependent upon Soviet aid for survival. To make regimes like that viable, the countries in question had to have indigenous Communist movements and be in a state of civil conflict. Austria and Finland didn't qualify, but the countries of Eastern Europe did.

Sixty years later, it is hard to estimate the actual support for native communism in Eastern Europe, but some studies have indicated that in the first postwar elections 30 to 40 percent of Eastern Europeans voted for the left-wing, pro-Moscow parties. The fact that the Soviets were certainly gun-happy in their support of leftists was a huge factor in the domestic power struggle, but hardly the only major one.

The resulting regimes were not Moscow puppets. Soviets and Eastern Europeans were often in tension with each other, and each country of Eastern Europe developed its own special brand of communism. Poland, for example, had just 10 percent of its farmland collectivized—in other words, the government left agriculture largely in private hands. In Hungary, János Kádár gradually built a hybrid economy that combined a free market with central planning, dubbed "goulash communism" by cheering Western observers. Nicolae Ceauşescu of Romania challenged Moscow's intervention in Czechoslovakia in 1968, and maintained friendly relations with China *and* the United States at the height of the cold war.

If we want to understand why communism in Eastern Europe lasted so long, we might look into the social contracts between the rulers and the ruled. No Communist state could have done without secret police—but people accepted the state not just because of terror and intimidation, but also because of free health care, free housing, and free education. Zlatko Anguelov, an activist of the 1989 revolution in Bulgaria, writes in his poignant memoir: "The stories of pain, blood, torment, and exile are true, but they are the lesser truth. They were not the essence and the meaning of the communist regimes. They skew the scenario of communism in Eastern Europe, distorting it into an image of heroic resistance crushed by merciless oppression . . . The story of abiding and compliance has not yet been written."

The revolutions of 1989 were infinitely more complex than the stereotypical image of the good masses overthrowing the bad regimes. If in 1945 communism hadn't exactly arrived at the point of a gun, 1989 was not really about throwing off Moscow, an outside power. For the Eastern Europeans, the 1989 revolutions were a domestic matter, and behind-the-scenes dealings with the old elites, compromise between the revolutionary leaders and the Communist old-timers, and, of course, chance shaped the revolutions at least as much as people's anger did— and each revolution's path was unique.

Unique, but still rooted in the experience of one particular country: Poland, the mother of the Eastern European revolution. No one can predict a revolutionary situation, and no one saw the Polish revolution coming in 1980, though already by the late 1960s communism had lost most of its appeal and proved unable to compete with capitalism at the level of store shelves—the most important level of all. Deeply dissatisfied and, maybe, historically doomed, the Eastern bloc still rolled on until the Polish revolution disturbed the inertia. Revisiting the fall of communism in Eastern Europe, one comes to the conclusion that all the other revolutions were products of a chain reaction originating in the Polish revolt.

It is important that the revolutionary movement in Poland, coming seemingly out of the blue in 1980 with the creation of the independent trade union Solidarity, led by Lech Wałesa, had been fermented not only by social critique and anger over shortages, but also by the mystical aspect of Roman Catholicism. The 1989 story would be incomplete without a look into the spirituality of Pope John Paul II, a native son of Poland, the nation that had crowned the Virgin Mary its queen in the seventeenth century and since then had been expecting her intercession, which—at least in the view of John Paul II—finally arrived in 1980–89. That triumph of liberation theology—though the pope would have emphatically disagreed with the use of the term—has to be kept in mind when we look at modern-day grassroots movements, sometimes finding them insufficiently secular for our taste.

There are good reasons for 1989, the year that John Paul II called an "annus mirabilis," to be reexamined. We are still living in the aftermath of that seminal year in more ways than one. Overestimating the benevolent effects of the 1989 revolutions, the West took them for the definitive solution to Eastern Europe's problems—instead of treating them as the mere continuation of history that they were. Before the advent of communism in 1945, the Eastern European nations had free-market economies and some had free elections, and, frankly, neither the free market in itself nor free elections per se can work as a magic wand. Yet, profoundly misled by the post-1989 euphoria, Western governments started aggressively pursuing the free market, free elections solution in other "nonfree" areas. Predictably, the results proved ambiguous.

Another lesson the liberation of Eastern Europe provided is to be careful when you invite someone to join the free world, for they might actually come. To many in Western Europe, the fact that hundreds of thousands of liberated Eastern Europeans chose to resettle in the wake of 1989 (six hundred thousand moved to Britain alone) came as an unpleasant surprise. The newcomers brought along their unresolved social issues and thus put them on the British, French, and German domestic agendas. One of the unexpected consequences of this mass migration was the spontaneous redefinition of "whiteness" in Europe that resulted in a new caste bigotry, in which domestic Caucasians divorced themselves from other Caucasians, newly arrived and disadvantaged.

Eastern Europe's journey through the twentieth century was a true odyssey: it ended where it started—with capitalism. In 1980, the Polish revolution came up with a slogan, "There is no bread without freedom"; the title of this book reverses that dictum. As the Eastern European saga of 1945–89 demonstrates, correlation between prosperity and liberty is never simple.

This book is not going to detail systematically the seminal consequences of the Eastern European revolution. It doesn't pretend to be a comprehensive history of 1989 either, but rather a more essayistic exploration of how 1989 looks when it's seen more as a domestic matter, in the light of civil conflict, rather than in the grand geopolitical terms that have come to define the conventional account.

Part One

1942–1979

1. War Brings License: 1942–48

The year was 1981, and if the world had ever cared about Poland, it was then. Three men had claimed the scene, and the protagonists of the emerging revolution had choices to make.

They couldn't have been more different. Karol Wojtyła was the son of a Habsburg officer raised in a rented apartment ("The extant furniture, china, cutlery, and decorations suggest solidity, piety, and a simple, but hardly impoverished, standard of living"); Wojciech Jaruzelski came from the gentry and grew up on an estate ("a deeply religious and patriotic upbringing"); Lech Wałesa was a carpenter's son born in a hamlet in the heart of a marshland ("Our neighbors had avoided it, deeming it too dreadful to live on"). The officer's son was fluent in several languages, and an acknowledged poet, academic, and playwright. The nobleman did what his ancestors had—he had joined the army. The working-class man was an electrician. Given their very different backgrounds, it would have seemed totally impossible for the three to ever meet, let alone interact, but their paths *did* cross and the collision would shatter what Marx dreamed up, Lenin planned, and Stalin executed.

Those looking for a providential plan wouldn't fail to notice that, strangely enough, the three had been exposed to similar misfortunes.

They all lost fathers to World War II, though the age gap between them, the sons, was tremendous—a quarter of a century. It is not unusual for a carpenter's son to do manual labor—like father, like son—but, surprisingly, his privileged brethren were forced into that as well, the middle-class boy working at a quarry, the nobleman in coal mines. At an age more appropriate for courtship and partying, each of the three saw multiple violent deaths, massacres that spared them only by chance. They were all children of war.

In the era before missiles, the war reached people first as a nighttime glare on the horizon; the light was a no-nonsense messenger, the reflection of fires in the war zone. The glare was disturbingly soundless and lasted for a night or two or three, depending on the force of the resistance the army was putting up in the area in question, and then the people started hearing the cannonade. In a few hours, the first wave of refugees hit the town. By that time, they had lost most of the bags they had carried with them, and many had lost family. Now the people in town had to decide—to flee or to stay.

If they chose to stay, they discovered shortly that the enemy, when he arrived, had a human form. He needed food and lodging, and everything else his nature might have demanded. In an instant, everyday life ground to a halt: banks, hospitals, and schools were shut down, money was more or less useless, the town thrown back to a time before abstractions—and its people had better have something valuable to barter for food. The enemy put up street signs in his language—*Nach* this and *Nach* that—but he used the local alphabet on the cardboard placards attached to the necks of executed resistance fighters.

The streets were empty, the people very quiet. Noise was the privilege of the occupying force. But in that silence, opportunities were born.

In 1942, one of the young men negotiating the silence was the future pope, Karol Wojtyla.

War has circles, like hell. This is how a witness described the Wehrmacht's arrival in a French town: "They [the German soldiers] smiled from afar at the young girls and the young girls walked by, proud and scornful . . . So the Germans looked down at the crowd of kids around their knees: all the village children were there, fascinated by the uniforms, the horses, the high boots. However loudly their mothers called them, they wouldn't listen. They furtively touched the heavy material of the soldiers' jackets with their dirty fingers. The Germans beckoned to them and filled their hands with sweets and coins." In Poland, the arrival looked very different: "Of the houses, all that remained were brick chimneys and a few walls amid the smoldering ruins and glowing embers. The stench of fire and death was in the air . . . People still walked among the ruins, searching dazedly. They picked their way through, looking, perhaps, for what remained of their belongings and their kin."

In September 1939, Nazi Germany and the Soviet Union dismembered Poland. About one million Poles on the Soviet side of the border lost their property and shortly thereafter their freedom, deported to Central Asia and Siberia, where they were forced to work in mines and construction sites. Hitler did the same with his share of Poland. In the western part of the country, designated by Hitler as the area to be claimed by German settlers, half a million Poles were stripped of their land and evacuated. All in all, about three million Poles were sent to the Reich to work on farms and factories. Hitler's viceroy in Poland, Hans Frank, a man with "cold, fishlike" eyes who made Wojtyla's city, Kraków, his base, banned schools and Chopin concerts; he ordered libraries destroyed, monuments taken down. "The Pole has no rights whatsoever," Frank announced. Poles would work for the Reich and "in the end they will die out. There will never again be a Poland." His colleague in Prague had seven Czechs executed and proudly posted notices announcing the accomplishment. Frank smiled. "If I wanted to order notices posted every time seven Poles were shot, there wouldn't be enough forest in Poland to make the paper."

Like many others, Wojtyla fled Kraków in September 1939 and then, frightened by the chaos on the highways, turned back. Like every Polish male over the age of fourteen, he was now obliged to work for the Reich—and the philology major did, first at a quarry and then at a power plant. Like many, he lost family when the wartime malnutrition and distress killed his father, the last surviving Wojtyla other than himself. But unlike many other young men, he was not interested in materialistic interpretations of the catastrophe that had befallen Poland, like the Luftwaffe superiority in the air, the Blitzkrieg of the German panzer corps, the Red Army backstabbing Poland, Britain and France not rushing military help to their Polish ally. He argued metaphysically: at the age of twenty-two, single, poor, and orphaned, he felt like Job—a fine man scorched by God for no obvious reason.

Poland was often called the most Catholic country in Europe. An American traveler visiting shortly before the war admired peasants walking to church barefoot wearing "their very best" and carrying "bouquets of flowers mixed with sprays of wheat." The main Polish shrine was the church at Jasna Góra Monastery in Częstochowa, where, in "a chapel on the N.E. side, above the altar, hangs the celebrated and wonder-working picture known as the 'Black Madonna' (Regina Regni Poloniae). This consists of a painting of the Virgin and Child on cypress-wood, much darkened by age and adorned with costly jewels." The dry description comes from a Baedeker the visitor was likely using, and it doesn't even remotely hint at what she saw in the actual location. "Inside the church," she wrote,

> when the large bronze gates leading to the altar were thrown open, there was a regular stampede. People shoved wildly, raising their hands in the air to grab the doors by which to pull themselves in, or to keep their arms from being broken in the jam. People grabbed each other to get near the altar rail. One looked into faces that bore signs of tragedy, and tears were rolling down many cheeks . . . The Church means much to the people of Poland where extreme poverty exists. Church days are almost their only days of fete, their only hours of freedom. The fine architecture of church building, the richness of the ecclesiastical treasures and of the Mass—these are about the only things of beauty that enter into the lives of most of these communicants.

The visitor's analysis sounded unwittingly Marxist. But the irony was that the wealthy in Poland were equally devoted. When in 1920 Józef Piłsudski defeated the invading Red Army on the Vistula River in a classic maneuver, sending his best forces into the gap between two Red Army groups, many Poles attributed the victory to God's intervention, dubbing it the "Miracle on the Vistula." The losers proposed a different explanation for the strategic blunder: not God but tired troops (incidentally, one of them was Joseph Stalin) and supply shortages.

In Kraków, the portal of Wawel Castle bore the inscription *Si Deus Nobiscum Quis Contra Nos*—If God Is With Us Who Can Be Against Us? This "if" suggested the possibility of abandonment by God. With Hans Frank in the Wawel, the Poles were forced to address a dilemma: Accept? Rebel? Approximately four hundred thousand Poles took up armed resistance. Millions did not.

Despite what his apologists would have to say forty years later, the only act of defiance Karol Wojtyla allowed himself was to perform in the clandestine Rhapsodic Theater, a company performing patriotic dramas for a select audience—basically, preaching to the converted, and in a whisper, too. The young man wrote a play called *Job*, the stern title somewhat compromised by a baroque subtitle:

A Drama from the Old Testament
The Action Took Place in the Old Testament
Before Christ's Coming

The Action Takes Place in Our Days
In Job's Time
For Poland and the World

The Action Takes Place in the Time of Expectation,
Of Imploring Judgment,
In the Time of Longing
For Christ's Testament,
Worked Out
In Poland's and the World's Suffering.

The play followed the Book of Job closely: there *was* a reason behind the trial, as, unknown to Job, God had made a bet with Satan about Job's "integrity," and all the deaths and loss of property were one huge test of Job's faith that Job almost failed, because, finally overwhelmed, he loudly questioned God's wisdom: "I cry to you, O God, but you don't answer me. I stand before you, and you don't bother to look." God's response to the rebel's objection was very compelling: "Where were you when I laid the foundations of the earth? . . . Have you ever commanded the morning to appear and caused the dawn to rise in the east? . . . Do you know where the gates of death are located? . . . Have you visited the treasuries of the snow? Have you seen where the hail is made and stored? . . . Can you hold back the movements of the stars? Are you able to restrain the Pleiades or Orion? . . . Can you shout to the clouds and make it rain? Can you make lightning appear and cause it to strike as you direct it?"

On hearing the frightfully specific list of things he couldn't do, Job repented and howled: "I take back everything I said, and I sit in dust and ashes to show my repentance." Satisfied by the humbled man's cooperation, God "blessed Job in the second half of his life even more than in the beginning," giving him "fourteen thousand sheep, six thousand camels, one thousand teams of oxen, and one thousand female donkeys," and also seven sons and three daughters, and let him live until the age of 140 "to see four generations of his children and grandchildren."

The Book of Job addressed the issue of theodicy head-on, and the answer it gave to the question of why bad things happen to good people—there is always a cosmic reason for everything, and an individual, if he wants to keep his integrity, has to accept that—is a cornerstone of all three Abrahamic religions. But unquestioning devotion like that demanded a lot of strength, particularly from a young intellectual struggling in an occupied country. Also, Abrahamic theodicy suggested that a human might eventually get an answer to the why-is-this-happening-to-me question. Wojtyla was determined to go all the way through the trial and do everything humanly possible to get an answer. At work, he prayed on his knees, "unafraid of ridicule and seemingly able to tune out the racket around him to concentrate on his conversation with God." He joined a group called the Living Rosary run by Jan Tyranowski, a tailor by occupation, which had about sixty young males, ages fourteen and up. They were secretive like early Christians, and like an apostle, their leader lacked any formal training. Tyranowski put Wojtyla in charge of a team of fifteen. The immersion in spiritual work—reading, meditating, tutoring during a foreign occupation—was what later generations of Eastern European dissidents would call "inner emigration," retreating inward and washing one's hands of the state and its evils.

Wojtyla was Tyranowski's favorite, and the tailor introduced the young man to a hallowed treasure: the writings of St. John of the Cross, a poet-saint best known for wrestling with the Dark Night of the Soul, a three-o'clock-in-the-morning type of angst that should not be fought but rather embraced, as the surrender leads the sufferer into sweeter depths, where Jesus shines.

How well I know the spring that brims and flows,
Although by night.

This eternal spring is hidden deep,
How well I know the course its waters keep,
Although by night.

Its source I do not know because it has none
And yet from this, I know, all sources come,
Although by night.

In the fall of 1942, the portal to the depths had a location: Franciszkańska 3, in Kraków, where Archbishop Adam Stefan Sapieha ran an underground seminary.

Sapieha, the father figure of Wojtyla's life, was a "short man of iron will." Arrogant, curt, and unforgiving—in one word, princely—he presided over the Polish church during the war after its official shepherd, August Cardinal Hlond, followed the government into exile. When Hans Frank invited himself to dinner, the archbishop served him beet jam, acorn bread, and ersatz coffee, declaring that that's what the rest of the nation was having. After an uprising began in Warsaw on August 1, 1944, and the Nazis retaliated massively, Sapieha ordered all the seminarians into his residence. They would stay there until the Red Army marched into Kraków five months later. An eyewitness wrote:

The Red Army soldiers seemed strange, haunted, their faces endlessly weary. They moved lethargically, a gray mass that little resembled an army, their earflaps flapping, their eyes voids, their gray overcoats almost down to their ankles. They wore quilted jackets and trousers, and clumsy, misshapen felt boots. Some of them carried rifles with protruding bayonets; others carried submachine guns with cartridge drums, a piece of rope where the strap should have been.

The Poles smiled at the Soviet soldiers, but they did not respond. Seeing how weary they were, Poles handed them food. They ate without stopping or even slowing their pace. Trucks followed pulling long-barreled antitank guns. "On to Berlin" signs were scrawled in Russian on their sides.

The number of vulgarities written about the origins of communism in Eastern Europe is insulting to the dignity of the nations in question. It is not fair to assume that Marxism reached Eastern Europe dressed in a Red Army trench coat. It arrived earlier and looked different, and to understand that we must look to Franz Kafka.

"As Gregor Samsa awoke one morning from uneasy dreams," "The Metamorphosis" famously begins, "he found himself transformed in his bed into a gigantic insect." Samsa, Kafka's grotesque double, is a "commercial traveler" by occupation, so alienated from everyone and everything that his horrid metamorphosis seems to be the culmination of a journey, not the beginning of a new one. Looking at his "armor-plated" back, "domelike brown belly divided into stiff arched segments," and "numerous legs"—a centipede, in the opinion of Vladimir Nabokov—Gregor asks himself a question: "What has happened to me?" But he instantly switches to the breadwinner's concerns: he has to catch a seven o'clock train, having already missed his regular one, as he had inexplicably slept through the "ear-splitting noise" of the alarm clock, "properly set for four o'clock." "Oh God, he thought, what an exhausting job I've picked on! . . . The chief himself would be sure to come with the sick-insurance doctor, would reproach his parents with their son's laziness, and would cut all excuses short by referring to the insurance doctor, who of course regarded all mankind as perfectly healthy malingerers."

Though Kafka personally had no interest in Marxism, "The Metamorphosis" echoes *The Communist Manifesto*: "The bourgeoisie, wherever it has got the upper hand, has put an end to all feudal, patriarchal, idyllic relations . . . It has drowned the most heavenly ecstasies of religious fervor, of chivalrous enthusiasm, of Philistine sentimentalism in the icy water of egotistical calculation." In principle, Gregor's metamorphosis should've evoked exactly that—religious fervor ("Is that the

Devil messing with our boy, Mother?"), chivalrous enthusiasm ("Don't you worry, son, we *will* find a cure no matter what!"), and sentimentalism ("Scratch his back, *there*, between the plates. The poor darling seems to like that"). Yet "In the course of that very first day," the story informs us, "Gregor's father explained the family's financial position and prospects to both his mother and his sister." Obviously, with Gregor unable to go to work anymore, they didn't look good.

The capitalist grinder that several generations of Europeans—from Marx to Kafka—were forced to live through mauled everyone; but each Job crushed by injustice had a choice of how to react. Gregor the bug spent days at the window—"he nerved himself to the great effort of pushing an armchair to the window, then crawled up over the window sill and, braced against the chair, leaned against the windowpanes, obviously in some recollection of the sense of freedom that looking out of a window always used to give him"—staring at the street but not daring to escape. He eventually starved himself to death. Other bugs of Kafka's generation abused by the system went straight through the window—and into rebellion. In Bulgaria, Communist fighters arranged a very special funeral for the country's elite: they had good bait—the corpse of an important general they had assassinated—and then detonated a bomb at the funeral mass, raising the death toll from one to one hundred fifty.

Albert Einstein wrote: "One strength of the Communist system . . . is that it has some of the characteristics of a religion and inspires the emotions of a religion." Like Christ, Marx talked about the rich versus the poor. Like Christ, Marx thought that the poor were virtuous while the rich were not. Like Christ, Marx believed in equality. Like Christ, Marx promised a new beginning. Again, like Christ, Marx said that there should be a transitory authority between the present and God's Kingdom on Earth (Marx said Party, Christ said Church). Had Marx incorporated Christ into his theory, Marxism would've gone down in history as a revisionist Christian cult.

With Marx dead, Engels, visibly relaxed (Marx had been a bossy co-author and a needy friend), admitted, "The history of early Christianity has notable points of resemblance with the modern working-class movement." He went as far as endorsing a catchphrase by Ernest Renan, a popular revisionist historian of Christianity: "If I wanted to give you an idea of the early Christian communities I would tell you to look at a local section of the International Workingmen's Association." The International Workingmen's Association, also known as the First International, was a quarrelsome debate forum in which Marx (and Engels) fought anarchists, but in 1894, when Engels's endorsement came, the *Second* International was the leading force of the European left and Lenin was forging the Bolshevik movement in Russia.

Seriously unaware of the fact that he was building a new cult, Marx made a number of insightful observations about religion. He did *not* actually say, "Religion is the opium of the people"—a phrase that when taken out of context makes him look incredibly lacking in sympathy. What he said was "Religion is the sigh of the oppressed creature, the heart of a heartless world, just as it is the spirit of a spiritless situation." Only then did he add: "It is the opium of the people." In hindsight, we have every right to see communism as the opium. But it began as a sigh.

The terms Marx used to describe the condition of the lower classes in Europe—"a heartless world," "a spiritless situation," "the oppressed creature"—definitely rang true for Poland. Prior to the dismemberment of the country by Russia, Austria-Hungary, and Prussia in the late eighteenth century—or after 1918, when the collapse of the three empires in the course of World War I let Poland regain independence— the thing that defined Polish society was its sharp class division. The nobles, locked in a rigid caste, derived their wealth from the land, which they owned and the peasants worked. The upper-class Poland looked modern, prosperous, and flamboyant. An American diplomat praised "a gaiety of the soul" on the streets of prewar Warsaw, "one of the most beautiful capitals of all Europe" (he stayed at the American legation in the Blue Palace, an "architectural gem," the property of Count Maurice Zamoyski). The thing that impressed him most was the prime minister's visit to the legation, where the good-natured playboy inscribed in the guest book "a bar of music, composed extemporaneously, by way of signature." But another American prewar visitor, Anna Louise Strong, a writer of socialist persuasion, reported: "Ragged, half-starved peasants lived in dirt-floored hovels on the edge of a swamp. Practically every inhabitant shook with malaria . . . Behind the village rose healthy wooded slopes—the landlord's estate of thousands of acres. Its owner lived in

Paris, coming here for a few weeks' winter hunting with his friends. There was no way for the peasants to move to that healthy land; if they so much as entered its woods for berries or mushrooms, the foresters set dogs on them." (Wojtyla's sponsor, Archbishop Sapieha, was *actually* a prince, and his aristocratic background was appropriate to lead a church that owned about a million acres of land in a poor country.)

Yet another American, Louise A. Boyd, an author and photographer, wrote: "In 1935 there were 0.7 motor cars per 1000 inhabitants in Poland as contrasted with 11.9 in Germany, 22.6 in Sweden, 7.4 in Czechoslovakia and 1.8 in Rumania . . . Horses and wagons or carriages and boats and rafts on the navigable waters are the principal means of transportation and travel away from the railways . . . for no small part of the population the only means for travel is on foot and the only means for transporting goods their own backs.

"It was like a return to conditions in the United States previous at least to 1906 . . ."

The land reform of the 1920s left the bulk of it in the hands of the gentry, and by 1930, seeing no future in the home country, more than one million Poles had moved to the United States; three hundred thousand emigrated to France.

Predictably, there could be no political accord in a society like that. The two brutal experiments in social engineering unfolding in Europe at that time—communism and fascism—appealed to Polish radicals. While Western democracies struggled with the Great Depression ("The sky was dark with millionaires throwing themselves out of windows," Quentin Crisp remarked sarcastically thirty years later), Nazi Germany built autobahns and "people's cars" (Volkswagens), and the Soviet Union constructed mega power plants and new cities. The Polish right and left developed extremist wings with paramilitary units. With the radicals clashing with each other over the heads of the powerless centrists, the founding father of modern Poland, Józef Piłsudski, ordered the army into Warsaw. Despite Piłsudski's moral authority, the fighting in the streets of the capital lasted for three days. Later, Piłsudski had all the opposition leaders arrested and subsequently jailed, thrown out of the country, or put into a "camp of isolation"—a modest but true sibling of Stalin's Gulag camps and Hitler's *Konzentrationslager*. Piłsudski called his system Sanacja—clearly, from the Latin root *sanitas*;

nowadays, Polish historians define his regime as a "secular authoritarian system of government of a nonfascist type," or rule of a "military clique." In 1935, over half of Poles eligible to vote boycotted the general elections.

Sanacja froze riots but not critical thinking. Here is a description of a childhood in a left-leaning family breeding an agent of change (much later, the boy, Romuald Spasowski, would become Red Poland's ambassador to Washington). Like Lenin, the boy's father grew up on a small estate; now he was "left-wing," "a decided advocate of materialist philosophy and a recognized intellectual force in Poland." When the son was seven, the father decided he was turning into a bourgeois brat and enrolled him (for a reasonable six months) "in a boarding school for orphans."

The father read European newspapers, yet every night "at ten o'clock he would switch the dial to long wave in order to pick up Moscow." It's hard to believe that a cultured person could fall for Stalin's base interpretation of Marx, but in teaching his son Russian he used not Turgenev or Tolstoy, but *The History of the Communist Party*, drafted by Stalin; the boy, who had long forgiven his father the orphanage, now forgave Stalin his primitive style and liked the book "for its clarity and logic." The father said, "Only the Soviet Union could defend Poland and Europe from Nazism." The privilege of class sheltered the boy from economic hardship—but not from the ideological pressure of the Sanacja regime. When he went to a military camp for high school students and refused to attend mass, he was "sent directly to clean latrines and work in the kitchen." He was a budding Communist before his prom.

But something Gothic was happening to the Communist cause. In 1935–39, Stalin put the old party elite through show trials and then had them executed. He did the same to thousands of foreign Communists wintering in Moscow. A former student of the boy's father was executed as a spy. All in all, five thousand Polish Communists were shot, and the Polish Communist Party itself was disbanded on Stalin's orders. Yet the boy and his father kept their faith.

Wasn't Stalin's purge horrific enough to make most Communists realize that they had been fooled? No, it was not. Here we come across the Job theme again: the Communist deity punishes the faithful for no apparent reason—and those who survive take the indignity as a legitimate trial, a test imposed by Stalin for reasons too high for mere mortals to understand ("Where were you when I laid the foundations of the earth? . . . Have you ever commanded the morning to appear and caused the dawn to rise in the east?").

The way state communism had evolved in the USSR looked legitimate to left-leaning intellectuals. What was happening in Poland on the eve of war did not. Typically for a regime built around a military figure, Sanacja ran on extreme forms of patriotism, often breeding revanchist sentiment.

Much later in life, Karol Wojtyla would write: "Poland is part of Europe. It is a clearly defined territory located in the European Continent . . ." This was self-deluding. There were no clearly defined territories in Eastern Europe, and Poland, Bulgaria, Hungary, and Serbia had had empires of their own—and the Polish one was the biggest and lasted the longest. Twenty years after Ivan the Terrible's death, in 1604, Poland occupied Russia's core land, including Moscow, and put an impostor on the Russian throne. The impostor was Russian, claimed to be Ivan the Terrible's son, and married a legendary Polish beauty, Marina Mniszek. After rioters killed him in the future Red Square, Polish swords brought to power another pretender, who repeated his predecessor's career (including marrying Marina Mniszek). The Polish intervention thrust Russia into chaos, remembered since as the Time of Troubles, from which a new dynasty, Poland's nemesis, the Romanovs, was born.

As soon as Poland regained independence after World War I, its army occupied the better half of Ukraine, the capital, Kiev, included. When Lenin sent the Red Army into Poland, the move was driven as much by the desire to retaliate as to sovietize. For Soviet leaders such as Stalin (who, as we remember, participated in the abortive 1920 Polish campaign), Poland was historically a military threat, and, at the peak of the Great Terror in 1937-39, he had many enemies of the people executed as "Polish spies."

Like many other governments unable to reach social accord through economic development, the Sanacja regime believed that territorial expansion would substitute for domestic reform. When on October 1, 1938, after the Munich Accords, Hitler's troops marched into the Sudetenland, Polish troops occupied the Czech part of the town of Cieszyn in Silesia (the town had been divided after World War I) and the government's decision met with popular support. Here is how Spasowski remembered a patriotic rally in Warsaw: "The dense crowd waited tensely, and as darkness fell over us, torches were lit, dozens, then hundreds and thousands. A band struck up the national anthem, and we all stood at attention. Searchlights glided across the blackness overhead. The speeches began, and the masses responded with applause and cheers. Gradually, the atmosphere became heated, and chanting began: 'Si-le-sia, Si-le-sia, Si-le-sia,' and 'Cie-szyn, Cie-szyn, Cie-szyn.'"

World War II canceled the existing social contract in Poland. The limitations Hans Frank imposed on the Poles were oppressive and barbaric, but for once a person was truly beyond state, society, class, institution, law, nation, or any semblance of order; in other words, free—not butterfly free, of course, but, let's say, mole free, meaning free to dig through the dirt and rock of war in any direction he or she desired. Some stories were uplifting—a tailor became a church leader, and a college sophomore started acting in a prized theater. Some people chose to join the dark side. A woman started working for the Gestapo, turning in Jews because the Germans would let her keep the victims' possessions; a man helped the Germans to round up slave labor because he could rape women before shipping them west; a girl, unhappy about her father's second marriage, betrayed her stepmother and half brother "to death, reporting that they took food to the partisans in the woods."

The license of war meant much more to the people belonging to repressed political movements, be they Marxist or ultranationalist, particularly when they looked at what had happened in Russia during World War I: in nine months, one sad ex-pat, Vladimir Ulyanov, remade himself as V. I. Lenin, revolutionary.

The Polish resistance remained shockingly disunited, as each cluster of fighters had a different set of expectations for the postwar settlement. After Poland fell in September 1939, the government evacuated to Paris and then, after France folded nine months later, to London, and inspired (if not exactly led) the resistance from there. Meanwhile, in Stalin's Soviet Union, the "Moscow Poles" assembled and in due time started *their* underground ring, grossly inferior to the London group. No ideologue or ideology could erect an insurmountable barrier between the two insurgent armies, and they joined forces now and then, but a fault line existed as early as 1942. One Polish historian cites the year as the beginning of a civil war in Poland.

The biggest force, the Armia Krajowa (Home Army), stayed loyal to the exiled government and, at four hundred thousand men, was the backbone of the "Polish Underground State" that, as the London Poles claimed, existed in Poland. The rural resistance, Bataliony Chlopskie (Peasant Battalions), professed loyalty to the government-in-exile, too, but demanded that it commit itself to radical land reform after the war—something that the government didn't want to grant. Meanwhile, the Communist-led Armia Ludowa (People's Army), learning from Lenin's revolution, made land reform the centerpiece of its program. The ultraright Narodowe Sily Zbrojne (National Armed Units), hunted down Communists, on one particular occasion finishing off a rival partisan group with axes. All the armies fought with one another over territory and resources.

In March 1940, purging the Gulag of the potentially rebellious groups, Stalin ordered executions of twenty-one thousand Polish officers captured during the 1939 campaign. When in 1941 the Soviet Union found itself under German attack and Stalin realized that the country wouldn't survive without an alliance with Britain, he recognized the London Poles, freed Polish prisoners, and encouraged one of them, General Wladyslaw Anders, to form a seventy-thousand-strong army and take it to Iran to join ranks with the British armed forces there.

But cooperation with the London Poles was short-lived. In the spring of 1943, the Germans discovered mass graves of Polish officers on Soviet territory and made the fact public. The London Poles demanded an investigation. Stalin responded by suspending diplomatic relations with the Polish government-in-exile.

He did that readily, as by that time he had organized the Moscow Poles into a viable political force. As early as January 1942, he allowed Polish survivors of the Great Terror to reestablish the Communist Party, this time called the Polish Workers' Party. A year later, he let Polish Communists build an army led by a former Gulag prisoner, Colonel Zygmunt Berling, and it joined the Red Army at the front.

The outcome of the fratricidal conflict, uncertain in 1942–43, became predictable after the Red Army entered Poland in July 1944. On July 26, in the recently liberated city of Lublin, the Polish Committee of

National Liberation, chaired by a socialist, Edward Osóbka-Morawski, proclaimed itself the provisional government of Poland. The Home Army knew that there would be no space for it in Poland under Soviet occupation and on August 1 responded with an uprising in Warsaw—as Polish historians have written, "with a view to establishing an independent Polish administration in the city before the arrival of the Soviets."

The Red Army sat out the uprising just several miles away across the Vistula River, engaged in positional warfare with the Germans. The Soviet commander watched Warsaw burn: "clouds of smoke," "blazing houses," the "flashes" of German explosives. Could the Red Army have entered Warsaw to save the Poles? Or was it too entrenched? It was a deliberate betrayal, most Poles said: Stalin wanted the Germans to cleanse Poland of all the resistance forces he didn't control. A higher strategic necessity, Stalin's generals and later revisionist scholarship suggested. But, frankly, for the purposes of our inquiry the real motive isn't important. What matters most is the fact that Poles *believed* they had been betrayed—and perceptions often have more salience than the underlying reality.

In any case, in 1944 the Red Army brought a new wave of destruction to the already overwhelmed nation. Poland did not suffer anything similar to the rape of Germany (up to two million victims), but the Soviet ambassador to Poland openly said to his American counterpart that he was "most perturbed over the robbery, rape and murder which had been perpetrated by undisciplined members of the Red Army. He said that these occurrences were bound to affect adversely the relations between the Soviet Union and Poland, but, because of the sudden relaxing of military discipline at the end of the war, it was a development which, however regrettable, was not unnatural."

Talking to Josip Broz Tito, the new—Marxist—leader of another Eastern European country, Yugoslavia, which also had to deal with the Soviet occupying force, Stalin referred to Dostoyevsky: "Do you see what a complicated thing is man's soul, man's psyche? Well, then, imagine a man who has fought from Stalingrad to Belgrade—over thousands of kilometers of his own devastated land, across the dead bodies of his comrades and dearest ones. How can such a man react normally?" Then he added good-naturedly: "And what is so awful in his having fun with a woman, after such horrors?"

What made many Poles put up with the Red Army's war crimes was the fact that the Soviets encouraged a new economic order. In September 1944, the Soviet-supported Polish Committee of National Liberation launched a radical land reform, distributing among the rural poor all private estates with more than 125 acres of land. Also, by historical necessity, Poles had learned the ropes of collaboration long before. With the exception of the brutal, arrogant Reich, all the empires that had marched onto Eastern European soil believed in cooptation—and Eastern Europeans believed in survival. For Poles, given the long history of the Russo-Polish conflict, this as often as not implied collaborating with Russia.

Prince Adam Jerzy Czartoryski, crème de la crème of European aristocracy, brought to the Russian court after the final partition of Poland in 1795 practically as a hostage, charmed three successive Russian monarchs—Catherine the Great, Paul I, and Alexander I, who made him Russia's shadow foreign minister. Another nobleman, Michał Kleofas Ogiński, who represented independent Poland in the Netherlands, fought Russian invasion, and composed the famous patriotic polonaise "Farewell to the Homeland," later spent several years at the court of the tsar as a legislator. In his official biography of Karol Wojtyla, George Weigel writes, referring to the Red Army's onslaught on Poland in 1920: "To make sure that any resistance would be summarily crushed, the Provisional Polish Revolutionary Committee, the puppet regime to be installed in the wake of the Red Army's inevitable victory, would be led by Feliks Dzerzhinskii, head of the Cheka, the Soviet secret police, the most feared man in Bolshevik Russia." Apart from the dubious usage of the words *puppet* and *inevitable*, everything in the sentence is correct, but one important thing is missing. Dzerzhinsky—"the most feared man in Bolshevik Russia"—was a Polish nobleman and a founder of the Communist movement in his home country.

The commander of the army group that lingered at the Vistula during the Warsaw uprising, Marshal Konstantin Rokossovsky ("taciturn and expressionless," giving the "impression of granite strength," according to the American ambassador to Poland Arthur Bliss Lane), was born in Warsaw and worked at a quarry there before joining the Imperial Russian army to fight with it in World War I. During the same war, Wojtyla's father, Karol senior, was with the other side—the Habsburgs. Teaching his son German (which, of course, was not mandatory in the independent Poland), he supplied the future pope with a lifelong Austrian accent. When years later Weigel asked the pope whether his father had given him his middle name—Józef—in honor of the national icon, Marshal Piłsudski, it turned out that, to the contrary, the name honored Emperor Franz Josef I of Austria—a man whom many other Poles hated just as much as they hated Tsar Nicholas II.

Stalin was persistently ambivalent about what to do with Poland. Thriving throughout his whole life on ad hoc alliances (with Zinoviev, Kamenev, and Bukharin against Trotsky; with Bukharin against Zinoviev and Kamenev; with Hitler against Britain and France; with the United States, Britain, and France against Hitler), he now applied this winning principle to Poland and the rest of Eastern Europe. Though he didn't give it a name, *that* was the Stalin doctrine. First let the leftist coalition marginalize the prewar establishment and its political parties. Then we will see.

At the Big Three meetings, Stalin took up the Moscow Poles' cause. With Poland out of reach of British and American ground troops, all Churchill and Roosevelt could do was make Stalin promise free elections after the war that would hypothetically give the London Poles a chance to share power with Socialists and Communists. Churchill, actually, privately acknowledged that Stalin would have the final say on Polish matters. In October 1944, he reported to his wife from Moscow: "The two sets of Poles have arrived & are being kept for the night in two separate cages. Tomorrow we [Churchill and Stalin] see them in succession. It is their best chance for a settlement. We shall try our utmost. I have had vy nice talks with the Old Bear [Stalin]. I like him the more I see him. <u>Now</u> they respect us here & I am sure they wish to work w us—I have to keep the President in constant touch & this is the delicate side." On June 21, 1945, in the Kremlin, with Stalin in attendance, Polish leaders established a coalition government. Chaired by Edward Osóbka-Morawski, who had presided over the Committee of National Liberation, it now included six London Poles.

The United States and Britain recognized the new government. It was not independent from the Soviet Union, but nor was it its puppet. Something in between the two, it existed in a gray area of sovereignty, now affirming Stalin's wishes, now contesting his judgment. Its army was now a real force of four hundred thousand men and had participated in taking Berlin. Its security apparatus worked hand in hand with Stalin's secret police, but its employees were Polish. The agenda of the young government was almost impossible: rebuild the country, reform the economy, and bring the civil war to an end.

Responding ferociously to the Warsaw uprising, the Germans had "destroyed the city methodically, block by block and house by house," Arthur Bliss Lane wrote. "I could see only a handful of houses left unharmed; all others were bombed or gutted by fire . . . the smoky smell of long-dead fires hung in the air. The sickening sweet odor of burned human flesh was a grim warning that we were entering a city of the dead." Anna Louise Strong seconded that: "What had once been one of the liveliest capitals of Europe was an almost uncanny desolation, worse than the lost Pompeii or an Assyrian excavation, because the human bits remaining were so recent."

If reconstruction would take years, the redistribution of property could be done quickly—and it was. In the cities, the government nationalized all industrial enterprises employing more than fifty workers. In the country, farmers implemented the reform themselves. A witness wrote: "These last days of war were the easiest time for the transfer. The absence of many owners—those killed by the Germans and those who fled with the Germans—made an economic vacuum in which some owners must be found quickly to till the soil." The anger at the ancien regime ran deep: Count Potocki owned a palace ("thirty-seven rooms in a big park and all just for one man"); he had entertained Goering on his property, and before the Red Army came, the Germans sent eight trucks to help the count "take away his fine rugs, pictures, and antique furniture."

"Two thirds of the land in prewar Poland was owned by landlords" and now it was divided among the farmhands.

The smallest "estate," a farm of only one hundred and fifty acres, presented an interesting problem. Its owner, a Pole, had lived in America and had come back to Poland to buy land with the money earned overseas. The Germans drove him out but he hid in the villages. He now claimed his land on the ground that the land reform applied only to "feudal heritage," and not to farms bought "with a man's

29

own savings" . . . The peasants' commission had decided that the returned American couldn't farm so much by himself since he was sixty years old with no son and only a daughter. They left him his home and fifteen acres, somewhat more than a peasant share.

For farmers, making decisions like that *was* freedom.

But one person's freedom often curtails another person's rights. The brazen redistribution of property prolonged the civil war. As late as March 1946, the antigovernment forces killed eighteen Soviet soldiers, forty-five Polish troops, and eighteen Polish policemen, and destroyed eight bridges and an oil depot. The rebels' cause was lost from the start, as they were disunited: some came from the fascist Fallanga, others from the Home Army, but the group that fought the fiercest represented a mistreated ethnic minority: Ukrainians.

The infamous 1939 Nazi-Soviet division of Poland has become an epitome of Stalin's crimes against humanity. But his justification of the Red Army's march into Poland—a "liberation" mission to rescue Ukrainians and Byelorussians from the Polish "yoke"—wasn't just a good campaign slogan. The annexed territories did not belong to the core of the Polish state and did have an anti-Polish national liberation movement. Before the war, five million Ukrainians lived in Poland as an oppressed minority. The land reform of the 1920s, limited as it was, excluded Ukrainian farmers completely.

The Organization of Ukrainian Nationalists, an underground network based in and around Lviv, waged a campaign of terror against Poles there for years. Warsaw responded with punitive raids. During the war, the Ukrainian Insurrectional Army, a force of at least thirty thousand led by the passionate and charismatic Stephan Bandera, fought Poles, Russians, *and* Germans. Other Ukrainians, believing the Nazis would grant them independence, formed the SS Galicia Division—one of the very few non-German units of Hitler's war machine.

When Hitler's invasion of the Soviet Union brought the USSR, Britain, and the United States together, Stalin forced Roosevelt and Churchill to consent to the incorporation of eastern Poland into the USSR. Both the Moscow and London Poles accepted that as a fait accompli, but both groups expected reimbursement: the German lands in the west—Pomerania, Silesia, Western and Eastern Prussia. Stalin arranged the swap, in Yalta. Compared to 1939, the Poland of 1945 was 20 percent smaller, but no matter how badly the war had hit German Pomerania and Silesia, the basic infrastructure there remained superior to that of the eastern Polish provinces lost to the USSR, and the three-hundred-mile-long Baltic Sea coast offered opportunities for new industries such as shipbuilding.

As soon as the war ended, the Polish government started deporting the Germans west and Ukrainians east. "In areas inhabited by a Ukrainian community," Anita J. Prazmowska writes, "conflicts with the Poles increased dramatically . . . Ethnic violence overwhelmed whole areas, creating a situation comparable to that of a civil war . . . To the Polish units fell the task of rounding up the Ukrainian population living in areas designated as Polish territories and implementing a forced exchange of population with the Soviet Union. The Ukrainians fought back, presenting the Poles with a multiplicity of difficulties for which they were scarcely prepared." Meanwhile, Polish communities in the area "exploited the army's action to plunder Ukrainian villages."

In 1945–46, 3.5 million Poles moved to the "Recovered Lands" in the west. To make that possible, the Polish army had to remove the German nationals from the region first. "Pillaging and rape . . . inevitably accompanied the army's actions," Prazmowska writes. "One of the difficulties encountered by the Poles at this stage was the Russian commanders' anger at being faced with thousands of Germans removed from territories held by the Poles and being herded into areas under the administration of the Red Army. With the Poles pushing the Germans across the border and the Russians on the other side refusing to accept them, the river banks became congested with unwanted humanity." Following the Soviet example, Polish authorities kept about fifty thousand German prisoners of war in captivity until 1950, using them at coal mines and in other labor-intensive industries.

The postwar redistribution of property also involved Jews, who before the war made up 10 percent of the population. About three million Polish Jews died in the German concentration camps, and Oskar Schindler, for one, got a factory in Kraków from a dispossessed victim. The prewar republic hadn't minded Jew-bashing, often originating in the Roman Catholic clergy. During the war, the Home Army ignored the Holocaust, while the ultranationalists actually welcomed it. Prazmowska writes: "Although no organizational collaboration was established between the nationalist organizations and the German administration, it was known that they made it difficult for Christians to harbour Jews and might have killed Jews in hiding." Jerzy Lukowski and Hubert Zawadzki suggest: "Reports that some Jews in eastern Poland had welcomed the Soviets in 1939 also strengthened the widely held stereotype of 'Judaeo-communism' which had been promoted by right-wing parties before the war. Contemporary accounts suggest that numerous Poles easily came to accept the dispossession of the Jews and their isolation in the ghettos."

After the war, the Holocaust survivors—about two hundred thousand—were still widely believed to be doing too well for their own good. "Among the workers, the view that Jews enjoyed a high standard of living was so strong that evidence to the contrary made little impression," Prazmowska says.

The medieval belief that Jews used Christian children's blood to make Passover bread was now coupled with a new legend—namely, that Jewish doctors "drained Christian children of blood to treat wounded Soviet soldiers." The first postwar pogrom occurred in Kraków in August 1945; the second in July 1946, in Kielce, where an eight-year-old boy, absent from home for two days for an unclear reason, invented a cover-up tale about being "a prisoner in the cellar of a Jewish home" with "the bodies of Polish children there." Children's lies often reflect the zeitgeist, manipulating adults by tapping into their prejudices and fears. Provoked by the boy's claims, the mob lynched forty Jews and also several police officers trying to stop the riot.

The government didn't want embarrassments like that and, to the affirmation of the people, started encouraging Jewish emigration. Lane reported: "Although it was most difficult for a Polish Gentile to obtain permission to leave the country unless he had legitimate business abroad which would benefit the government, Polish Jews might leave quite freely, without passports and without any restrictions at the frontier." Shortly after the war, the vast majority of Holocaust survivors left Poland, their property and jobs taken over by ethnic Poles.

The writing of a new social contract in Poland was still a work in progress. The government proceeded with caution, exploring the public's reactions as things changed. After two years in power, its only major reforms were distributing land among private farmers and taking over bigger industrial enterprises. The new limitations on freedom hadn't been clearly defined yet, and no elections had been held to test the new system's willingness to be of the people and by the people. However, it was already becoming obvious that nationalism might serve the new Polish regime just as well as it had served the Sanacja. The grassroots violence against Jews and Ukrainians in the process of the redistribution of property gave the government hope that promotion of "Polishness"—a totally un-Marxist concept, by the way—would help in bonding the masses. The fact that nationalistic anger largely originated in the material concerns of the Polish street seemed to suggest that if the government made the Poles better off it could get away with undemocratic rule.

On March 5, 1946, at Westminster College in Fulton, Missouri, Winston Churchill declared: "From Stettin in the Baltic to Trieste in the Adriatic, an Iron Curtain has descended across the continent. Behind that line lie all the capitals of the ancient states of Central and Eastern Europe. Warsaw, Berlin, Prague, Vienna, Budapest, Belgrade, Bucharest and Sofia, all these famous cities and the populations around them lie in what I must call the Soviet sphere."

Historians will never agree whether the Fulton speech was an eleventh-hour warning or a self-fulfilling prophecy provoking Stalin's insecurities. In March 1946, Churchill was a bitter politician kicked out of office by war veterans, and it is possible that the strong words were rooted in a desire to enhance his own public persona. In March 1946, the Iron Curtain *was* descending, no doubt, but it *hadn't* fully descended yet, and the situation in Poland could best be described as fluid. There was little doubt that the coalition government would not last, as the London Poles had very few resources to secure a permanent place in Polish politics, while the Moscow Poles had all the support of the occupying force. Yet it was still not clear how close the Poland-Moscow relationship would be—and Communists and Socialists in the government were little wiser about that than the Polish street. Two questions still had to be answered: first, to what extent did Stalin expect the government to mimic the Soviet model, and second, would he be comfortable with pluralism in the Marxist camp, with Communists and Socialists sharing power?

In May 1946, the leftist leaders of the coalition government visited Stalin in the Kremlin, the Socialists led by Edward Osóbka-Morawski, the Communists by Bolesław Bierut. Competing for the patron's ear, Socialists and Communists bad-mouthed each other *and* the opposition parties. There was also a practical question to discuss: Stalin had promised the West there would be free parliamentary elections in Poland, and if the Polish government was to keep its standing in the international arena, the elections would have to be held soon.

Stalin listened for about three hours, then said that Poland did not need a dictatorship of the proletariat. The wealthy, he continued, had failed the nation during the war and a "democracy," "a new type of democracy," he clarified, was capable of dealing with them. It was okay to have small businesses in the country, as "the middle class has never defined a society." Political opposition was necessary, but it would be a "tame opposition." The West, he continued, wanted all Polish political parties to run independently in the forthcoming parliamentary elections, but he, Stalin, would have rather seen the Communists and Socialists running in a bloc. At this point, the transcript of the session notes, a Socialist delegate "gave a deep sigh and stirred uneasily in his chair."

The sigh was prophetic. In the bloc, Communists piggybacked on the Socialists' popularity in rural areas, promoting their candidates and their agenda. When only three months later the Socialists visited Stalin separately and complained that the Communists had begun ousting them from power, Stalin slyly replied that he couldn't pronounce a verdict because the Communists were not present: "Even in bourgeois countries, the jury can't decide without listening to the accused first."

The Socialists, very nervous in this dog-eat-dog situation, stayed on course. In the fall of 1946, Poland was heading for the parliamentary elections scheduled for January—Socialists, Communists, and two smaller leftist parties acting in a bloc, as Stalin wanted. By that time, Ambassador Lane rightfully noticed, freedom of speech had become "an empty term," as the government disqualified and sometimes arrested the opposition candidates, suppressed their bulletins, and employed an unlikely activist force—the army, which was deployed to campaign for the government.

The elections went as planned: the ruling bloc announced victory, and the nation, according to Western observers, was calm and apathetic. According to research conducted fifty years later and described by modern-day Polish historians as just "fragmentary studies," the opposition could have received between 60 and 70 percent of the vote. Revisiting any election that occurred half a century earlier is a daunting task, but, given the natural anti-Communist bias of contemporary Polish scholars, one can assume that any possible margin of error in the studies favors the 1947 opposition, so the leftist government would have received at least 30 to 40 percent. Frankly, in many Western-style democracies that would be sufficient to form a government. The redistribution of property and the promise of more material benefits to come gave Polish Marxists an acceptable public mandate for further change.

Joining the seminary in 1942, Wojtyla found himself in a parallel reality, calmer and safer than in the real Poland. As for the fateful vote of 1947, he didn't participate in it. Having ordained Wojtyla on November 1, 1946, Sapieha sent him to Rome.

Contrary to what Ambassador Lane reported ("it was most difficult for a Polish Gentile to obtain permission to leave the country unless he had legitimate business abroad which would benefit the government"), the clergy still traveled freely, and Wojtyla boarded a train to the West. Ironically, his trip could have actually benefited the government. Under Sapieha's leadership, the Polish Church pragmatically chose to coexist with Red Warsaw, and the regime seemed to be encouraging the emergence of Sapieha's new generation of priests. Jerzy Lukowski and Hubert Zawadzki write in *A Concise History of Poland*:

> [The Church] retained full freedom of worship, and proceeded, not without a touch of triumphalism, with the creation of new parochial structures for the millions of Poles settling in the so-called "Recovered Lands" and with taking over the ruined churches of the departing, mostly Protestant, German population. Indeed, as a result of the

frontier and population changes, and for the first time since the four-teenth century, Poland was now an overwhelmingly Catholic country . . . Little wonder that the authorities moved cautiously in their rela-tions with the Church; the Stalinist Bierut even used the traditional formula "So help me God" at his presidential inauguration in 1947.

The Vatican, in fact, didn't recognize the legitimacy of the "Recovered Lands"—understandably, given the German Catholics' feelings—and barely tolerated Polish activities there, let alone the "triumphalism" the Church displayed.

The relationship between the Polish government, the Polish Church, and the Vatican became intricate. Clearly, despite the individual lead-ers' idiosyncrasies, the Marxists regarded atheism as an integral part of their program. That definitely endangered the position of the Church, which had traditionally perceived itself as the keeper of Polish spiritu-ality and identity; also, it was just a matter of time before the govern-ment would nationalize the agricultural lands owned by it. But what was also clear was that the Polish Church would not be persecuted to the extent the Russian Orthodox Church had been after Lenin's revo-lution. Ironically, what bound state and Church together in Poland was revanchism—a quest for territories lost by the Polish empire over the centuries. True, Poland's territorial losses in the east were extensive, but in the lands lost to the Soviet Union the Eastern Orthodox outnum-bered Roman Catholics anyway, and that made the loss less painful. In the "Recovered Lands," meanwhile, the Church was given an opportu-nity to oust an ancient foe, German Protestantism. The Vatican, viru-lently anti-Communist since 1917 and now clearly displeased with the emerging coexistence of state and Church in Poland, was still reluctant to condemn it: a Church compromised by collaborationism was better than a martyred Church.

One definition of faith given by Marx was "Religion is the self-consciousness and self-esteem of man who has either not yet found himself or has already lost himself again." This could hardly be applied to the future pope, as he was born into an unwavering Catholicism and, to the best of our knowledge, had never departed from it. What did torture him throughout the 1940s was the Job dilemma. Personally, he was ready to live a Job's life, but his home country, Poland, which had lost one fifth of its population to the war and was now convulsed by civil conflict, was a *land* of Jobs, and he was looking for a meaning to this upheaval.

After the war, some Western European princes of the Church, alarmed by the onslaught of a materialism that had led to agnosticism, atheism, or simply spiritual indifference, started aggressively modernizing Catholicism. One of the best-known examples was the archbishop of Paris, Emmanuel Suhard: angry with postwar secularists such as Sartre, he proclaimed France a mission territory and ordained worker-priests, the hammer-and-sickle apostles. But at this point in his life, Karol Wojtyla wasn't particularly interested in social teachings. His focus was on the metaphysical aspects of Roman Catholicism such as miracles and the rituals facilitating them—something very similar to what the secular world would call "magic."

Applying the word *magus* to a Roman Catholic priest, let alone a future pope, sounds wrong, as the Church condemns magic in no uncertain terms and in the past has sent people to the stake for practicing it or being accused of practicing it. However, the border between Catholic miracles and un-Catholic magic is blurred, as both concepts imply something unnatural happening to people or objects. Technically, the difference is that a Catholic miracle happens through divine intervention, while the folk concept of magic concerns a person manipulating the natural world on his own. But nothing is unambiguous in the realm of the supernatural.

Catholicism has never really gotten rid of idolatry and polytheism. When a believer kisses the box containing the severed finger attributed to St. John the Baptist—a veneration encouraged by the Church—he obviously attributes certain magical qualities to one particular piece of mummified organic matter. Of course, Catholic dogma holds that saints answer prayers only through their intercession with God, but for the believer who kisses the box, St. John the Baptist is still a deity—a minor one and subordinated to God, but an individual deity nonetheless. Not every prayer is answered, but the believer knows that prayers coming from *some* people are, reportedly, noticed on high. Hypothetically, if his faith is intense, one day his prayers might be answered, too, and he will become another conductor channeling divine intervention to where, he thinks, it's needed most.

Visiting Paris, Wojtyla stayed just twelve blocks from the place where the Virgin made an appearance in 1830 to present the faithful with the Miraculous Medal, an oval coin bearing her image, since worn by millions. The core of Western European Catholicism—Italy, France, Spain, and Portugal—was as fixated on the cult of the Virgin Mary as was his homeland. In Poland, the Black Madonna icon shed blood tears; in Portugal in 1917, in the village of Fatima, the Madonna talked to three children, the last apparition attended by seventy thousand people, some of whom saw a multicolored sun leaping over the sky (the Madonna revealed that there *was* a heaven and that Russia should be converted to Catholicism; the third prophesy was officially secret, its transcript held in the Vatican). In Lourdes, France, the Virgin made herself visible eighteen times and blessed local water springs to produce healings recognized by the Church.

Wojtyla stayed in Rome for two years. Weigel says: "Distance, budgets, and Karol's responsibilities" made it impossible for him to visit Poland. But Sapieha paid for his trips all over Europe—and it looks as though the young man was under orders from the prince not to return home until the dust settled. The sweet maze of Catholic mysticism kept unfolding—startling, inspiring, perplexing. Wojtyla went to the poor Italian south to the town of San Giovanni Rotondo to meet Padre Pio, whom millions of Italians believed to be a living saint. The Capuchin carried the five stigmata of Christ on his body and was known to occasionally struggle with the Devil, who punched him, posed as a crucifix, the Virgin Mary, *or* dancing girls, and on particularly bad days messed with his books.

For Wojtyla, encounters with miracle workers like Padre Pio meant something very practical: the world on high *could* be reached and asked to step in to alleviate human misery. In his mind, it was this ethereal world—and not any social teaching or economic plan—that would define what was going to happen to Poland. Wojtyla met Padre Pio in 1947. Twenty years earlier, Pope Pius XI had temporarily banned Padre Pio from saying mass and denied any evidence of divine intervention in his life. Fifty-five years later, in 2002, as Pope John Paul II, Wojtyla would proclaim Padre Pio a saint.

During the fateful stay in Rome, he unexpectedly found his solution to the Job dilemma. A young Flemish priest told him: "The Lord allowed the experience of such an evil as communism to affect you . . . And why did he allow it? We were spared this in the West, because perhaps we could not have withstood so great a trial. You, on the other hand, can take it."

Reassured, in summer 1948, Wojtyla returned to Kraków.

2. Communism Rises: 1949–77

Communist regimes were often called "Kafkaesque" for their labyrinthine bureaucracy and atrocious system of justice (guilty until proven innocent). But let's revisit "The Metamorphosis" from a different perspective. Assuming Gregor Samsa was born in 1915, when Kafka wrote the story, in 1948 he would be thirty-three. Now, with Communists in power, the Samsa family situation would look very, very different.

In the original story, the family, disgusted with the bug largely because his metamorphosis has deprived them of a steady income, is on its own in the world. The retired father has to find a job, the mother turns the house into a bed-and-breakfast, the sister has to abandon her plans of going to a conservatory and becomes a housemaid, progressively angrier at the bug who has caused all this deprivation and now expects to be taken care of. The sad insect, feeling guilty indeed, starves itself to death—but the family's fortunes still do not look good, as money is and always will be in short supply; judging by the way the parents ogle the daughter's womanhood at the end of the narrative, they now hope to marry her off to a life of unpaid bills and bad jobs of her own. Had the

Samsas been living in Kafkaesque Eastern Europe, the outcome could have been different.

All the family would have had to do to get rid of the insect would have been to make a phone call. In no time an ambulance reeking of body fluids and emissions would have arrived and ferried Gregor to an asylum for bugs, as the state had an elaborate network of facilities for every sort of outcast—not just mental institutions and orphanages, but also hospitals for infectious patients and hospices for mauled war veterans. Gregor's parents would've received meager but generally adequate pensions allowing them to pay the subsidized rent and utilities and to cook meat on Sundays. His sister (let's assume she *was* gifted, as entrance exams were extremely competitive) would have gone to the conservatory for free. For the Samsas, the welfare that communism generated would have been a perfect resolution to an ugly domestic crisis.

Equating "bread" with "freedom"—that's what made communism appealing in Eastern Europe after the war. Stalin's marshals did not escort Eastern European Communists to the presidential and ministerial offices straight through the battlefields, with German tanks still smoldering in the streets; Stalin's economists did. (An Eastern European in the Metropolitan Museum in the 2000s, paying a quarter as the nominal admission fee under the steely glance of a cashier, says with much disdain: "A nation that wages wars should be able to support its own museums.")

Of course, Poles never forgave the Soviets the 1939 aggression, the 1940 executions of Polish officers, or the betrayal of the 1944 Warsaw uprising. Brutalities like those simply did not belong in the realm of forgiveness. Instead, Poles learned to live with painful memories and to expect more to come their way. Soviet army bases all over Poland; monuments to the Soviet liberators; new street signs commemorating Lenin and Stalin; a neo-Gothic, Soviet-built skyscraper in Warsaw, an alien ziggurat transforming the cityscape once and for all—all that simply had to be endured. And it was—again, not simply because the Soviet-leaning government forced the people under threat, but also because the new Polish state, in many ways modeled after the Soviet Union, was able to feed everyone.

On the ruins of the Warsaw ghetto houses for the Polish have-nots were built; the ugly ziggurat in the capital was, actually, the Palace of Culture and Science, not just paid for but also literally built by the Soviets as a gift to the reborn city; it had three thousand rooms, a swimming pool, and a theater in which the Rolling Stones would later perform; in the west, the Poles developed a whole new swathe of territory obtained from Germany through Stalin's intercession, and as early as 1946, the old German city of Breslau, now called Wrocław, had 170,000 Poles and no Germans.

This is how the Polish historians Jerzy Lukowski and Hubert Zawadzki describe the new social contract:

> Its triumphal showcase was the Lenin steel mill in Nowa Huta, a new "socialist" town that was intended to dwarf the neighboring ancient city of Kraków, that bastion of Polish conservatism . . . Hundreds of thousands of young, mostly poor, peasants were uprooted from their village communities, lodged in workers' hostels at the industrial sites, and promised a share in a glorious proletarian future. Their often genuine enthusiasm was dampened by drunkenness, low productivity, and a sense of dislocation. The state provided a basic welfare system, although it favoured those who were economically active in the industrial sector at the expense of the elderly and the rural population. Nevertheless, the pre-war curse of unemployment seemed to have gone for good. For thousands of peasants and workers there was the prospect of social advancement in the new urban centres, and in the new vast economic and administrative structures created by the state . . . Culture was made available to the masses on an unprecedented scale through the heavily subsidized expansion of publishing, of the cinema, the theater and of concert halls. By 1957 Poland could boast twenty-seven symphony orchestras and nine major opera houses.

Another historian, Anita J. Prazmowska, wrote in 2004:

> In admission to secondary schools and universities children from peasant and working-class families were favoured. Scholarships and student accommodation were offered to children from poor backgrounds, thus making it possible for them to gain an education. Technical schools, evening schools and correspondence courses were established to en-

able the workforce to improve its qualifications. Adult illiteracy was rapidly eliminated. The composition of the professional classes was thus altered in future years. Foreign visitors and the old elites frequently scoffed at these people's uncouth manners and lack of grooming; nevertheless investment in education provided opportunities for those who sought them . . . for the first time in their lives, workers were given subsidized holidays, and were encouraged to enjoy some leisure activities . . . The health system, destroyed during the war period, was rebuilt at great expense. A point of pride for the Poles was the fact that tuberculosis among children was eradicated.

Like every other achievement in the Communist bloc, the victory over tuberculosis came at a price: restrictions on freedom, placed upon the people by the omnipotent and omnipresent state.

In August 1917, two months before the Communist revolution in Russia, Lenin wrote, with aggressive use of italics, "*Together* with an immense expansion of democracy which *for the first time* becomes democracy for the poor, democracy for the people, and not democracy for the rich folk, the dictatorship of the proletariat produces a series of restrictions of liberty in the case of the oppressors, the exploiters, the capitalists. We must crush them in order to free humanity from wage-slavery; their resistance must be broken by force; it is clear that where there is suppression there is also violence, there is no liberty, no democracy." The state, Lenin wrote angrily—and, one must add, insightfully—"is an organ of domination of a definite class," and he promised no peace for those identified by the Communist state as exploiters.

One can ask, though, how is the fight on a disease like tuberculosis related to violence? Can there be a connection between a health care system and restrictions on freedom? Sadly, the answer is yes. A fight against a contagious disease involves different things in different systems. In the Communist bloc, the fight against TB included mandatory registration of the infected with local health centers and mandatory treatment in hospitals and sanatoriums both enforced by the police, if necessary. Building the system of free health care involved violence: buildings for clinics had to be confiscated and doctors were made state employees with meager salaries. To make that possible, the state limited or banned private practice, and the police kept an eye on medical professionals, making sure they did not build up a clandestine clientele and did not sell the free medications they had access to at work. As police efforts alone were not nearly sufficient, the state encouraged citizens to watch over one another and report misdeeds to the authorities, guaranteeing that even anonymous calls and letters would be taken seriously.

In the fall of 1948, Georgi Dimitrov of Bulgaria walked into the lounge of a tuberculosis sanatorium to catch forty students playing bridge. "His face changed color, his Adam's apple started to jump up and down, his eyes blazed and the next moment he shouted in a high-pitched piercing voice: '. . . Shame on you! Is that why the nation has sent you here? You are playing cards with the people's mone-e-e-ey . . .'" Dimitrov was a model authoritarian in whom aggression displaced reflection. Yet he *did* have a point, because free public health care *was* a heavy burden on the postwar government budget and, frankly, there are more productive ways to spend time than holding bridge tournaments.

Dimitrov was not a Soviet puppet without any merit of his own. Fifteen years earlier, in 1933, he had stood up to the Nazi leader Hermann Goering. A month after Hitler became chancellor of Germany, there was a fire in the Reichstag building in Berlin. Very likely orchestrated by the Nazis but blamed by them on a Communist conspiracy, the arson gave Hitler a welcome pretext to assume emergency powers. Ordered to prepare a show trial, the police arrested Dimitrov, at that point the chief Comintern representative in Europe. During the hearings, Dimitrov, who by that time had spent seven months in jail (five of them in chains), had an exchange with Goering that made him an international celebrity.

> GOERING: It was my task to expose the [Communist] Party, and the mentality, which was responsible for the crime.
> DIMITROV: Is the Reichsminister aware of the fact that those that possess this alleged criminal mentality today control the destiny of a sixth part of the world—the Soviet Union?

Dimitrov's brazenness made him the brightest star of the Eastern European Communist movement (it also impressed the German court, as it found him not guilty.) But practically all the Communist leaders of Eastern European countries had done time in jail as political prisoners of the domestic prewar regimes: not only Dimitrov, but also Walter Ulbricht of East Germany, Bolesław Bierut of Poland, Mátyás Rákosi of Hungary, Klement Gottwald of Czechoslovakia, and Gheorghe Gheorghiu-Dej of Romania. All swore by egalitarianism, though of course ended up becoming privileged. When during the war Churchill flew into Moscow and, knowing the perilous state of the Soviet economy, brought sandwiches so that he wouldn't be a burden for the hosts, Stalin laughingly served him one lavish meal after another, while the famished people of Leningrad were dying. But compared to the lifestyle of the dominant minority of any given Western country at the time, theirs was modest. Stalin used four country residences on a regular basis—a divine luxury no one else in the Soviet Union could afford; yet, before the revolution, his contemporary Prince Felix Yusupov, "the man who killed Rasputin," had used *fifty*.

Incomprehensibly, personal exposure to incarceration and torture had not taught Ulbricht, Bierut, or Rákosi any compassion, and coming to power, they started implementing their utopia through terror. The mechanism of Eastern European justice consisted of four simple steps straight out of Kafka. One: "Someone must have slandered Josef K., for one morning, without having done anything truly wrong, he was arrested." Two: "It's the figure of Justice . . . actually Justice and the goddess of Victory in one." Three: "With failing sight K. saw how the men drew near his face, leaning cheek-to-cheek to observe the verdict. 'Like a dog!' he said; it seemed as though the shame was to outlive him." Four: "The party secretary ordered my mother not to be difficult" and not to wear black.

The four steps were simple, but the repressive mechanism behind them was not. Of course, Stalin shared the know-how of establishing and maintaining secret police, and Soviet advisors descended on Warsaw and Budapest to show the natives the ropes, but then each country created a Gulag of its own—seemingly an oxymoron, given the countries' size. Bulgaria, for example, hosted a hundred prison camps. Belene was the biggest and the deadliest; its inmates were kept in chains "for two whole weeks in a boat stuck in the ice of the river during the coldest February," or "confined for several days and nights in a solitary cell with water" up to their necks. Between 1945 and 1960, 2,700 Bulgarians were executed, 17,000 more sent to labor camps, 25,000 deported to rural areas—not a small accomplishment for a country the size of Tennessee. Needless to say, the guards, interrogators, and executioners were native.

The border between "state" and "people" was blurred, and, as often as not, the rank and file acted as agents of repression, too. Peasants who used to walk to church barefoot now wanted revenge on those who had worn patent leather shoes. In order to feed the poor the state had to rob the haves, and as for the "masses," many people would denounce friends and family to increase their own rations: "somebody at the party committee had got his eye on [our flat]"; "We were literally kicked out of the flat"; "the confiscation of assets was also part of the sentence" (all the quotes come from Hungarians who grew up in the forties).

The darkest years were between 1948, when Tito took Yugoslavia out of the Soviet bloc, and 1953, when Stalin died. After the loss of Yugoslavia, Stalin feared the domino effect of "Titoism." Firmly believing in the inevitability of World War III and expecting it to start during his lifetime or shortly thereafter, Stalin wanted military bases along Western Europe's borders. Tito had deprived him of access to the Mediterranean, and if "Titoists" prevailed in Poland or Hungary, Stalin reasoned, the gateway to central Europe would be lost as well. To secure the western strategic theater, any possibility of dissent in Eastern Europe had to be nipped in the bud.

In Poland, in 1948, the creative and independent Władysław Gomułka, an advocate of the "Polish way to socialism," was placed under house arrest, and the person who replaced him as party leader, Bolesław Bierut, relied blindly on force and intimidation. The Socialist party wisely chose to "unite" with the Communists; other parties got marginalized or disbanded. The security force grew to two hundred thousand, files were kept on 30 percent of Polish adults, and people suspected of disloyalty were arrested and sometimes executed.

To ensure the vassal's strategic loyalty, in 1949, Stalin sent his favorite Pole, Marshal Konstantin Rokossovsky, to Warsaw to serve as minister of defense (a provocation to the Poles who remembered only too well that Rokossovsky's army had "stood and watched while Warsaw fought, burned, and died"). By Stalin's lights, Poland was an invaluable strategic asset: among all Eastern European countries, it had the longest border with Germany. The Polish officer corps would pay for that dearly: in 1952, 75 percent of Polish generals held Soviet citizenship.

Still, the purge was infinitely milder in Eastern Europe than in the Soviet Union. Gomułka would return to lead Poland again; a Slovak Communist, Gustáv Husák, put on show trial in 1949, later became head of the Communist Party of Czechoslovakia; in Hungary, János Kádár followed the same path. Stalin's trial and Gulag system had no such process for rehabilitating those who had been identified as enemies of the government. In Eastern Europe, Anne Applebaum notes, the majority of the Gulags "did not last, and many had closed even before Stalin's death." In 1950 in East Germany, to "improve the new regime's image," "the East German secret police actually nursed prisoners back to health before their release, and provided them with new clothes."

Stalin monitored Eastern European leaders closely, wanting to be 100 percent sure that they remained good hosts for his troops. But, contrary to popular belief, in Eastern Europe Stalin did not clone regime after regime after regime—not even in the darkest hours, 1948–53. During the 1930s, the Soviet Union failed to export the revolution to Eastern Europe and elsewhere, and so Stalin realized that the cookie-cutter approach to communism didn't work. In Poland, only 10 percent of the land was collectivized—a totally anti-Marxist situation, as agriculture is believed to be the breeding ground of exploitation and capital accumulation. Stalin had killed or exiled or starved to death anywhere between three million and seven million peasants during the epic Soviet collectivization campaign, and in a conversation with Churchill he called *that* the biggest challenge of his lifetime, yet in postwar Poland he let the petite bourgeoisie be. Moscow was not in simple terms an "occupying power." Each Eastern European regime formulated its own version of communism, and as for the Soviet troops, intimidating as they looked, their primary task was not to pacify Eastern Europe but to threaten the West.

Franz Kafka's story "In the Penal Colony" has been called a premonition of many things: death camps, Hitler, Stalin, Mao Zedong, Pol Pot. It also predicted Khrushchev's Thaw.

In the story, a nameless traveler visits a Devil's Island whose government is in transition from brutality to a more humane modus operandi. The "apparatus," an elaborate death-through-torture machine, invented by the "former Commandant," a man who was "soldier, judge, mechanic, chemist, and draughtsman," falls apart before the traveler's eyes. Now dead, the former Commandant lies in a secret grave under a table in the teahouse; the new Commandant, influenced by "women," advocates a "mild doctrine." Basically, the 1914 text tells one all one needs to know about what happened in the USSR after Stalin died: a tyrant passes away, a reformer takes his place, the terror stops. As for "women," those were party intellectuals who (unlike Khrushchev) had read Marx and now struggled to salvage his teachings from the Stalinist abomination.

Years later, in front of a tape recorder—ironically, preparing his memoirs for publication in the West—Nikita Khrushchev said: "When Stalin died there were literally a million agents [in the Soviet Union]. One agent watches another agent, and all of them report. If you are an agent then you have to justify your existence with activity. They reported. Everything was overflowing with paper. People were arrested and sentenced. The prisons were filled up and all the agents' mouths had to be fed besides.

"When we approached the Twentieth Party Congress [in February 1956] we faced the question head-on."

In a closed session of the congress, Khrushchev delivered his so-called secret speech denouncing Stalin. In his definitive biography of Khrushchev, William Taubman writes: "Khrushchev's speech denouncing Stalin was the bravest and most reckless thing he ever did. The Soviet regime never fully recovered, and neither did he." The text of the speech was given to the heads of foreign Communist Party delegations present at the congress, says Khrushchev, "so they could study it. Comrade Bierut received it and sent it back to Warsaw. This document was particularly bitter for Poles to read because it described how the Polish Communist Party was dissolved and what kind of accusations were made against it [by Stalin]." The Stalinist Bierut died in Moscow, succeeded by the faceless Edward Ochab, and, according to Khrushchev, "After Bierut's death there were divisions in the Polish leadership, and as a result copies of the speech became accessible to the public. I was told that in Poland you could buy two copies in the market for one ruble. In this way it became available to the forces of world reaction."

Indeed, in early April, the secret speech reached the CIA, and in May the U.S. State Department released it to *The New York Times.* On June 28, 1956, workers and students rioted in the Polish city of Poznán.

The clashes were about low wages, overtime pay, and food shortages. It was hardly a revolutionary challenge to the regime, but the government sent the army in and killed about seventy people. One of the leaders responsible for the crackdown, Prime Minister Józef Cyrankiewicz, had a "weakness for toys and ingenious Western gadgets, which his friends would bring him from abroad. Those toys and gadgets inhabited an entire room in his apartment, and it was said that he played with them for hours." Yet another involved in the massacre, Stalin's Pole, Minister of Defense Konstantin Rokossovsky, was a Gulag survivor who had endured two mock executions.

The massacre did not pacify the rioters, and the rebellion spread. Facing chaos or, possibly, Soviet intervention, the new leader, Ochab, professed his inability to cope with the crisis, and the Polish Politburo brought back Gomułka, purged earlier as a right-wing deviationist.

In the Communist vernacular, a left-wing deviationist is a nutcase, while a right-wing deviationist is someone who is too smart. Gomułka was very smart. Guns wouldn't help. The Church would.

The Polish state might have been Kafkaesque, but Poland's soul was not: it had faith. One of Bierut's gravest mistakes had been falling out with Primate Stefan Wyszyński. A son of a church organist and a schoolteacher, early in his career Wyszyński was dubbed a "labor priest," publishing articles on the workers' conditions and even acting as counsel in labor disputes; during the Nazi occupation, he worked secretly under the alias Sister Cecilia and survived a Gestapo arrest. When Bierut took away a major Church right—the authority to appoint bishops—Wyszyński responded with a thunderous sermon: "We teach that it is proper to render unto Caesar the things that are Caesar's and to God what is God's. But when Caesar seats himself on the altar, we respond curtly: he must not." Caesar had him arrested but not exactly martyred. Three years of internment were not a stake.

Now Gomułka brought him out of internment and promised that the Church's rights would be restored to her. Back in Warsaw, in his first sermon, Wyszyński said: "I am a little late—only a little more than three years," but it looked like he was not late at all. He prevented the escalation, telling the people: "Poles know how to die magnificently. But, my dear ones, Poles must learn to work magnificently." When told of a group of students in Warsaw planning a march on the Soviet embassy in the middle of the night, Wyszyński put his clothes on, went to the rallying point, said mass, and then told the young men and women that heroism of perseverance was higher than heroism of "the newsstands."

On his side, Gomułka sent Rokossovsky packing. Khrushchev came to visit, showered him with insults, and threatened to use military force; Gomułka persevered. According to Khrushchev, what reconciled him with the Polish reformer was Gomułka's "anxious but sincere declaration: 'Poland needs friendship with the Soviet Union more than the Soviet Union needs friendship with Poland. Can it be that we failed to understand our situation? Without the Soviet Union we cannot maintain our borders with the West.'"

In May 1957, *Time* magazine called Wyszyński "the most remarkable prelate in the Roman Catholic Church today," "a prince of the church who threw away the Vatican rule book in his dealings with the state," and "the embodiment of the fervent faith of more than 27 million Poles." "Today," the *Time* article continued,

> the cardinal [Wyszyński] and the commissar [Gomułka] lean on each other in a breathtakingly precarious balancing act, protecting each other against extremists in both the Catholic and the Communist camp, personally opposed in everything except Polish patriotism and a talent for tough-minded compromise. It is a strange coexistence between the cross and the hammer-and-sickle. But Masses are crowded, public schools are swamped with applications for religious instruction that is once again permitted without interference. Everyone seems to be wearing crosses and holy medals, and even the prosperous red bourgeoisie of state officials can occasionally be seen bundling their children to church . . . No country in the Roman Catholic world knows such a flowering of the faith as Poland today.

Five hundred thousand Poles turned out at the national shrine of Częstochowa—the keep of the Black Madonna—when Wyszyński celebrated mass. As an American correspondent wrote, the cardinal was "a mere speck of red to most of the crowd"—but he was surely a speck that had made a difference. In his "breathtakingly precarious balancing act," he wrestled a better social contract from the Communist government—and persuaded the Polish street to accept it as the best possible compromise.

His Hungarian counterpart, József Cardinal Mindszenty, didn't win anything similar to that praise. Released from jail during the 1956 Hungarian uprising, he sided with the insurgents—and by doing so contributed to the civil war.

The turbulence in Hungary began a few months after Stalin's death, when one true believer, Imre Nagy, clashed with another, Mátyás Rákosi. Both leaders had done some dirty work. Between 1948 and 1952, Rákosi had purged the real or imagined enemies of Hungarian communism; in the 1930s, Nagy had worked for Stalin's secret police, reporting on his fellow exiles in Moscow and delivering many a one-way ticket to the Gulag. After Stalin's death, Rákosi was not repentant, but Nagy was. Supported by Khrushchev's Kremlin, and elevated to the post of prime minister, Nagy released political prisoners previously targeted by Rákosi and allowed collective farms to dissolve themselves so that those who wanted to could start private farming. The novelist Michael Korda, a visitor to Hungary in 1956, wrote: "Life was better, and food more plentiful; though Hungary was still a police state, the worst excesses of the terror were ended, and a certain freedom of thought in the arts was permitted once again." The hard-liners, led by Rákosi, angered by what they called Nagy's right-wing deviationism, struck back. Korda continues: "In April 1955, Nagy was removed from office, and all power was once again in Rákosi's hands. Nagy was even expelled from the Communist Party, and obliged to hand over his party card—the ultimate humiliation. Yet here, too, there was a sign of weakness. Stalin would have had Nagy executed; but instead Nagy merely retired to his country house to live comfortably."

In the summer of 1956, the impact upon Hungary of Khruschev's speech proved tremendous: the country had a long tradition of intellectual Marxism, and it had already enjoyed a "thaw" introduced by Nagy and then cut short by reactionaries. Now bravely defying

Rákosi and his infamous secret police, the AVH, in Budapest groups "of anti-Rákosi communists and intellectuals held debates on the most controversial of social issues, some of which were broadcast into the street by loudspeaker." Before Rákosi could crush them, Khrushchev stepped in. In July 1956, he forced Rákosi to resign, had him flown to the Soviet Union, and put him under house arrest there. The person who succeeded Rákosi, Ernö Gerö, knew that in order to appease the population he would have to bring Imre Nagy back (a maneuver like that—pacifying the public by bringing in a popular purged moderate— had worked in Poland with Gomułka).

But it seemed already too late. On October 23, one hundred thousand people participated in a state funeral for László Rajk—Rákosi's minister of the interior, accused of treason, executed, and buried secretly in 1949. The funeral exemplified the intellectual confusion and emotional turmoil of the fall of 1956: Rajk had been a Stalinist par excellence and had purged hundreds of people before Rákosi purged him. But before this paradoxical commemoration could have been properly analyzed by Nagy and Gerö, let alone Khrushchev, two more rallies took place in Budapest later in the day.

> By the early evening a mass of people—perhaps as many as 250,000—had assembled in Parliament Square, shouting for Nagy to appear. At first the government attempted to disperse the crowd by turning the lights off in the square, but the demonstrations grew so unruly that they were switched back on again. Eventually, sweating and nervous despite the cold night air, Nagy, who had been persuaded with great difficulty to address the crowd, appeared on a balcony, and was cheered for many minutes. "Comrades . . . ," he started off, but the people shouted him down with cries of "No more 'comrades'!" Nagy, who had been a communist all his adult life, had to start again, with some embarrassment, addressing them instead as "young Hungarians."

> Meanwhile, in a different location—outside the central radio station headquarters—a crowd assembled to listen to a recorded speech by Gerö.

Gero's speech was harsh, threatening, and unconciliatory, and it sparked off the first moment of real violence. The crowd demanded a microphone to broadcast their demands and repudiate Gero's speech; the woman director of the radio station refused; people began to throw bricks through the windows of the building; and then somebody backed a van into the big wooden gates at the entrance and knocked them down. At this the AVH guards in the building fired tear gas into the crowd and opened fire with automatic weapons . . . As the hated AVH fired into the crowd, the soldiers in the trucks or standing on tanks began to hand their weapons down into the crowd. The weapons were passed overhead from hand to hand, gleaming dully in the light of the streetlamps, until they reached the people in front, who began to fire back on the AVH . . . At last those of the crowd who were armed managed to break into the radio building. AVH members who were trying to change into stolen civilian clothes were shot, as were some who had hidden in the women's lavatory. Others were thrown out the windows into the street, and killed there.

That was the beginning of the Hungarian civil war. That night, Nagy accepted the post of prime minister   and either contacted Mos cow himself, asking for military intervention, or let someone else place the fateful call. In a few hours, Soviet tanks and armored personnel carriers left their bases in the Hungarian countryside and rolled into Budapest. At least four thousand Hungarians, mostly college and high school students, met them with fire and Molotov cocktails.

Tank crews like open country, with areas of good cover from which to shoot; and like all soldiers they have a particular dislike of fighting against amateurs who don't take prisoners. And from the very beginning, nei ther side was inclined to show mercy. Anybody who tried to surrender was likely to be shot, and while the medical students very bravely picked up the Hungarian wounded under fire, they did not bother trying to save the Russians, who, for their part, didn't pay much respect to people in white coats, or to ambulances marked with a red cross . . . To the hor ror of the Kremlin, Imre Nagy, and the Western powers, the morning of October 24 saw Budapest in the throes of a full-scale battle.

Unbelievably, the Kremlin capitulated. Khrushchev decided that Hungary would be better off with a reformist Marxist, Nagy, supported by popular vote, than with a Stalinist government restored to power by Soviet armor. On October 28, the Kremlin ordered its troops out of Budapest and started negotiating a complete withdrawal from Hungary—on one condition: Hungary should stay inside the Warsaw Pact.

> The streets [of Budapest] were littered with broken glass, debris, rubble, and spent cartridge cases—one proceeded slowly to avoid driving over a corpse, or bursting a tire on shards of armor from damaged tanks or unexploded artillery shells. Some of the tanks were still burning, filling the air with dense diesel fumes and the smell of charred human bodies. If one looked—though one tried hard not to look—the crisp, blackened bodies of tank crews and gunners hung out of open hatches, clawlike hands still reaching for safety, or perhaps mercy.

But Soviet withdrawal did not bring peace to the city, and neither did Nagy's desperate calls for national unity and reconciliation. The civil war intensified. In the center of Budapest, dozens of AVH officers were "shot at point-blank range and the half-naked body of one of the officers strung up from a tree, doused with gasoline, and set on fire." Only a week earlier, Budapest had said heartfelt goodbyes to a bad Communist slain by other bad Communists; now Hungarian revolution started destroying the Communist state. Stressed out, Nagy miscalculated. On October 30, in an attempt to curb the violence, he promised a multiparty system and free elections. When that didn't work, on October 31 he announced that Hungary was quitting the Warsaw Pact. That was a fatal mistake. Michael Korda later wrote:

> This was, of course, to deny the reality of Hungary's geography. If the Poles had tried to leave the Warsaw Pact, there were half a million Russian soldiers in East Germany to keep them separated from the West—Poland could be attacked from East and West simultaneously, squeezed like the filling of a sandwich. But an independent Hungary would roll the Iron Curtain all the way back to the border of the Ukraine, and for the first time directly expose Soviet soil to

the possibility of an attack by the West. Seen from the point of view of anybody standing in front of a map in the Kremlin, this must have seemed like a direct threat.

That was how it was taken. Meanwhile, Hungarian leaders who had fled to the USSR, led by János Kádár, persuaded Khrushchev that the remaining AVH and army forces were enough to restore the regime— provided that the Soviet troops stepped in again. After painful deliberation, Khrushchev reversed course. In the small hours of the morning of November 4, Soviet troops returned, this time under orders to stay until the uprising was crushed.

Nagy was arrested, taken to Romania, held there for more than a year, and then executed. The overall toll of the civil war was twenty thousand Hungarians and fifteen hundred Soviet soldiers. In the wake of the bloodbath, one hundred thousand Hungarians crossed into Austria. The AVH and the Soviet occupying force looked the other way. Everyone agreed that restoration would proceed more smoothly with the dissenters gone.

The answer to the question of why the people of Eastern Europe and not the Soviet Union rebelled is obvious: as mentioned before, the purge there had been Stalinesque, not Stalinist, suppressing but not paralyzing free will. But there is another question to ask: What did the rebels want to achieve? The conventional answer, "They wanted to get rid of communism and liberate themselves from Soviet power" won't do. By the mid-1950s, the Soviet Union and its version of communism had lost luster—but not so Marxism itself, with its powerful message of egalitarianism. As Korda, who saw the 1956 revolution in Hungary firsthand, writes, most rebels did not envisage "a full-scale return to capitalism and private ownership of land. Ten years of communism had changed people's mind-set. Some wanted Marxism without the errors of Leninism and Stalinism; some wanted a more human form of communism without Russian domination and police terror; hardly anybody was as yet aware that the whole system was a sham and a failure, and would lead nowhere." The leading Polish philosopher of the time, Leszek Kołakowski, was described as "an antitotalitarian socialist, a supporter of social reforms and the emancipation of labor."

As for the truly anti-Communist camp, its ambition was not to build a modern free-market democracy, but rather to restore the archaic prewar social arrangement. In Hungary in 1956, rebels of that persuasion demanded restitution of the Church's property and aspired to build a new Hungary around its Catholic Church. The Polish intellectual Adam Michnik, the most distinct voice of the liberal opposition from the 1970s and on, upset by similar reactionary trends in the anti-Communist movement in his country, angrily wrote: "Yesterday's Party member becomes today's champion of the Middle Ages: out of hatred for communism he now espouses the virtues of serfdom. As someone has aptly put it, such a person merely replaces 'yesterday's stupidities with those from the day before yesterday.'"

From the first attempts at a rebellion in 1956 until 1989, when communism actually fell, the opposition in Eastern Europe and the Soviet Union didn't really address the question "What kind of freedom is it that you want?" The 1956 rebels claimed freedom from want and freedom from fear—but at that their program stopped. Nothing like the Bill of Rights existed in the imagination of the dissenting East. As the opposition craved freedom from fear, it seems fair to assume that they would have welcomed the Fourth Amendment—"The right of the people to be secure in their persons, houses, papers, and effects, against unreasonable searches and seizures, shall not be violated, and no warrants shall issue, but upon probable cause, supported by oath or affirmation, and particularly describing the place to be searched, and the persons or things to be seized"—but mass lynchings in Budapest demonstrated that while people longed to be free from fear themselves, they would grant their opponents no rights at all. With a better society uncharted either by the neo-Marxists or anti-Communists, Eastern Europeans negated communism without suggesting any specific alternative to it. Tribalized and disunited, they fought fear in the dark.

They were more coherent and united in demanding freedom from want, though. An emblematic case is the outstanding Polish journalist Ryszard Kapuściński, an internationally acclaimed writer. His position is fascinatingly mainstream: now left-leaning, now anti-Marx, now angry, later resigned. Unlike many other Eastern Europeans critical of their regimes, from Joseph Conrad to Milan Kundera, Kapuściński did not emigrate, instead becoming the respectable face of "Communist"

Poland on the world stage from the sixties onward. In 1956, the year of trouble, he made his first trip overseas and later described it in a book called *Travels with Herodotus.*

Interestingly, the narrator's anti-Communist critique is not exactly focused on terror. In 1956, people were already coming out of the gulags, and in a newspaper article one could write that store shelves in a village were "always bare." When Stalin was alive, "one could not write that a store was empty—all of them had to be excellently stocked, bursting with wares." Ultimately, the control the state exercised over him was very mild, because it sent him to the "free world" on his own, unsupervised, unwatched, unmonitored, practically free to do whatever he wanted. It gave him the money to travel, too.

On assignments at home, he rattled along "from village to village, from town to town, in a hay cart or a rickety bus, for private cars were a rarity and even a bicycle wasn't easily to be had." In his own words, the thing he wanted most—he actually uses the phrase "I wanted one thing only"—was to cross the border. "To cross it and come right back—that, I thought, would be entirely sufficient, would satisfy my quite inexplicable yet acute psychological hunger." And so finally he did. The state sent him to Rome.

Below me, the entire length and breadth of the blackness through which we were flying was now filled with light. It was an intense light, blinding, quivering, flickering. One had the impression of a liquid substance, like molten lava . . . The entire luminous apparition was something alive, full of movement, vibration, energy.

It was the first time in my life I was seeing an illuminated city . . . Bustle, traffic, lights, and sounds—it worked like a narcotic . . . I must have looked like a creature of the forest: stunned, a little fearful, wide-eyed, trying to take in, understand, distinguish things . . . I did not notice the architecture, the statues, the monuments; I was fascinated only by the cafes and bars . . . One day I spotted an empty table, sat down, and ordered a coffee. After a while I became conscious that people were looking at me. I had on a new suit, an Italian shirt white as snow, and a most fashionable polka-dotted tie, but there must still have been something in my appearance and gestures, in my way of sitting and moving, that gave me away . . . I had changed my suit, but I apparently could not conceal whatever lay beneath it that had shaped and marked me as a foreign particle.

Stalinism had dismissed feelings like that as "idolatry of the rotten West," but, shaken by 1956, many Eastern European leaders now chose to listen. In this sense, the 1956 rebellions did not fail altogether. The governments of Poland, Czechoslovakia, and even the bleeding Hungary introduced market reforms and more lenience toward contacts with the West. The citizens of the Soviet Union would not get anything like that for thirty more years. Visiting Hungary, junior party apparatchiks of the Soviet Union, still sufficiently insignificant to be able to roam foreign cities without much protocol, "spent a long time at the Budapest farmers' market, stricken by what we saw" (by the way, that's Mikhail Gorbachev talking). Gone were "fashions à la Warsaw Pact" and bleak cities without bars and cafés.

In 1959, *the* anti-Communist, Vice President Richard Nixon, visited Warsaw, where an estimated quarter of a million people greeted him. Flowers, waving, clapping, cheering: "Long live America!" "Long live Eisenhower!" and (hold your breath) "Long live Nixon!" The trip followed close on the Kitchen Debate—a public shouting match between Khrushchev and Nixon at the American National Exhibition in Moscow. Allowing the exhibition—an unprecedented show of the archenemy's achievements—Khrushchev had made a goodwill gesture and was annoyed beyond words when Nixon showed him around a model American kitchen equipped with all sorts of gadgets, insisting that every American family could afford a house like that.

KHRUSHCHEV: Your American houses are built to last only twenty years so builders can sell new houses at the end. We build firmly. We build for our children and grandchilden.

NIXON: American houses last for more than twenty years, but even so, after twenty years, many Americans want a new house or a new kitchen. Their kitchen is obsolete by that time . . . The American system is designed to take advantage of new inventions and new techniques.

KHRUSHCHEV: This theory does not hold water. Some things never get out of date—furniture and furnishings, perhaps, but not houses . . .

In another seven years, we'll be at the level of America, and after that we'll go farther. As we pass you by, we'll wave "hi" to you, and then if you want, we'll stop and say, "please come along behind us."

Khrushchev's bragging made him a laughingstock at home, but if the Soviets kept their jokes private, the Poles turned Nixon's visit into a political demonstration of sorts. Unlike the Soviet Union, as early as 1959 Poland was getting close to being free from fear—and it definitely aspired to be free from want.

———

The edifice of authority crumbled very slowly because millions of Eastern Europeans didn't really want it to. Though the Wall was the most obvious symbol of Eastern European disunion, there were other and more significant—walls dividing Eastern European societies.

The generation of Eastern European leaders that came to power in the sixties was a study in degradation. Too young to have benefited intellectually from the cosmopolitan Marxist discourse at the turn of the twentieth century, the only skill they had was political manipulation. Also, they did something the populace could not forgive: they created a different lifestyle for themselves and their families.

Nicolae and Elena Ceauşescu ordered fresh orchids flown to Romania from Thailand and used eighty-four properties all over the country (again, Stalin had used four), including twenty-three hunting lodges, where Nicolae shot thousands of animals a year, some of them imported from as far as Alaska. Eventually, his collection of trophies would include 244 deer and 385 bears. In that hobby, his chief competitor was a neighbor, Todor Zhivkov of Bulgaria, who claimed to hold "the world record for antler trophies of stags he had killed personally," taking hunting trips as far away as Mongolia. Even the ascetic Erich Honecker of East Germany, when deciding on an annual event for foreign ambassadors, chose a hunt.

They all grew up in the time when hunting was the privilege of the rich and famous, and when they finally made it, not daring to imitate the Romanovs or the Habsburgs by bedding ballet dancers, they imitated them by getting expensive rifles. Feeling very regal after each hunt,

Brezhnev distributed the dismembered kill: "This is for Gromyko, this is for Kosygin, this is for Andropov"—one wild hog feeding all the wise men of the Evil Empire.

The world of luxury they created for themselves was still a far cry from that of Imelda Marcos or John F. Kennedy, and their wealth was not hereditary or even for life, because a leader ousted from power lost most of the material benefits the day he was sacked, and every person in Romania knew that the Ceaușescus' prosperity was exactly as lasting as the orchids they imported.

These were elites whose dacha furniture had metal tags nailed to it, so that when the person fell out with the leader or retired, an inventory team could count and account for every chair he left to his successor (in 2006 in the United States, a severance package for a "failed" chief executive of Home Depot was $210 million). Moguls drove around in Soviet-made Chaika limousines, their windows covered by arrogant curtains, but their children could not inherit them. Here, privileges were like fiefs and had no monetary backup: you lose power, you lose its spoils.

In 1968, the conqueror of Warsaw, Marshal Rokossovsky, diagnosed with terminal cancer, begged a doctor to send him to the subtropical Crimea on the Black Sea, to the Ministry of Defense dacha: "I know that I can die at any moment, please make my last year good." The doctor counterfeited the paperwork, and the retired war hero got clean bedsheets, free meals, and a room with a view. When one of the most powerful men in Bulgaria, a secretary of the party's Central Committee, had a fling, he asked a subordinate—in his case, a writer, for the secretary supervised arts and literature—to lend him his apartment for the night because he couldn't take his date to a hotel: the management would have reported him to his very own Central Committee, which would have been only too happy to shred him to pieces for "moral decadence." In principle, Eastern European elites were as shackled by the rules as were their subjects, and, doubtlessly, whispered the names of freedoms *they* would've wanted.

The greatest spymaster of Eastern Europe, Markus Wolf, chief of East German intelligence for thirty years, wrote in his memoir:

People who could leave the country were greatly envied by the population at large; travel fever was acute in this country of nontravelers. I had traveled less widely for pleasure than most middle-class American college students, which is something that Western commentators tend to forget when they talk about the lives of the members of the nomen-klatura. For all my privileges, I had never visited the Prado, the British Museum, or the Louvre . . . I was privileged to have a fine apartment, a car and driver, and pleasant holidays at the invitation of other secret services in the Eastern bloc. But these were always connected to my job and status; in the end, the wider world was sealed off to me, too.

Yet there *was* a new gap between the top and the rest that people such as Zhivkov, Brezhnev, and Ceaușescu promoted, and it didn't go unnoticed below. As early as 1955, a leader of Yugoslavia, Milovan Djilas, wrote a book maintaining that the privileges and power of the dominant minority in the East had become totally un-Marxist. The title of the book was its concept: *The New Class.*

According to some estimates, in Eastern Europe state bureaucra-cies accounted for more than 10 percent of the total labor force. Add the families. Add an amorphous group of those who fed off the domi-nant minority, an astonishingly diverse body—drivers, party writers, poets and artists, secretaries, bodyguards, entertainers, interpreters, babysitters, journalists, maids, academics—and maybe the second tier of privilege (a very unusual, socialist middle class) would account for another 15 percent. A simple look at the Communist Party member-ship in Eastern Europe reveals a stupefying degree of support for the system, with Stalinists, idealists, and, of course, opportunists joining in huge numbers. As late as the mid-1980s, 11.6 million Eastern Euro-peans—about 10 percent of the population—were card-carrying party members.

Then there were people who had successfully carved out a niche for themselves somewhere in the shadows—black-market profiteers trading in American jeans, French perfume, and rare (in other words, banned) books, hotel and restaurant managers serving not the party but the backdoor clientele, gigolos and hustlers ambushing foreigners on the beaches. All in all, likely, close to 30 percent of the population had a stake in the survival of the regime and were largely "free of want."

Though, in the poet Anna Akhmatova's words, communism turned "vegetarian" after Stalin's death, no one was completely free

of fear in the Eastern bloc. Of course, an obvious wall separated political pariahs from the good citizens (a child of the 1956 Hungarian
rebellion remembered: "[Relatives] began to withdraw from us and
then, when we visited them one day, they told us we had better not go
there again"). But even the elites never felt safe. After Djilas published
his critique of state communism, his comrade-in-arms, Tito, put him in
jail for five years.

But honest allegiance, not just fear, held the regimes together. No
matter how many opportunists joined the party, the true believers were
still there. In 1956, a Czech intellectual pronounced her astonishment
at a writers' conference that the twenty-year-old Václav Havel was talking about "some forgotten poets while socialism was fighting for its life
in the streets of Budapest." Our traveler, Ryszard Kapuściński, did not
need a party pep talk to avoid taking a rickshaw in India in that same
year: "the very idea of sprawling comfortably in a rickshaw pulled by a
hungry, weak waif of a man with one foot already in the grave filled me
with the utmost revulsion, outrage, horror."

In each country of Eastern Europe, the same group of people
thought of themselves as the agents of change—intellectuals, often
calling themselves the intelligentsia, Russian-style: not bookworms or
professionals, or operagoers; more like a self-appointed order, the only
group *that knows*. Eastern Europe was a very educated island. Due to
the Communist version of affirmative action in favor of workers' and
peasants' children, young people were getting college degrees in increasing numbers. With palpable admiration, Anatole Broyard says in
the memoir of his rebellious youth in New York: "There were people
in the Village who had more books than money"—but if the Village
was exceptional, *all* intellectuals of the Eastern bloc had more books
than money and took special pride in the fact.

Each college graduate was a potential samizdat customer. Thanks to
increasing exchanges with the West, samizdat got a sibling—*tamizdat*,
an acronym literally meaning "published *there*." As often as not subsidized by Western governments, small publishers in North America and
Europe began releasing numerous titles in Eastern European languages
to be smuggled into East Berlin, Warsaw, and Moscow: the Bible, Orwell, Solzhenitsyn, Brodsky. The literary front of the cold war was of

paramount importance because banned literature was not just about the misdeeds of communism (Orwell and Solzhenitsyn), but about the open world in general—a tantalizing glimpse of a utopian space of endless opportunities.

The *tamizdat* was part of a successful (though not necessarily perfect) campaign, sometimes referred to as the propaganda war. Most families now had radios, and powerful transmitters placed along the borders of the Eastern bloc brought anti-Communist broadcasts into almost every household, the "anti-Communist" content ranging from news to religious sermons, literary readings, and rock concerts. Suppressed in the East as "decadent," rock was in huge demand—and turned political. Tom Stoppard, a native of Czechoslovakia and a friend of Havel's, in the introduction to his play about Eastern European dissent incidentally named *Rock'n'Roll*, called "the rock'n'roll underground" an "attack on the official culture." The dissident group that would make Havel famous in the seventies, Charter 77, started as a bunch of Czechs protesting the arrest of an underground rock band, the Plastic People of the Universe.

The West, on air 24/7, was winning people over—if not by dissidents' pleas then by the music of Deep Purple and the Rolling Stones. Radio broadcasts were a far cry from the present-day networking power of the Internet, yet they did help the opposition in Eastern Europe to feel connected. A phone call placed by a dissident in Romanian Transylvania to Budapest ultimately reached the headquarters of the Voice of America, the BBC, Radio Free Europe, Deutsche Welle, Vatican Radio, and every obscure partisan station like the Voice of the Andes (a small Christian network supposedly broadcasting from Ecuador). It wasn't a James Bond but a Jamie or Jimmy at the studio who now undermined communism.

By the late 1960s, the Eastern European societies had largely recuperated from the pain of 1956. The young people, who came of age in the times of "vegetarian" communism, were naturally freer of fear than the generation of their parents. Again, by definition freer from want, the young people expected even more goods and services to come their way, as the increased contacts with the West encouraged their pursuit of material comfort. The discontent of the generation that hadn't been exposed to Stalinism was bound to result in a new revolutionary outburst.

It promptly arrived in 1968 in the shape of a short revolutionary cascade in Czechoslovakia and Poland.

———

The Prague Spring began with generational change and ended with bloodshed. In the 1960s, the Czechoslovakian economy performed better than the Soviets' due to a more lenient attitude toward small private businesses and a stronger work ethic. There was no crisis the government could claim to be confronting, yet the top leadership chose to reform. By that time, the party leader, the conservative Antonín Novotný, had been in charge for ten years, and the Central Committee policy makers embodied stagnation, an old-fashioned authoritarian personal style, and lack of creativity. The Czechoslovaks invited the Soviet leader, Leonid Brezhnev, to Prague for consultations.

Brezhnev was no fan of change, but he also didn't like to quarrel. The Czechoslovaks showed him respect and trust, and—though without much enthusiasm—he approved a leadership change in the Czechoslovak Communist Party.

The new leader, Alexander Dubček, was fifteen years younger than Brezhnev—forty-seven in 1968—but no one could say that he was inexperienced. Like Brezhnev, he was a World War II veteran (fighting the Germans in the Slovak underground), went to school in Moscow, and since 1958 had belonged to the top party echelon. Elected first secretary shortly after Brezhnev's visit, in January 1968, and supported by the majority in the Politburo, he set about giving the Czechoslovak economy a jump start. "Decentralization" of the planned economy had been the reformers' mantra all over the Eastern bloc since the late 1950s, and János Kádár of Hungary had already started dismantling the leviathan. But if Kádár was known as an iron fist in a velvet glove, Dubček argued that economic reform would work best when backed up by the freedom of criticism. He was less cynical than Kádár, who was introducing elements of the free market while paying lip service to the Soviet version of Marxism-Leninism. Together with other Czechoslovak reformers, Dubček came up with the concept of "socialism with a human face." The freedoms he bestowed on the Czechs and Slovaks within five months—including freedom of speech and foreign travel—overwhelmed the nation. By early summer, Dubček found himself in the position of Imre Nagy in 1956—the people, particularly younger intellectuals, started demanding more: alternative political parties and withdrawal of Soviet troops.

Unlike in Hungary in 1956, there was no antigovernment violence, and Dubček kept reassuring Brezhnev that things were under control. But rallies in Prague, at which thousands of young people often chanted anti-Soviet slogans, proved they were not. The Czechoslovak reformers did not think of themselves as part of a global revolutionary movement, which in 1968 consisted not just of Vietnam War protests and civil rights riots, but also of Black Panthers, the Chinese Cultural Revolution, Baader-Meinhof terror attacks in Germany, and street fights in Paris. Dubček was a good Communist, not attracted in the least to the radicalism of Mao Zedong or modern-day Trotskyites. But the Prague youth, dying to become part of the open world, seemed energized by the extreme forms of global revolt, and no one could vouch that the nonviolent spirit of the Prague Spring would last. Actively supported by the leaders of East Germany, Poland, and Bulgaria, the Kremlin decided to intervene militarily.

On August 20, Soviet, East German, Polish, and Bulgarian troops invaded Czechoslovakia. Dubček chose to collaborate. The Soviets flew him and other Czechoslovak leaders to Moscow, where they signed a document accepting and justifying the invasion and temporary occupation of their country. When Dubček returned to Prague, he still was first secretary of the Communist Party of Czechoslovakia.

About seventy Czechs and Slovaks were killed in street fights with the occupying force—still nothing compared to the twenty thousand who had died in Hungary in 1956. Devastated, Dubček embarked on a policy of "normalization"—explicitly dismantling the freedoms his earlier reforms had brought. Back from Moscow, he addressed the nation in a radio broadcast. Kieran Williams writes in his analysis of the Prague Spring that Dubček offered people "a deal: in return for their good behavior and cooperation, he and other leaders would arrange the withdrawal of foreign soldiers as soon as possible and continue the basic reform course . . . What made Dubček's speech so effective, however, was the manner in which he spoke: his halting, eggshell voice, minute-long pauses, and sobs conveyed a sense of his own physical and emotional ordeal during the past week, and convinced listeners that he shared their anger and grief."

Yet spontaneous resistance continued. On January 16, 1969, a student, Jan Palach, set himself on fire on Wenceslas Square in Prague and died in a hospital three days later. Within the next four months, two more men committed themselves to self-immolation—but their suicides were not reported in the media.

The event that eventually forced Dubček into retirement was not the Palach crisis, but an ice hockey victory. On March 21, the Czechoslovak team beat the Soviets at the World Championship, and half a million Czechs and Slovaks poured into the streets for a celebration that turned into a countrywide anti-Soviet manifestation, with random acts of violence against the occupiers, such as the sacking of the Aeroflot office in Prague. Livid, Moscow threatened to send more troops. Unable to bear the pressure any longer, Dubček stepped down. The new leader, Gustáv Husák, pursued "normalization" aggressively.

During the months of "normalization," three hundred thousand people left the country. Like in Hungary twelve years earlier, the regime wisely chose to let the malcontent go.

In Poland in 1968, students took to the streets, too, but for the government the crisis did not get out of hand. Young intellectuals did not appeal to the majority of Poles; furthermore, Gomułka cleverly played the anti-Semitic card, blaming unrest on Jewish intellectuals and accusing them of unpatriotic behavior. Jews had long been a scapegoat for the working class all across Eastern Europe and Russia, and the tactic worked one more time. A history of Poland says: "All over the country, orchestrated demonstrations of hatred . . . were staged against 'Zionists' . . . Gomulka next tried to limit the wild anti-Semitism, but the damage was done: up to 20,000 people of Jewish descent, in the main fully assimilated and almost all belonging to the intelligentsia, and some non-Jewish intellectuals were pressured into leaving the country."

With intellectuals marginalized, two years later, in 1970, workers rebelled on their own. The incentive couldn't have been more basic: in December, the government announced price increases on essential foods. But what else could the government do? Not just hospitals and schools, but *museums* had to be maintained. Of course, the timing couldn't have been more ill conceived—ten days before the Christmas feast season. On the fourteenth, protests started in the Lenin Shipyard in Gdansk.

One activist, however, was unwilling to attribute the 1970 rebellion solely to increased food prices, and attempted to paint a broader picture, focusing on the economic innovations that had fomented the laborers' anger. "In the new system," the activist complained, "the worker wasn't simply assigned the job of making a table, for example, but was also required to finish it within a specified period of time. He was no longer being paid for making a table, but for devoting a certain number of work hours to this task."

Deadlines, productivity, costs, time management, competitiveness, efficiency—all that was immaterial to him. On the one hand, this was the cynicism of a person forced to survive in a perverted economic system: you pretend to pay, we pretend to work. On the other, this was the naïve voice of a true child of state communism: from each according to his abilities, to each according to his needs. His name was Lech Wałesa, and accepting his logic of labor-wages dynamics would make Eastern European tables the most expensive in the world.

"Drinking on the job," he continued, "picked up again, and since we were checked at the gates to prevent us from sneaking in alcohol from outside, the men started making it right in the shipyard"—sometimes in places as unlikely as "on the top of construction cranes."

Let's assume someone watched the December 14, 1970, events at the Lenin Shipyard from the top of a construction crane. A hundred feet below, a crowd was heading to the management's offices; the workers walked fast, but to the brewer above their progression seemed relaxed and slow. On reaching the offices, the crowd stopped. From his vantage point, the brewer could see a little head in the window, the director talking to the workers. Soon, the man noticed that the crowd left the shipyard premises, heading (seemingly slowly again) to party headquarters. Even from the top of his crane, he could hear them singing the "Internationale," "Poland Has Not Perished," and "God Protect Poland."

Preoccupied with his potion, the brewer learned the rest of the story only at the end of the day. At party headquarters, the workers, chanting "Give us bread!" (which was an exaggeration totally appropriate in a revolutionary situation), overwhelmed a loudspeaker car and then started roaming the city, clashing with the police and looting. Yes, looting, which is part of every revolution. After Lenin's Red Guards stormed the Winter Palace and discovered the Romanovs' wine cellar, they started breaking bottles and barrels to the point where people began drowning in wine.

The following day the rebels invaded party headquarters and took prisoners. Army units started crawling into downtown Gdansk, but at first they didn't look particularly threatening. Coming across two tanks, a group of workers stuck "mud onto the slits of the tanks, which then advanced blindly some distance before coming to a standstill." But the government troops grew in numbers.

According to Wałesa, "One worker then stepped out of the crowd and spoke to the soldiers. The people behind him couldn't hear what he was saying and pushed closer; it must have looked as if the front rows were advancing. The workers strained to get a better look to make sure the men in uniform were Poles, not Russians in disguise. An officer gave the order to charge; people began to panic; inevitably, a burst of machine gun fire answered the shouts of panicked workers."

Presumably very anti-Russian, the rebels still used the Soviet vernacular to describe their plight. The scenes of the carnage looked "like a film by Eisenstein" (obviously referring to the Odessa Steps sequence from *The Battleship Potemkin*). As for their rebellion, they likened it to the Kronstadt mutiny in Russia in 1921, when revolutionary sailors at the famed naval base demanded "Soviets without Communists." Chastened by the populist anger, Lenin responded to Kronstadt with the New Economic Policy—an attempt at a milder social contract allowing small businesses and cultural diversity. Would an NEP of sorts take root in Poland in 1970?

It would. With forty-five workers killed, Gomułka resigned. The new leader, Edward Gierek, visited Gdansk. He said that he had been a coal miner and understood that the workers had been "provoked beyond endurance." He promised price cuts and wage increases—he would deliver on both—and was well received. The fact that calm was restored so easily suggested that the Polish street was not yet interested in dismantling communism in its entirety, and believed that the utopia could still deliver wages and bread.

The era of stagnation that followed the tumultuous 1960s—under Brezhnev in the Soviet Union, Kádár in Hungary, Husák in Czechoslovakia, Honecker in East Germany, Zhivkov in Bulgaria, and Gierek in Poland—was almost beneficial. Numb after rebellions and crackdowns, the Eastern European societies took a break to rethink their past and formulate agendas for the future.

Václav Havel wrote: "The seventies were bland, boring, and bleak . . . I can't say any longer how 1972, for instance, differed from 1973, or what I did in either of those years." Every person who lived through the seventies between the Oder River and the Pacific couldn't agree more. But even stagnations have a philosophy. The seventies in Eastern Europe are, probably, best described by the dichotomy of *Candide*. If the generation of native idealists still argued that "Everything is connected in a chain of necessity, and has all been arranged for the best," the generation of their children seemed to cling to the final sentence of the novel, "we must cultivate our garden." Havel called the "garden" pole of Candide's dichotomy withdrawal "into a kind of internal exile."

The invasion of Czechoslovakia in 1968 was the last act of Soviet aggression in the Eastern bloc. The era of stagnation made the stick unnecessary, and as for the carrot, Moscow started applying it liberally. The discovery of rich oil and gas fields in Siberia led to the spectacular rise of the energy sector of the Soviet economy, and the USSR quickly became a major exporter. Part of the petrodollar income now began to be used to subsidize Eastern Europe's economies through direct loans; as for oil and gas, Moscow delivered them to Eastern Europe at prices well below the world average.

Soviet economic aid notwithstanding, Eastern Europeans still suspected their nations were getting ripped off. A popular Bulgarian joke: "What is Soviet-Bulgarian friendship? It is a cow that grazes in Bulgaria, but is milked in the Soviet Union." Interestingly, there was a Soviet joke that answered this criticism: Brezhnev commissions his portrait and gets very perplexed when the artist delivers a canvas with him wearing nothing but underwear and having two feminine breasts. "What the hell is that?" Brezhnev asks. "One breast is for Cuba to suck," the artist says, "another for Bulgaria." "Why then keep the underwear on?" "I didn't want to show what the Soviet people get."

Folklore like that suggested something very important about the state of mind in the metropolises of the Eastern bloc. Obviously, the Soviets now regarded Eastern Europeans as people on welfare, and as the Soviet Union's resources were limited, the foreign aid provided by the government for strategic reasons impacted domestic standards of living. Not only did Soviet citizens feel animosity toward Eastern Europe and Cuba, they also deemed the strategic concerns of their own government unwarranted. Attitudes like that indicated that the Soviet grass roots, needing freedom from want just as badly as Poles or Bulgarians, thought domestic living standards—and not empire-building—should come first. Fear still chained them to the Soviet state machine, but the new awareness promised that at some point in the future the empire would lose its foot soldiers.

The Russians were among the hungriest in the Eastern bloc. They always were. Marquis de Custine, 1839 (quoting the owner of a German hotel): "Sir, [the Russians] have two faces. I do not speak of the valets, who have only one; but of the nobles. When they arrive in Europe they have a gay, easy, contented air, like horses set free, or birds let loose from their cages: men, women, the young and the old, are all as happy as schoolboys on a holiday. The same persons when they return have long faces and gloomy looks; their words are few and abrupt; their countenances full of care. I conclude from this, that a country which they quitted with so much joy, and to which they return with so much regret, is a bad country."

The greatest Russian poet of the last fifty years, Joseph Brodsky, wrote in "Spoils of War": "Among flags we preferred the Union Jack; among cigarette brands, Camel; Beefeater among liquors . . . I remember the roar produced by the then newly opened, imported from Lord-knows-where, American-made laundromat in Leningrad when I threw my first blue jeans into a machine. There was joy of recognition in that roar; the entire queue heard it. So with eyes shut let's admit it: we recognized something in the West, in the civilization, as our own: perhaps even more so there than at home."

A visitor to the United States: "New York impressed me tremendously because, more than any other city in the world, it is the fullest expression of our modern age." The visitor's apartment "was equipped with all sorts of conveniences that we Europeans were quite unused to: electric lights, gas cooking-range, bath, telephone, automatic service-elevator, and even a chute for the garbage." Who is talking? Ryszard Kapuściński in 1956? No, this is Leon Trotsky in 1917.

In 1944–45, Eastern Europe saw Ivan, but Ivan saw it, too, to be completely blown away by the beautiful things those people possessed. The spoils of war brought home by fathers in 1945 left an undying imprint on the memory of the sons. Not terribly spectacular in the country of origin, these exotic artifacts took on a luminous quality in the bleak Soviet Union. "It could be a set of binoculars (Zeiss!), or a German U-boat officer's cap with appropriate insignia, or an accordion inlaid with mother-of-pearl, or a sterling-silver cigarette case, a gramophone, or a camera." (The son's narrative here is Brodsky's, again.)

The people of the "metropolis" looked at the "colonies" in awe and envy; countries such as Poland were poor when compared with France, but affluent compared with the USSR. They sat on the periphery of Europe but—unlike the Soviet Union and its predecessor, Russia of the tsars—they *were* Europe. Despite Peter the Great's famous attempt at westernizing his country, Russia spent the next two centuries merely catching up. Meanwhile, Hungary and Poland had *lived* European history.

A trip to Hungary or Czechoslovakia was not a colonizer's weekend trip. It cost two months' salary and had to be approved by a local party committee (KGB "consent," as the security clearance was called, was a separate matter). The party insisted that tourists show respect to their Eastern European hosts, and to pass the exit visa interview, Soviets memorized the names of the heads of state, government, and party of all Eastern European countries, with "Gustáv Husák," "Edward Gierek," "Todor Zhivkov," "Erich Honecker," and a dozen other names growing into row after row after row of prayer beads.

A person could not travel to a "capitalist" country before he had done a trial trip to a "socialist" one. Unsupervised trips to the West were reserved only for older, trusted cadres. And the rules got more absolutist: Do not wear shorts and cork helmets—repeat, shorts and cork helmets (What is it about it that you didn't understand? That's what the British colonizers wear). Do not take rickshaws (again, that's what the British colonizers do). Do not take rides from foreigners. Do not drink alcohol. If in a compartment of a train or in a cabin of a boat you find yourself with a person of the opposite sex, ask to be transferred to a different compartment or cabin (we don't want to hear anything about the homosexual opportunities travel might produce, as there are no homosexuals in the USSR). These regulations lasted through the early 1980s.

One hundred fifty years after de Custine, one still couldn't be sure whether the state would let a person out. Most trains to Eastern Europe crossed the border at a Ukrainian station called Chop, hence a popular saying: "Don't cry 'Hop!' till you've crossed Chop."

Robinson Crusoe is fictional; Alexander Selkirk, Daniel Defoe's inspiration, who spent 1704–1709 on an uninhabited island in the South Pacific, is not. There are different ways to survive a shipwreck. Visiting Selkirk's island three hundred years later, the contemporary travel writer Thurston Clarke wrote with understandable admiration: "He flavored his goat stews with wild turnips, parsnips, and parsley; boiled his lobsters with a native pepper berry; gorged on black plums; sewed together a goatskin cap and coat, using a nail as a needle . . . He entertained himself by carving his name into trees and by singing and dancing with his cats and kid goats." Other men in Selkirk's situation, Clarke adds, reacted differently—hence the "skeletons clutching rusted revolvers" on many a lone island.

Eastern European countries did become castaways, cut off from the West, to which they traditionally belonged or wanted to belong, and not really connected to the Soviet Union because most Eastern Europeans regarded it as inferior culturally and, of course, materially. On visiting Selkirk's lookout on the island, Clarke wrote: "I decided I could have met the physical challenges of clubbing seals, chasing goats, hiking this trail, and lighting signal fires. But could I have made myself climb here every day, and hope?"

All Eastern Europeans did something similar to "clubbing seals" (in their case, overcoming shortages) and hiking difficult trails (bypassing secret-police traps), but Poland seemed to be the only one to climb the cliffs every day, and hope. When other Eastern European nations suffered a defeat, they had nothing to fall back on. The Poles did. To paraphrase Oriana Fallaci, even atheists in the country were Christian atheists. In all other countries of the Eastern bloc, the keepers of national tradition were intellectuals, largely isolated from the people; in Poland, the keepers were priests.

By the mid-1970s, Poland *had* socialism with a human face. No other country in the bloc gave its citizens as much freedom and as many possibilities to vent their anger. But for the government, the task of filling store shelves remained difficult. For the Soviets, a trip to Poland was one big shopping tour, as their expectations were low and their image of the good life rather basic; for the Poles, their material situation looked dismal, since they compared their shelves with those in New York and London. Intent on stocking the shelves with quality goods, Gierek started borrowing heavily. Deeply in debt, he was investing thoughtlessly, and "people were saying that Poland was fast becoming one great construction site. Fiat was building a car plant; Britain's Leyland would be producing a great variety of engines; France's Berliet would produce buses; the German firm Grundig would be supplying us with state-of-the-art electronics." For all intents and purposes, in Poland, the Iron Curtain had become a thing of the past.

Of course, this came with the Kremlin's consent. In the aftermath of World War II, Moscow forbade Eastern Europeans from participating in the Marshall Plan because Stalin rightfully thought that it would pull them into America's orbit. Now, in the seventies, not liking the idea of Polish-Western cooperation at all, the Kremlin still agreed because Gierek's dealings kept Poland reasonably stable. A Polish ambassador to Washington, Romuald Spasowski, testifies: "There was no question that the Soviets had given Poland the role of blazing the trail of economic détente. No other socialist country had intruded itself on the West as Poland had."

In 1972, President Nixon returned to Poland. Henry Kissinger, who personally found Gierek very impressive, wrote: "What drew Nixon there was a combination of nostalgia, domestic politics, and foreign policy. Nixon was nostalgic about Poland because in 1959 it had given him a tumultuous welcome." Nineteen seventy-two was an election year, and in the hope of bolstering his foreign policy agenda, he wanted "to encourage sentiments of national independence in Eastern Europe." The latter formula was a misnomer—the crowds giving Nixon an enthusiastic welcome were already independent from Moscow in all but name.

A few days after Nixon's visit, Fidel Castro descended on Poland. Spasowski remembered: " 'We came to see friends, and what do we see?' asked Castro, straight out in the conference room, his eyes darting in all directions. 'Nixon's been here! An imperialist whose planes are bombing Hanoi! *You had that criminal here.* And I've heard about the welcome he got,' he said, with another defiant look around the room. 'Where's your internationalism?' " Gierek, his chin "trembling with anger," advised the revolutionary to change his tone.

No one will ever know precisely whether Castro was an ideological Communist or simply a rebel wearing a practical (Marxist) costume, but it is obvious that he was a true believer, even if not entirely clear in what. Like a voodoo priest detecting possession, he demanded a chance to purge the demon.

The subject of his exorcism was the students of Kraków. He took the stand in the university square to speak about Poland's future. According to Spasowski, who accompanied Castro on the trip, Castro said:

> "All of capitalism's rotten temptations don't matter to you, the automobiles, the flashy poison!"
> He broke off. There was an angry whistling from the windows, and the crowd on the square had begun to boo.
> "But we do want cars!" shouted a student standing nearby.
> "We want to live like anyone else!"
> Castro was struck dumb.

The revolutionary couldn't go to sleep that night. Followed by his security detail, he started cruising the medieval city in moonlight.

> Castro walked over to an old man sitting on the steps of a building and called over the interpreter.
> "Tell him I'm Fidel Castro."
> The old man did not understand. "Who are you?" he asked.
> "My name is Fidel Castro, and I'm the first secretary and premier of the revolutionary government of Cuba."

The old man still could not make heads or tails of him. "Sorry, never heard of it."

Castro began explaining to him what Cuba was and what revolution was.

The old man heard him out and then rasped, "Cuba? Good, so there's a Cuba. But I'm in Kraków, and we've had it up to here with revolution."

In June 1976, seeing that foreign credit was not enough and that the government desperately needed new sources of revenue, Gierek announced a sharp price increase: sugar went up by 100 percent, milk by 50 percent, sausage by 90 percent. This time, workers' strikes spread all over the country; in the town of Radom the workers ransacked party headquarters and clashed with the police. Within forty-eight hours, the government backed off the price hikes.

In September, a group of intellectuals from the New Left announced the formation of KOR, the Workers' Defense Committee. That's what Lenin did in Russia circa 1900, ushering in a "Workers' Party" to guide the grassroots labor movement. Many years later, a Catholic intellectual wrote, "for the first time intellectuals, students, and farmers joined with the workers who faced police harassment because they were marching for their rights . . . The founders of KOR belonged to different schools of thought. Some were Catholics and some weren't. This showed that people were beginning to cross ideological boundaries and set aside entrenched prejudices in the name of solidarity and the common good."

When a character in Hemingway's *The Sun Also Rises*, a book incredibly popular in Eastern Europe, is asked how he went broke, he answers: in two ways, first gradually and then suddenly. Clearly, in hindsight, we are entitled to exclaim, *here* is the writing on the wall! The problem is, since the wretched Nebuchadnezzar, no one has ever, ever seen the fiery letters. In 1976, we did not see anything, and Western publishers still commissioned books like *The Eastern Bloc in the Year 2000*.

3. The Pope Arms 150 Divisions: 1978–79

In the 1970s, not just Western publishers but pretty much everyone else was sure that communism would last. Military experts prophesied concern over Soviet military growth, their apprehension based on the numbers of Soviet tanks, aircraft, and missiles. Economists emphasized the unsolvable problems of the Communist system but saw no signs of its impending disintegration. People looking at communism from a metaphysical perspective and waiting for a sign from on high did not feel encouraged, either. That was how the future pope, Karol Wojtyla, felt.

His ecclesiastical career was brilliant: a priest at twenty-six, a bishop at thirty-eight, a cardinal at forty-seven. But what was almost certainly more important to him, by the time he reached middle age he had formulated a theodicy, and, despite his stunning smile, everything in his mind had been set in stone. Like Pangloss in *Candide* he accepted that everything was necessary in this best of all possible worlds. In a poem addressed to the "God-Man" he wrote:

I approach you saying, not "Come"
But simply "be."

As we remember, shortly after the war, a young Flemish priest told him in Rome: "The Lord allowed the experience of such an evil as communism to affect you . . . And why did he allow it? We were spared this in the West, because perhaps we could not have withstood so great a trial. You, on the other hand, can take it." The explanation grew on him, and thirty years later he was positive that the Poles were a new chosen people. "When the war was over," he later recalled, "I thought to myself: the Lord God allowed Nazism twelve years of existence, and after twelve years the system collapsed. Evidently this was the limit imposed by Divine Providence upon that sort of folly . . . If communism had survived for longer and if it still had the prospect of further development to come, I thought to myself at the time, there had to be a meaning in all this." "The harm done by fascism or communism," Wojtyla argued, can "somehow enrich us and lead us toward good . . . From this point of view, we in Poland have a contribution to make."

The "contribution" he had in mind had one big precondition: "This will happen if we learn to go beneath the surface, without yielding to the propaganda of the Enlightenment. We managed to resist this in the eighteenth century, and thereby in the course of the nineteenth century we were able to acquire the determination necessary to regain independence after the First World War . . . The *cogito, ergo sum* (I think, therefore I am) radically changed the way of doing philosophy," he complained. "In the pre-Cartesian period, philosophy, that is to say the *cogito*, or rather the *cognosco*, was subordinate to *esse*, which was considered prior." In other words, with the advent of the Enlightenment, God began to be taken out of the equation or "was reduced to an element within human consciousness."

Never mind that managing to resist "the propaganda of the Enlightenment" in the eighteenth century, Poland fell behind its neighbors. Had it allowed as much science as Russia under Catherine the Great, it might not have been dismembered by Russia, Austria, and Prussia and, therefore, there would have been no necessity whatsoever "to regain independence" after World War I—and, with the balance of power in Europe totally different, maybe there would have been no Great War at all.

In Wojtyla's eyes, Poland remained unspoiled by modernity, rationality, the wretched *cogito* (or *cognosco*)—and that made her special, a beacon of spirituality in the mechanical, disenchanted, materialist world. (But what about "But we do want cars!" What about the obsession with foreign travel? What about the blue jeans and Marlboro cigarettes popular with younger priests?)

He lavishly endowed the homeland with all sorts of adjectives suggesting a very vain quality—greatness. Like many Poles, Wojtyla believed that Poland had actually saved Europe and had done so twice: first, in 1241, when, as he put it, it "halted the Mongol invasion" at the Battle of Legnica, and then in 1683, when King Jan III Sobieski "saved Europe from the Ottoman threat at the battle of Vienna" (every other nation in Central and Eastern Europe would strongly disagree on both accounts). Whenever possible, he promoted the homeland's cultural legacy, readily enumerating writers "of genius" like "Adam Mickiewicz, Juliusz Slowacki, Zygmunt Krasinski, Cyprian Norwid"; an "extraordinary genius in several fields," Stanisław Wyspiański; "the great Wojciech Boguslawski"; and so on and so forth.

But much more important, he researched and emphasized a "deep bond between the spiritual and the material, between culture and territory. Territory seized by force from a nation somehow becomes a plea crying out to the 'spirit' of the nation itself. The spirit of the nation awakens, takes on fresh vitality, and struggles to restore the rights of the land." The *cognosco* has crept in the back door: the concept of "nation-state" was not something natural or God-given, but rather a philosophical innovation of the early nineteenth century. Meanwhile, in Poland restoring the "rights of the land" was dangerously explosive: Lithuania, Byelorussia, and Ukraine sat on pre-1939 Polish land, and after 1945 Germany lost land *to* Poland.

In 1978 Wojtyla didn't advertise his idiosyncrasies, doubly cautious as an Eastern European and as a member of a corporation. Appointed bishop in 1958, he got the news in Warsaw and, not particularly liking the capital, a reasonably secular city, walked into an obscure convent and asked to be let alone in the chapel. When after a few hours the nuns started wondering what the handsome priest had been doing there all that time, they found him prostrate on the floor. "My train doesn't leave for Kraków until after midnight," he said. "Please let me stay here. I have a lot to talk about with the Lord." Describing his residence, his secretary would later say, "The chapel was where he would carry on a dialogue with God and listen to what the Lord had to say to him." The secretary added: "He was in love with God. He lived on God."

The Vatican insiders thought he was a Marian—a mystic placing Mary practically as high as Jesus (a "Co-Redemptrix" in the vernacular), the touching but precarious continuation of the pagan tradition of worshipping the Goddess. He cleverly acknowledged the fascination— and he had better, because as a Pole he was suspect. The national shrine, the Jasna Góra Monastery in Częstochowa, was built around the Black Madonna; in 1655, after the invading Swedes failed to take the monastery during a forty-day siege, the then Polish king dedicated his throne and his country to "The Virgin Mary, Queen of Poland"—and that's how she had been known since then. In another shrine, Kalwaria Zebrzydowska, twenty-four chapels commemorated Jesus and twenty-one Mary. Each page of the essays Wojtyla submitted to his teachers in the seminary had an inscription "To Jesus through Mary" or "Jesus, Mary, and Joseph."

He emphasized his awareness of the possible conflict, saying that as a young man he had even tried to distance himself from Mary, feeling that the fixation was taking him away from Jesus until he happened to read an eighteenth-century French theologian who reassured him that devotion to Mary was still properly focused on Christ. Now he would often go to Kalwaria Zebrzydowska and Częstochowa, as he put it, "to hear the Mother's 'heartbeat.'"

He taught philosophy, hiked, skied, and kayaked with young Catholics, wrote and published essays, poems, and plays. The authorized biography says that he continued "to be utterly uninterested in what passed for 'politics' in Poland." What "passed" for politics included the rebellions of 1956, 1968, 1970, and 1976—the cataclysms regulated and eventually smoothed out by Primate Wyszyński.

Wyszyński didn't appreciate Wojtyla's escapism. When death vacated the archbishop's seat in Kraków, Wojtyla was only eighth on the primate's wish list; when Rome made the appointment nevertheless and someone asked what he thought about the new archbishop, Wyszyński responded dryly: "He is a poet."

Wojtyla found himself at Franciszkańska 3, in Kraków, again. His secretary remembered:

The entire archbishop's residence, including the study, the dining room, the parlor, and even the cardinal's bedroom, was bugged; the whole place was "wallpapered" with listening devices. They were in the telephones, of course, but they were also stuck behind the wall coverings, or under the furniture.

We knew perfectly well that electronic ears were eavesdropping on us. Plus, the spies were so incompetent that we couldn't help knowing. A party of workers would just show up without warning and tell us that the telephone was out of order or that there was a problem with the electrical system. That was their ruse for planting the bugs.

The cardinal even made a joke out of it. He would speak in a loud voice to make sure they could really hear, and he would tell them what he wanted them to think. But when he had sensitive conversations, he would leave the residence . . . If foreign bishops came to visit, he would even take them to the mountains.

His car was shadowed, too, and Wojtyla jokingly blessed the agents in the black vehicles, calling them his "guardian angels." Yet his only documented act of defiance was ordaining priests for the persecuted Czechoslovak Church. His secretary remembered:

At night, the seminarians would bravely set out on their risky journey across the border. On the other side, there would be someone waiting to take them to Kraków. The next step after that was the 'recognition.' Every young man had half of the certificate authorizing his ordination, and it had to match up with the other half, which the archbishop would have received in the meantime. Finally, there was the ordination ceremony in the cardinal's private chapel, which would obviously be performed with the utmost discretion. The cardinal would lay hands on the young men and make them ministers of Christ. And then, as soon as it was dark, they would begin the journey home—without knowing what to expect when they got there.

Defiance, yes, but not completely out of line, as he didn't do the same for the persecuted Catholics of the Soviet Union.

According to his spokesman thirty years later, it was very clear to

Wojtyla that around 15 percent of Polish priests, monks, and nuns collaborated with the secret police—though perhaps he didn't know that some of them were his close friends. He never passed harsh judgment on the "collaborators," quietly acknowledging the fact that they operated in a gray area of loyalty and morality. Some handed in purely formal reports worthless to the government, some actually tried manipulating the secret police officers they "worked" for. Surviving communism meant compromising.

The Holy See understood that, too. Under Paul VI, the Vatican diplomat Agostino Casaroli constructed *Ostpolitik*—sort of a "don't touch, don't spread" arrangement: the Communist regimes of Eastern Europe agreed not to purge the clergy as long as they didn't attempt proselytizing or politicking.

Meanwhile, all across the world, the Catholic Church was in turmoil. Liberation theology spread in Latin America, where Che Guevara was a new St. Sebastian. The Luther-like Hans Küng preached against papal infallibility, and the reactionary of the Church, Marcel Lefebvre, against ecumenism and other innovations. But he, Wojtyla, was with the establishment. Received by Pope Paul VI, he brought a gift: a photo album consisting of pictures of tearful ecstatic crowds worshipping the statue of Our Lady of Ludźmierz, known as the Shepherdess of Podhale, an area south of Kraków. The pope, whose pontificate of 1963–78 coincided with the growing secularism worldwide, murmured to his secretary wistfully: "This is Poland. Only there is this possible."

Wojtyla visited Polish communities in America and Canada; he traveled to Australia and the Philippines; he hosted European cardinals in Kraków and befriended a number of Germans, particularly Franz Cardinal König, the archbishop of Vienna. Starting in the 1960s, the two Churches forged a special relationship. Refusing to honor or even recognize the post–World War II territorial reshuffle arranged by the USSR, USA, and Britain in 1945, West Germany didn't acknowledge the new Oder-Neisse border with Poland and, consequently, the legitimacy of Polish authority over Pomerania and Silesia. Relations between Warsaw and Bonn remained very strained, so it came as a shock when in 1965 Polish bishops sent a letter to the German bishops saying, "We extend our hands to you, forgiving you and asking you to forgive us." The

German episcopate responded along the same lines, and that ecclesiastic rapprochement eventually paved the road to reconciliation on the state level. The German clergy had one more reason to like the Polish Church. It was one of the few in Europe not rubbing salt into the German wound over the Holocaust. For Polish bishops, Auschwitz was not about one million Jews, but about a fellow Roman Catholic priest, Maximilian Kolbe, who volunteered to die there instead of a "stranger"—incidentally, a Polish gentile.

Still, in 1978, Wojtyla remained unknown to the global Catholic community, and in Poland, he was the number two clergyman.

Nineteen seventy-eight came to be known among Catholics as the Year of Three Popes. Paul VI died on August 6; the patriarch of Venice, Albino Luciani, who succeeded him under the name of John Paul I, on September 29. Celebrating the funeral mass for John Paul I in Kraków, Wojtyla said: "The whole world, the whole Church, is asking, Why? . . . We do not know what this death means for the See of Peter. We do not know what Christ is trying to tell the Church and the world through this event."

Preparing for a potentially long conclave, he packed a copy of a Marxist philosophical journal, sharing an interest in the field with a number of important contemporaries, including the KGB chairman Yuri Andropov. Together with a group of liberal academics, Andropov planned to update Marxism if one day his Politburo colleagues, who had never touched Marx, voted him into the position of general secretary of the Communist Party of the Soviet Union.

In Rome, Wojtyla paid a visit to a hospital where a friend, Bishop Andrzej Maria Deskur, lay unconscious in an intensive care unit after a stroke. Later, Wojtyla would reveal that the sudden illness "had gotten him worried" because "he had read it as a sign." Reading signs like that had a history. Twenty years earlier, shortly after another friend had lost an arm in a train wreck, Wojtyla was ordained bishop.

On the conclave's eve, Cardinal König asked Wyszyński: "Perhaps Poland could present a candidate?" "My goodness," Wyszyński exclaimed, "you feel *I* should go to Rome? *That* would be a triumph for the communists."

König, who had never particularly liked Wyszyński, was delighted. Wyszyński's remark echoed that of Franco three years earlier, when on his deathbed, hearing the mourners outside chanting "Farewell! Farewell!" the generalissimo asked with great bewilderment: "Where are they going?"

"No, not you," König responded sweetly. "But there is a second . . ."

Wyszyński was appalled. "No, he is too young, he's unknown, he could never be pope."

The conclave opened on October 14, and the first rounds of voting became a gridlock between two Italians, Giuseppe Siri of Genoa and Giovanni Benelli of Florence. With the impasse clear, Cardinal König suggested his candidate. An influential and rich clique, fed up with Italians but unable to nominate one of their own (thirty-three years after the war a German pope was still a joke), still wanted to break with tradition. Of course, the German cardinals were not the only ones who thought that the Italians' monopoly on the papacy should be terminated, and other nationals joined König's agenda. Wojtyla was young. Very close to the Germans, he still didn't belong to any clique. He was white and European, but he came from a suffering and relatively poor country.

On October 16, 1978, he left the conclave a pope. The world was stunned. On the square outside St. Peter's, most people, a witness reported, "don't seem to know who he is. They're silent, dead silent, angry, disappointed. Someone just asked me if the pope was black. No, I said. 'Asiatico?' No, I said. 'Un Polacco.' 'Un *Polacco?*'"

Basically, it was now or never. Standing on the balcony over St. Peter's Square, in the shiny new clothes that didn't really fit, he began in Italian (which was still pretty bad). He seemed to be "very close to tears and he had to grip the railing of the balcony to control himself," yet he made a joke. Then he brought up the Madonna—a no-brainer in Italy. He was also very, very handsome and athletic. To an American in the crowd he looked like a "pro football linebacker." Wisely, he did not ad dress politics in any way. In the end, the square gave him a "huge ovation." The ovation would roll on for almost thirty years.

On hearing the news, Andropov allegedly called the KGB station in Warsaw and snarled, "How could you possibly allow the election of a citizen of a socialist country as pope?" The anecdote might not be true, as Andropov was probably too smart to phrase his reproach in this way, let alone address the criticism to the Warsaw bureau instead of Rome; but the spymaster's concern was genuine. Was it possible that the CIA had put the man into the Vatican? On October 22, at the installation ceremony in St. Peter's Square, the Soviet ambassador to Italy sarcastically told the Polish head of state, Henryk Jabłoński: "The greatest feat of the People's Republic of Poland has been to give the world a Pope."

How many divisions does the pope have?

Poland and the Polish diaspora abroad met the miracle with tears, confusion, and joy. In Washington, the Polish ambassador rushed to the celebratory mass and announced that he was proud to be Polish that day. Legends were created: during the German occupation Wojtyla "was married and lost his wife to Nazi killers shortly afterwards"; he was "taking Jewish families out of the ghettos and providing them with new identities and hiding places." Both accounts were not true, of course, but it didn't really matter to the Poles what Wojtyla in actuality was and whether he had participated in the resistance; whether his love affair had ended in the woman's death or there had been a woman at all; whether he could indeed speak all the languages people said he could or how good a poet and philosopher he was or an actor he had been. All that really mattered was that he was a Pole.

It is difficult for powerful nations to understand what Wojtyla's election meant for Poland. For Poles, Wojtyla's ascension brought infinitely more than international fame, respect, or interest. Since 1795, Poland had been living with the concept of a missing king. Now the king had returned and he was perfect.

Had he been like Paul VI (dry, fragile, and professorial) or Benedict XVI (Gucci, Prada, and emerald crosses), he would probably have made a smaller splash. But he looked down-to-earth, modest, and vigorous. And very Polish.

Until he found a haven at Prince Archbishop Sapieha's palace, he had been a Job. He survived and moved on—a living illustration of the pronouncement from the national anthem, "Poland Has Not Perished."

In principle, becoming a pope and taking a new name, he was expected to shed his birth nationality, so that no ethnic bias would ever interfere with his judgment. He didn't. Making the Curia very angry, he refused to accept any of the drafts of his papal coat-of-arms and started using the arms of an archbishop of Kraków—"a large capital M beneath a cross, representing Mary beneath the cross of Christ."

Then there was the secretary issue. The secretary to the pope is virtually a shadow prime minister. To emphasize the Church's global nature, popes often chose foreigners for the position. John Paul II brought in Stanisław Dziwisz, a boyish-looking priest nineteen years his junior, who had grown up in a village in the area where Wojtyla skied: Zakopane, the Polish Aspen. "The relationship between the two men," George Weigel writes, "is perhaps best described as that which every father wants from a son; love and duty without fear or sycophancy." Another authority calls Dziwisz the pope's "friend and confidant." Maybe. But *another* Pole at the helm?

Wojtyla revitalized the Vatican. The Rome Tourist Council reported record revenues: in the first six months of his pontificate, the pope had attracted five million tourists. What did all these men and women expect to get from the visit? What was there to *tour*, exactly?

One can only guess whether Wojtyla actually had a plan for Poland in October 1978. The government sent him a congratulatory telegram and agreed to broadcast the inaugural mass live, with the president of Poland in attendance. In principle, John Paul could have chosen to capitalize on that recognition and continue with Casaroli's *Ostpolitik*. In the late 1970s, prudence was what defined cold war diplomacy, and both Moscow and Washington swore by the "don't rock the boat" rule. Instead, the new pope chose confrontation with the Communist bloc.

He met with the exiled Josyf Cardinal Slipyj, head of the Greek Catholic Church in Ukraine, a legendary and unyielding anti-Communist and Russophobe. Receiving the Soviet foreign minister, Andrei Gromyko, in the Vatican, the pope meanly told the reporters that the audience had been "the most tiresome" in his few months in Rome. In March 1979, he released his first encyclical, *Redemptor*

Hominis, which, he explained, he had "brought with me from Poland." *The Redeemer of Man* was straightforward: religious freedom was the paramount human right, its curtailment an "attack on man's very dignity." The Church was the "guardian" of human freedom.

Because of Casaroli's politics of appeasement in Eastern Europe, the pope didn't like him, and Casaroli returned the sentiment. But Casaroli was popular, and instead of firing him Wojtyla tied him up with a promotion, making him the secretary of state. The gilded leash worked. Before, a roving ambassador for John XXIII and Paul VI, Casaroli had been the éminence grise of Vatican diplomacy, not even a cardinal. Now, incapacitated by his new formal rank, and finding himself ousted from day-to-day decision-making, the Realpolitik-school diplomat complained: "I would like to help this Pope more, but I find him so different." Following the example of the autocratic nineteenth-century monarchs, John Paul II became his own foreign minister.

On June 2, 1979, Wojtyla knelt at the Warsaw airport and kissed Polish soil—or, rather, socialist concrete. With the Vatican and Warsaw still negotiating the visit, Brezhnev had called Gierek. "Tell the Pope—he's a wise man—he can declare publicly that he can't come due to illness." Gierek said the visit couldn't possibly be cancelled. "Do as you wish," Brezhnev said. "But be careful you don't regret it later."

On the eve of the papal visit, white-and-red (Polish) and white-and-yellow (Vatican) flags hung from the balconies, candles burned in windows day and night, people from out of town poured into the capital. Warsaw gave its native son the biggest homecoming party in history. Three million people—in other words, every tenth person in the country—came to see him. True, Poland is just about the size of New Mexico, but Eastern European roads are brutal and bus schedules ugly, so it could've easily taken an old lady from a nearby town twenty-four hours to travel to Warsaw. Now Andropov got an answer to the proverbial question "How many divisions does the pope have?" Three million equals one hundred fifty.

Many people swore that during the masses, or during the slow progression of the pope's motorcade through Polish cities, Wojtyla had fixed his eyes on them to bless each of the witnesses individually. The nation, calling its victory over Lenin's armies in 1920 the "Miracle on the Vistula," had found a magus. Cardinal König called the pope's visit a "political earthquake," but the pope's secretary, Stanisław Dziwisz, chose to call the atmosphere "almost supernatural." According to him, during a mass celebrated on a square in the center of Warsaw usually reserved for state parades, the pope "practically shouted the prayer to the Holy Spirit, he was sincerely praying, but at that historical moment the invocation also had an obvious relevance to a Poland still living under oppression: 'Send down Your Spirit! Send down Your Spirit! And renew the face of the Earth. Of this Earth!'" Another witness describes the pope's meeting with Polish students:

> As soon as the Pope started speaking, the whole crowd was seized with excitement. And at the end of Wojtyla's speech, his thousands of young listeners, as if on cue, simultaneously raised their little wooden crosses toward him.
>
> At that time, I grasped only the political implications of what was happening. I realized that things had changed, that the rising generations of Poles were by now inoculated against communism, and that before long Poland would be rocked by an earthquake.
>
> But that sea of wooden crosses contained the seeds of something much greater than a popular revolution. They held a "mystery," which I wasn't completely aware of at the time.

At the time of Wojtyla's visit to Poland, the cold war looked tamed. According to Richard Nixon, the person who embodied the Soviet Union in Western eyes, Leonid Brezhnev, was "like a big Irish labor boss." When an aide cautiously said that it was difficult for people on low incomes to get by, Brezhnev responded kindly: "You don't know what life is like. Nobody lives on their wages. I remember in my youth when I was studying at the technical college we earned extra money by unloading freight trains. How did we manage? Three bags or a container would go to them and one to us. That's how everyone lives in this country."

Brezhnev had a good cry at war movies, and he was a collector, swapping watches with foreign guests and expecting presents from them. Knowing his passion, a group of American businessmen at a Kremlin dinner gave him a dog—but since they couldn't bring the dog itself they offered a photograph and a collar. Brezhnev got upset like a child on a disappointing Christmas morning. "Morons . . ." he mumbled. "They don't even know how I hunt . . . Now this dog, this stupid collar . . ."

Unbeknownst to a public still living the cold war myth, in which the USSR and the USA were gridlocked in suspicion and fear, the Kremlin and the White House went far beyond the public face of the détente, reaching an unprecedented level of personal trust and intimacy. On a flight to California, where the Nixon-Brezhnev summit was to take place, Nixon showed the Soviet leader the Grand Canyon, but Brezhnev said he had seen it already in a Chuck Norris movie. Shortly after they landed, Chuck Norris stopped by and gave Brezhnev two Colts. Brezhnev was happy like a child on a good Christmas but asked: "And where are the holsters?" At Camp David, Nixon walked in on Brezhnev and a Soviet flight attendant in flagrante. "Take good care of him," Nixon said to the girl.

In Vienna, signing an arms control treaty, Jimmy Carter embraced the Soviet leader. Brezhnev responded, and the embrace grew into a kiss. "Not my fault!" the terrified Brezhnev whined. "*He* started it!" Carter seconded: "To my surprise, we found ourselves embracing each other warmly in the Soviet fashion." You do not start a nuclear war with a guy like that.

Andropov was close to Brezhnev but he was very different. Orphaned at an early age, he made it through a community college, joined the party, and became an apparatchik. He was ambassador to Hungary during the revolution of 1956, then chaired the Party Central Committee department responsible for socialist countries, and had headed the KGB since 1967. Self-taught, he spoke Hungarian and read English and German. Talking to the people he trusted, he complained that living standards were low and cultural standards even worse, that the schools were horrible and socialist realism in literature stupid. The Soviets *would* have freedom of speech, he said, but first living standards—and, consequently, social awareness—had to go up.

Andropov met with popular poets, scientists, writers, performers; some got his direct phone number. He summoned the literary critic Mikhail Bakhtin, famous for his theory of the carnivalesque, who had been banned from Moscow and Leningrad; Bakhtin was seventy-two and sick, and Andropov ordered his men to bring Bakhtin straight to the Kremlin clinic. He asked modernist sculptors to install abstract pieces at KGB resorts; when Ernst Neizvestny decided to leave the country, Andropov arranged for his sculptures and archives to be safely evacuated abroad, too. Between 1976 and 1980, the KGB sent 347 people to jail for political reasons—a trifle compared to Stalin's or Mao Zedong's purges.

Andropov was anti-Stalin—or so he said. Talking to a detained dissident, he revealed that he himself expected to be arrested in the 1940s and that there would be no resurgence of Stalinism in the USSR (he succeeded in persuading the man to denounce his cause publicly before foreign reporters). He was definitely lenient toward the two most famous critics of the USSR—Alexander Solzhenitsyn and Andrei Sakharov. He admired Solzhenitsyn's earlier writings, finding his later pieces hard to finish (many a reader would sigh knowingly). When in 1974 the Politburo wanted Solzhenitsyn arrested and put on trial, Andropov arranged for him to go into exile instead. A bit later, he did the same for Sakharov. Andropov's old friends—mostly liberal academics—worried about the corruption by power he faced, and he responded with a poem suggesting that it was people who corrupted power.

One of the KGB chairman's unlikely protégés was the songwriter and performer Vladimir Vysotsky. Vysotsky was a cult figure: hippieish hair, bell-bottom jeans, a French wife, substance abuse. Few knew that Andropov admired the rebel and quietly protected him. Also, for Andropov, Vysotsky's lyrics were a barometer of the unofficial—in other words, authentic—public mood. Wojtyla's papacy prompted the creation of a hit, in which Vysotsky, like many other people all over Eastern Europe very excited about the election, sang: "He's Polish, he's Slavic, he's us."

But did Andropov perceive John Paul as an explicit threat to the stability of the Eastern bloc? Or more like a latent danger, a time bomb of sorts? Frankly, in 1978, things didn't look too bad to Andropov. Not too many people were interested in reading *The Gulag Archipelago*; unlike Western fellow travelers, the Soviets had learned Stalin's system the hard way and Solzhenitsyn had nothing to add. They had lived with the knowledge for four decades and never attempted a rebellion. As for samizdat, one of its hits was Orwell—but Tolkien and Mario Puzo, probably, beat him. The KGB did have concerns because now and then young intellectuals formed revisionist Marxist groups, and working-class boys neo-Nazi gangs, and lukewarm, short-lived strikes happened—but overall the USSR hibernated.

———

It is unknown why on March 17, 1979, Brezhnev asked the Politburo to discuss "the circumstances that have emerged in the Democratic Republic of Afghanistan" without him. Perhaps he didn't feel well, but it was also possible that the old man, not as dumb as many thought, wanted to see what the rest of the leadership had to say about the anti-government insurgency flaring in Herat.

Foreign Minister Gromyko informed the meeting that the 17th division of the Afghan army, sent to Herat to "restore order," had "essentially collapsed." An artillery regiment and an infantry regiment had defected to the insurgents' side. "Bands of saboteurs and terrorists," Gromyko continued, "having infiltrated from the territory of Pakistan, trained and armed not only with the participation of Pakistani forces but also of China, the United States of America, and Iran, are committing atrocities in Herat. The insurgents . . . have joined forces with a domestic counter-revolution. The latter especially is comprised of religious fanatics." Earlier in the day, he continued, he had had a conversation with the Afghan foreign minister, Hafizullah Amin. Amin "did not express the slightest alarm about the situation in Afghanistan, and on the contrary, with Olympian tranquility, he said that the situation was not all that complicated, that the army was in control of everything, and so forth." Now the collegium had to decide on a painful issue: whether to send ground troops to Afghanistan.

Send ground troops *where*?

"Now I shall go far and far into the North, playing the Great Game." *Kim*, a novel by Rudyard Kipling romanticizing the Anglo-Russian competition for Central Asia in the nineteenth century, was a favorite among Andropov's officers.

The Russians had not taken much interest in the loose conglomerate of tribes that made up Afghanistan until the 1830s, the start of the Russo-British rivalry over Asia's heartlands, or the Great Game, as the rivalry came to be called. Paradoxically, neither empire really needed Afghanistan, obviously destitute and barely accessible at that point. The conflict was motivated by the desire of each to prevent the other from gaining some advantage: Afghanistan was the borderland between Central Asia, Iran, and India, and common sense suggested that the power controlling it would be able to expand in the three above-mentioned directions.

The two countries spent a fortune in the process, Britain sending in troops, Russia secret service agents and saboteurs. Only in 1907, in a hurry to settle their disputes on the eve of the impending war with Germany, did London and St. Petersburg strike a deal: Britain would control Afghanistan's foreign affairs but not make it part of the British Empire.

The Bolshevik revolution of 1917 proved useful to the Afghans: one guardian, the tsarist government, was gone, and the other, Britain, weakened by the war. Amanullah Khan declared full independence for his nation, sent a diplomatic mission to Moscow, and even asked Lenin for technological assistance. Still, the Afghan people continued to be ruled for the most part by tribal warlords. It wasn't until the 1950s that a program of military cooperation with the Soviet Union was begun, in the hope that a stronger military might give the central government the muscle it needed to challenge the autonomy of the tribal chieftains. By 1973, 50 percent of Afghan officers had been trained in the USSR.

In 1973, an army coup led by a fellow royal, Mohammed Daoud Khan, dislodged the last king. In April 1978, the radical, Marxist wing of the army took over and pledged allegiance to the Soviet Union in return for aid.

Afghan Marxists were not an assembly of lunatics descending on their society like locusts from a KGB vault. Afghanistan had legitimate causes for the attempt at social engineering—extreme poverty, absence of freedom (no matter how you interpret it, Afghanistan had none), and the resulting anger.

The radical party was made of two rival factions—the bigger Khalq and the lesser Parcham. Even before the dust could settle, the Khalq leaders, Nur Taraki and Hafizullah Amin, instituted mass repression—not only against the assumed "counterrevolutionaries," but also against

Parcham. Worried, the Kremlin sent an envoy to Kabul. The choice was telling—Boris Ponomarev, the last Comintern fossil, the Politburo expert on indigenous revolution.

Ponomarev, whose world revolution expertise had started when Hitler was Reichschancellor of Germany, and who, by 1978, had advised at least sixty coups d'état, didn't like what he saw. "The attention of the Afghan leadership," he wrote in the report, "was focused on the fact that in recent times repressions have taken on mass proportions, are being carried out without regard to law, and are directed not only at class enemies of the new regime ("Moslem Brothers," supporters of the monarchy, etc.), but also at persons who could be used for revolutionary interests; that brings out discontent among the populace, undermines the authority of the revolutionary government and leads to the weakening of the new regime." Ponomarev concluded: "Our ideas were attentively heard out, but with visible tension." For all intents and purposes, in 1978 Moscow had no real say in Afghanistan.

Three weeks after Ponomarev's report, Wojtyla was elected pope. Three weeks after that, Andropov, practically inexplicably, got involved in the Afghan mess. Unable to tame the strong (Khalq), Andropov attempted to bring the feud to an end by silencing the weak (Parcham).

Parcham's leader, Babrak Karmal, was in Prague, exiled there as an ambassador. Removed from his post and ordered back to Kabul by the vengeful Taraki and Amin, he asked for political asylum. To Andropov's utmost displeasure, the Czechs, demonstrating a characteristically independent mind, granted it. Now Moscow asked Prague to make sure that Karmal wouldn't "participate in antigovernment activity and is not to incite his supporters to the same."

But the wretched Khalq, high on power, continued the purge. In a matter of months, the brutality led to an insurgency, or "disturbance," as the Politburo chose to call the popular uprising. The center of the "disturbance" lay in the town of Herat. On March 17, 1979, allying with the minister of defense, Dmitri Ustinov, and the foreign minister, Andrei Gromyko, Andropov argued that Soviet ground troops should be sent to Afghanistan to settle the civil war.

The first person to raise objections was the chairman, Andrei Kirilenko. "The question arises, whom will our troops be fighting against if we send them there? Against the insurgents? Or have they been joined by a large number of religious fundamentalists, that is, Muslims, and among them large numbers of ordinary people?"

Prime Minister Aleksei Kosygin—a "tough customer," in Richard Nixon's words, a member of every Soviet cabinet since 1939—asked: "What is the army like in Afghanistan—how many divisions are there?" Ustinov gave the number at ten divisions, one hundred thousand soldiers in all. Gromyko, who had survived forty years in the corridors of power due to his amazing ability to backpedal, immediately said that the situation in Afghanistan was "very unclear." To Andropov's rage, that left the field to the premier.

Kosygin didn't mince his words: "With whom will it be necessary for us to fight in the event it becomes necessary to deploy troops—who will it be that rises against the present leadership of Afghanistan? They are all Mohammedans, people of one belief, and their faith is sufficiently strong that they can close ranks on that basis."

The Afghan "Mohammedans," in the old-fashioned Kosygin's manner of speech, hadn't earned their reputation for nothing. In 1842, they decimated the British force of sixteen thousand in a matter of seven days, with just one person reaching Jalalabad to tell the tale.

But Andropov played deaf. The "political decision," he said, had to be "immediately prepared, because bands are streaming in from Pakistan." Ponomarev suggested a compromise: "We should send around five hundred persons into Afghanistan in the capacity of advisors and specialists." Annoyed, Andropov barked: "Around Herat there are twenty thousand civilians who have taken part in the rebellion. As far as negotiations with Taraki are concerned, we must get on with it. But I think it is best for Comrade Kosygin to speak with Taraki."

Here the transcript of the Politburo session records a Greek chorus: "ALL. Agreed. It is better for Comrade Kosygin to speak with him."

Then Andropov said something very strange: "We must finalize the political statement, bearing in mind that we will be labeled as an aggressor, but that in spite of that, under no circumstances can we lose Afghanistan."

What *were* Andropov's motives? Afghanistan was not on the Soviet foreign policy agenda, but he was stubbornly putting it there, clearly jeopardizing détente, the Soviet-American thaw and all the stability of the tamed cold war (remember that kiss between Carter and Brezhnev).

Was it nation-building and proselytizing? Kipling:

> *Take up the White Man's burden—*
> *Send forth the best ye breed—*
> *Go, bind your sons to exile*
> *To serve your captives' need;*
> *To wait, in heavy harness,*
> *On fluttered folk and wild—*
> *Your new-caught sullen peoples,*
> *Half devil and half child.*

Was it the Great Game? But against *whom*? The list of involved countries Andropov and his (wavering) allies came up with on March 17 (United States, China, Pakistan, Iran) suggested not Realpolitik, but, rather, Kafka's "The Burrow": Step One: "I have completed the construction of my burrow and it seems to be successful." Step Two: "But I am growing old; I am not as strong as many others, and my enemies are countless." Step Three: "An almost inaudible whistling noise that wakened me." Step Four: "The thing to do, really to do now, would be to go carefully over the burrow and consider every possible means of defending it."

On March 18, the Politburo session resumed, again chaired by Kirilenko. One more time, Brezhnev wisely passed. As agreed the day before, Kosygin had talked to Taraki, and now the premier sounded plainly enraged. Only twenty-four hours earlier, Taraki had reacted to the situation in Herat "with Olympian calm"; now he was saying that if "the Soviet Union does not lend its assistance at this time, we will not hold out . . . If Herat falls, then it is considered that the matter is finished." He said the regime needed "reinforcements in the form of tanks and armored cars for the infantry." When Kosygin asked, "Will you be able to muster enough tank crews to place the tanks into action?" Taraki "responded that they have no tank crews, and therefore he requested that we dispatch Tajiks to serve as crews for tanks and armored cars, dressed in Afghan uniforms, and send them here." When Kosygin asked, "Would it really be impossible for you to form part of a division from the population of Kabul to assist the various provinces, to equip them and, in like fashion, to arm them?" Taraki answered "that there was nobody to train them." "I then said to him, how is it possible, given how many people were trained in the military academies in the Soviet Union, given how many of the old military cadres have come out on the side of the government, that there is now nobody to do the training? How then, I asked him, can we support you? Almost without realizing it, Comrade Taraki responded that almost nobody does support the government."

The minister of defense: "What is the problem? Why is this happening? The problem is that the leadership of Afghanistan did not sufficiently appreciate the role of Islamic fundamentalists. It is under the banner of Islam that the soldiers are turning against the government, and an absolute majority, perhaps only with rare exceptions, are believers." The foreign minister: "The army there is unreliable. Thus our army, when it arrives in Afghanistan, will be the aggressor. Against whom will it fight? Against the Afghan people first of all, and it will have to shoot at them . . . And all that we have done in recent years with such effort in terms of detente, arms reduction, and much more— all that would be thrown back. China, of course, would be given a nice present. All the nonaligned countries will be against us. In a word, serious consequences are to be expected from such an action . . . One must ask, and what would we gain? Afghanistan with its present government, with a backward economy, with inconsequential weight in international affairs. On the other side, we must keep in mind that from a legal point of view too we would not be justified in sending troops. According to the UN Charter a country can appeal for assistance, and we could send troops, in case it is subject to external aggression. Afghanistan has not been subject to any aggression. This is its internal affair, a revolutionary internal conflict, a battle of one group of the population against another. Incidentally, the Afghans haven't officially addressed us on bringing in troops." Even Andropov reluctantly echoed the ambivalence: "The economy is backward, the Islamic religion predominates, and nearly all of the rural population is illiterate. We know Lenin's teaching about a revolutionary situation. Whatever situation we are talking about in Afghanistan, it is not that type of situation."

But in his heart, the KGB chairman hadn't recanted.

On March 19, Brezhnev attended and chaired the committee meeting. He pronounced "all of the measures that have been adopted in the course of Saturday and Sunday, in my view, are entirely correct. The question was raised as to the immediate participation of our troops in the conflict that has arisen in Afghanistan. In my view the Politburo has correctly determined that the time is not right for us to become entangled in that war." The next day, Brezhnev continued, Taraki would be brought to Moscow; he and Kosygin would talk to him.

On March 22, Brezhnev reported: "Comrade Taraki arrived in Moscow in a somewhat excited condition, but during the discussions he gradually cheered up and towards the end he behaved calmly and sensibly. In my conversation with Comrade Taraki I said that the main thing now is political work among the masses and with particular stress I repeated this . . . I directly said to Comrade Taraki that repressions are a sharp weapon and it must be applied extremely and extremely [*sic*] cautiously, and only in the case when there are serious legal grounds for it . . . At the same time it was directly declared that we consider the introduction of Soviet military detachments inexpedient, insofar as in the current situation this would only play into the hands of our common enemy."

Throughout the next several months, the party line on Afghanistan did not change. Then, in September, Hafizullah Amin killed Taraki and things started to change quickly. On December 1, 1979, Andropov sent a personal letter to Brezhnev.

> 1. After the coup and the murder of Taraki in September of this year, the situation in Afghanistan began to take an undesirable turn for us. The situation in the party, the army and the government apparatus has become more acute, as they were essentially destroyed as a result of the mass repressions carried out by Amin.
>
> At the same time, alarming information started to arrive about Amin's secret activities, forewarning of a possible political shift to the West. [These included:] Contacts with an American agent about issues which are kept secret from us. Promises to tribal leaders to shift away from the USSR and to adopt a "policy of neutrality." Closed meetings

in which attacks were made against Soviet policy and the activities of our specialists. The practical removal of our headquarters in Kabul, etc. The diplomatic circles in Kabul are widely talking of Amin's differences with Moscow and his possible anti-Soviet steps.

All this has created, on the one hand, the danger of losing the gains made by the April [1978] revolution (the scale of insurgent attacks will increase by spring) within the country, while on the other hand, the threat to our positions in Afghanistan (right now there is no guarantee that Amin, in order to protect his personal power, will not shift to the West). [There has been] a growth of anti-Soviet sentiments within the population.

2. Recently we were contacted by group of Afghan communists abroad. In the course of our contact with Babrak [Karmal] and [Asadullah] Sarwari, it became clear (and they informed us of this) that they have worked out a plan for opposing Amin and creating new party and state organs. But Amin, as a preventive measure, has begun mass arrests of "suspect persons" (three hundred people have been shot).

In these conditions, Babrak and Sarwari, without changing their plans of opposition, have raised the question of possible assistance, in case of need, including military.

We have two battalions stationed in Kabul and there is the capability of rendering such assistance. It appears that this is entirely sufficient for a successful operation. But, as a precautionary measure in the event of unforeseen complications, it would be wise to have a military group close to the border. In case of the deployment of military forces we could at the same time decide various questions pertaining to the liquidation of gangs.

The implementation of the given operation would allow us to decide the question of defending the gains of the April revolution, establishing Leninist principles in the party and state leadership of Afghanistan, and securing our positions in this country.

Had the plan been limited to those two battalions, and the plot to surround the palace, remove the despot, and establish a regime friendly to the Soviet Union, it is unlikely that the West would have done more than raise a protest at the United Nations. But within the Kremlin walls, Andropov made clear that he had in mind something more than a good-neighbor policy.

On December 10, the Politburo approved war. The only voice of dissent came from a guest, a professional soldier, Chief of General Staff Marshal Nikolai Ogarkov: "We will reestablish the entire eastern Islamism against us, and we will lose politically in the entire world." Andropov cut him off: "Stick to military affairs." "But I am Chief of the General Staff!" "No more."

That was barely nine months after the old men of the Kremlin had come up with a totally sound, and prescient, assessment of the situation in Afghanistan: "Their army is falling apart, and we are supposed to wage the war for them" (Brezhnev); "To deploy our troops would mean to wage war against the people, to crush the people, to shoot at the people. We will look like aggressors, and we cannot permit that to occur" (Andropov); "Our army, when it arrives in Afghanistan, will be the aggressor. Against whom will it fight? Against the Afghan people first of all, and it will have to shoot at them" (Gromyko).

These judgments were forgotten by December, and the troops went in on Christmas Eve to kill Amin and establish a new government in Kabul without great difficulty. Andropov, not Minister of Defense Ustinov, stayed up all night in Moscow, talking to the KGB generals in the field. In a matter of months, though, the little victorious war turned into a quagmire.

Kipling:

When you're wounded and left on Afghanistan's plains,
And the women come out to cut up what remains,
Jest roll to your rifle and blow out your brains
  An' go to your Gawd like a soldier.

No matter how "decisive" a Soviet battle victory, no matter how many towns the Soviets occupied, no matter how heavy the Afghan battlefield casualties, or how many Afghan leaders the Soviets managed to capture, imprison, or execute, the will to resist could not be crushed. Nor did the ranks of the resistance shrink. Just as Ogarkov predicted, the specter of a modern Christian/European crusade brought volunteers streaming into Afghanistan from all over the Muslim world.

Not all the supporters of the Afghan cause were Muslims. Among those committed to helping the Afghans throw out the invaders was President Jimmy Carter, who decided to support the "god-fearing Mujahideen" against the "godless Communists." A number of U.S.-run centers in Pakistan and elsewhere taught guerrilla warfare skills to Islamic fighters, one of whom was Osama bin Laden.

Afghanistan was the worst mistake the Soviets had ever made.

Kipling, again:

I could not dig: I dared not rob:
Therefore I lied to please the mob.
Now all my lies are proved untrue
And I must face the men I slew.
What tale shall serve me here among
Mine angry and defrauded young?

It's a safe bet to say that the mujahideen had never heard of Poland. Yet the Afghan war cloud shed its cinder there. By the time Soviet casualties in Afghanistan hit two thousand, in the summer of 1980, strikes began in Gdansk.

Part Two

1980–1988

4. The Working Class Strikes: 1980–81

On August 14, 1980, an electrician named Lech Wałesa climbed over a twelve-foot-high fence at the Lenin Shipyard in the city of Gdansk to lead seventeen thousand workers in a strike.

A physical man, who projected an imposing strength, Walesa was at his best when acting tough—a quality born out of a difficult life. He grew up in a house on the marshlands that neighbors avoided, "deeming it too dreadful to live on," and the "surrounding grayness" was interrupted only by mallows "up against the walls of the house, creating in our young eyes an illusion of abundance and profusion, of vigorous life" (the latter metaphor strikingly reminiscent of the opening of Tolstoy's *Hadji Murad*). After vocational school, he began work at the Lenin Shipyard, an enterprise that contributed to the national budget significantly but refused to provide showers for the workers or dryers for their clothes. No matter what, Wałesa refused to feel a victim. During the 1970 riots, finding himself locked up in a building by the police, he forced the doors with a wrench.

Wałesa's ascension to influence and, eventually, power in August 1980 was unexpected and difficult to explain: he was like Meursault in Albert Camus's *The Stranger*, who, when asked why he shot dead an Arab on the beach, answers: Because of the sun. That summer day, this charismatic man walked, or rather climbed, straight into history.

On July 2, the government raised prices on food, knowing only too well that labor unrest might follow. And it promptly did—in the city of Lublin, where train operators blocked communications with the USSR. The Polish Politburo acted quickly, and while the Lublin strike was settled, the unrest was far from over. A few weeks later, a crane operator and labor activist at the Lenin Shipyard, Anna Walentynowicz, visited a cemetery.

Walentynowicz cleaned the tombs of workers killed during the 1970 riots. She collected the old candles and melted the remains into new ones, not out of some exceptional frugality but because now the old wax had a kind of talismanic significance. Jumpy in the aftermath of the Lublin strike, the shipyard management accused her of stealing and fired her. A week later, the strike began: the Lenin Shipyard workers asked for a monument to the 1970 victims, reinstatement of Walentynowicz, and a pay raise.

Walentynowicz's name would be forgotten. It was a man, Wałesa, who laid claim to this historic moment. He was careful to emphasize his legacy: participation in the protests of 1970 and 1976, arrests, blacklisting. Prior to the 1980 strike, he said, "We began to draw up a plan of action in which all the various groups would find their place." Before he climbed the fence, a meeting of activists decided that he would become the "ringleader."

The news spread along the coast, other facilities joined in, and on August 16 the Interfactory Strike Committee, with Wałesa its leader, was born. In a matter of days, the workers started demanding independent trade unions.

It is still not clear how to explain the snowball phenomenon, but by August 21 most of Polish industry was paralyzed by strikes. Polish farmers were the most powerful in Eastern Europe, producing 93 percent of the eggs, 90 percent of the potatoes, 85 percent of the milk, and 73 percent of the cattle. If they went on strike, the Polish economy would collapse.

Clearly, in August 1980 there *was* a revolutionary situation in Poland. Structurally, though not ideologically, it echoed the *Communist Manifesto*: the lower classes were alienated from the means—and fruits—of production; the upper class was ineffective, weak, and disunited; a revolutionary class was ready to step in. As Ronald Reagan famously put it in his speech at the House of Commons in June 1982: "In an ironic sense Karl Marx was right. We are witnessing today a great revolutionary crisis, a crisis where the demands of the economic order are conflicting directly with those of the political order."

But the crisis still had to find a resolution; for that, a revolutionary party was needed, and Poland didn't really have one. The spontaneous Interfactory Strike Committee was a political toddler. The establishment of KOR had been of paramount significance because it was the first group in the Eastern bloc that attempted to organize the working class as a classical twentieth-century revolutionary party would have. But KOR was secular and occasionally anticlerical, like most twentieth-century revolutionary groups founded by intellectuals—and that was a handicap in an unmodernly religious country, Poland. Wałesa, meanwhile, was proudly Catholic and intended to marry faith and politics.

Very likely, that's why from day one Wałesa was the face of the Gdansk strike, commanding the admiration of the Polish working class. The mass that he and his confessor, Father Henryk Jankowski, planned for six thousand workers at the Lenin Shipyard was to resemble a mystery play. In front of journalists and cameramen, Father Jankowski blessed Wałesa, and the new leader carried a big wooden cross to the site chosen for the monument to the 1970 martyrs. The image of the Black Madonna was on the shipyard's gates. Andrzej Wajda, the world-famous Polish movie director, later remarked: "Wałesa speaks with the voice of the dead." Indeed, at its beginning, the working-class movement set the scene as a Calvary—not a Storming of the Bastille. The message it conveyed was that the riot had been about divine justice and that, until justice was done, measures such as pay raises or independent trade unions would not extinguish it. In a way, the fact that the strikers hadn't yet come up with a coherent set of demands made their case stronger: open-ended, the August 1980 drama could have possibly meant a total rejection of communism as a system.

For a movement like that, the participation of the Church as a national uniting force was imperative—but it hadn't yet assumed this role. Everyone in Poland was on hold. Everyone waited to hear what the pope had to say.

Years later, John Paul II would repeat, chuckling, that he had *not* brought down communism "single-handedly," therefore admitting and, maybe, hinting at the possibility that he actually had. But his initial reaction to the Polish revolution was guarded. In August 1980, he was in Castel Gandolfo, the papal summer residence outside Rome. Often called the best-informed person in the world and surely the one who longed most for change in Poland, he now, inexplicably, postponed his response. The Communist authorities could send tanks to Gdansk—like they had in 1970; the Soviets could order their troops out of the bases in Poland and into the streets. The nascent movement, which had a leader but not a program or structure, had to capitalize on the momentum or the people's enthusiasm would start to flag. It was now or never. But the pope procrastinated.

With the pope incommunicado, Primate Wyszyński was only too glad to signal that though the Church was sympathetic to the workers, it was not necessarily on their side. In a sermon on August 17, he talked about "workers who are striving for social, moral, economic, and cultural rights," but also about the necessity of "calm and reason."

There was no immediate response from Castel Gandolfo. Only a handful of people knew what the pope was waiting for: his secretary, Stanisław Dziwisz, to come back from vacation—in Poland. No hard evidence confirms a cross-and-dagger conspiracy theory and, of course, August was the best time of year for a pope's secretary to take a break because Vatican business was at its slowest; oppressed by a lingering heat wave, the Romans shielded their windows with shutters and, if they could, left the city. Then what? Did the pope trust his secretary more than anyone else and would he have rather believed his account than the information the Vatican and the Polish Church provided? He well might have. John Paul was authoritarian, and people like that prefer private dealings to public institutions they actually control.

Only when Father Dziwisz returned to Italy did John Paul address a Polish audience in the Vatican. According to Dziwisz, he found the pope very excited about the TV pictures of the Gdansk workers kneeling on the pavement in front of the image of the Black Madonna that hung on the shipyard's gates. "Maybe the moment has come!" the pope said. In the Vatican, he said two prayers ("regarding the news which has come from Poland") to the Virgin, whom he, following his homeland tradition, addressed as the Queen of Poland; one of the prayers was specifically directed to a magical piece of wood: the Black Madonna. The pope sent a message to Wyszyński commanding the Polish Church to "aid the nation in its struggle for daily bread."

But Wyszyński was stubborn. He was positive the pope was making a mistake in judgment and was romanticizing the rebels. On August 26, Black Madonna day, at her shrine in Częstochowa, the primate declared that Polish workers were notorious for poor productivity and emphasized that everyone—not just the state—was responsible for the economic collapse. But the next day, the pope publicly defended the strikers, and Wyszyński angrily backed off.

The government was overwhelmed and started negotiating with the rebels. The Kremlin panicked. On August 28, Minister of Defense Ustinov, actively backed by Andropov, presented the Politburo with the worst-case scenario.

The strike movement is operating on a countrywide scale.

Taking account of the emerging situation, the Ministry of Defense requests permission, in the first instance, to bring three tank divisions (1 in the Baltic M[ilitary]D[istrict], 2 in the Beloruss[ian] MD) and one mechanized rifle division (Transcarp[athian] MD) up to full combat readiness as of 6:00 p.m. on 29 August to form a group of forces in case military assistance is provided to the PPR [Polish People's Republic].

To fill out these divisions, it will be necessary to requisition from the national economy up to 25,000 military reservists and 6,000 vehicles, including 3,000 to replace the vehicles taken from these troops to help out with the harvest. Without the extra vehicles, the divisions cannot bring their mobile reserves up to full readiness. The necessity to fill out the divisions at the expense of resources from the national economy arises because they are maintained at a reduced level in peacetime. The successful fulfillment of tasks during the entry of these divisions into the territory of the PPR requires combat arrangements to be established some 5–7 days in advance.

If the situation in Poland deteriorates further, we will also have to fill out the constantly ready divisions of the Baltic, Belorussian, and Transcarpathian Military Districts up to wartime level. If the main forces of the Polish Army go over to the side of the counterrevolutionary forces, we must increase the group of our own forces by another 5–7 divisions. To these ends, the Ministry of Defense should be permitted to plan the call-up of as many as 75,000 additional military reservists and 9,000 additional vehicles.

In this case, it would mean that a total of up to 100,000 military reservists and 15,000 vehicles would have to be requisitioned from the national economy.

The document sounded ominous, but it wasn't, really. Unlike Poland, the Soviet Union did not have private farming, and at the end of the summer the army, students, and workers went to the countryside to "help out with the harvest." To take fifteen thousand vehicles from that forced labor pool would mean huge food shortages in the cities. Colossi can get around on feet of clay, but they can't walk on an empty stomach.

Undisturbed by Moscow, the two sides signed an agreement on August 31. Wałesa used a souvenir pen with a picture of the pope acquired during John Paul's June 1979 visit. The five hundred days of dual power in Poland began.

────────

Here we come across an ironic parallel to Lenin's revolution. Dual power—that's how he correctly defined the political regime of Russia between the antimonarchy revolution of February 1917 and his own of October later that year. Dual power—the Provisional Government versus the Soviets of Workers', Soldiers', and Peasants' Deputies, the grassroots bodies of self-government created by the people and then infiltrated, manipulated, and eventually abused by V. I. Lenin. In Poland in 1980, we have the Communist government, looking more and more provisional every day, and the grassroots labor movement yet unbridled by any established political force.

The August 31 agreement legalized independent trade unions but did little else. A few days later, Gierek stepped down to be followed by a dull apparatchik, Stanisław Kania, but that was not the real news. The real news was that the unions formed a national body, called Solidarity, and Wałesa was its symbol and leader. Solidarity's program: "History has taught us that there is no bread without freedom."

This was not the end but just the beginning. Freedom, anger, and empty store shelves pretty much summarized the rebels' agenda, but this was just an *agenda*, not a solution. So what to do about central planning? Private property? Free elections? Soviet troops on Polish territory? Did the rebels realize that things such as affirmative action for the working class, women's rights, and welfare were going to dissolve as soon as they rewrote the rules?

The result was immense confusion. Poland began freewheeling; it was not exactly clear who actually ran Solidarity, but it was obvious that Solidarity was not a political party.

Wałesa had become Solidarity's face, and this helped attract many to the movement. Not just working-class, he *looked* working-class. Short-tempered, a blunt speaker, proudly uncultured, he was as grassroots as grassroots gets. Where an intellectual would've blushed, Wałesa grinned. He had six children, and once, when asked at a meeting, "Are all the children yours?" answered: "My wife always tells me that they are mine." His dress code was equally pedestrian, as he felt most comfortable "in a sweater, a denim jacket and corduroy trousers." He was poor. The family used to share two small rooms, but after the August strike the government gave him a new apartment—or, rather, one flat made of three small ones: six rooms, two kitchens, and two bathrooms.

Within days of the August agreement, a cult of personality formed around Wałesa. Like the pope, he was seen as a saint. Hagiographic sketches, memoirs, and pictures flooded the opposition media. People wrote to him, calling him a "spokesman for the Catholics in Poland," a "Great National Hero," and even a "Sign of the Times."

The émigré Polish poet Czeslaw Milosz, living in the United States, won the Nobel Prize because the politicized Nobel Committee felt obliged to encourage the Polish revolution. Visiting Gdansk, Milosz said, "What I feel for Lech Wałesa and the shipyard workers can be expressed in one word—gratitude." To prove this, he wrote several poems to or for Solidarity.

The people who didn't appreciate Wałesa in the West were intellectuals, for whom anticlericalism was a natural element of any rebellion. Seeing him with a rosary on television, Luis Buñuel scowled, "No, this is improbable. How can a workers' leader be religious? This is a contradiction in itself."

Exactly. But contradictions like that were what made the Polish revolution happen. All previous Polish revolts (1956, 1968, 1970, 1976) had been secular and materialistic. The imagery of 1980 revolved around the Cross, the Rosary, and the Black Madonna. Paradoxically, it was very close to the Latin American liberation theology that John Paul II fiercely condemned: the gun and the cross, the prayer and the insurgency, the Virgin Mary on the barricades. Now the whole of Poland knew that Wałesa started his day with a 7:30 mass. He said, "I am an ordinary worm on this earth. Don't provide me with glory." He told a foreign journalist that between the ages of seventeen and nineteen he had lost God and started partying and dating. "And then something happened: one day I had a cold, was very tired and I looked for a place to sit down. And as there was no such place nearby except a church, I entered the church. I sat there on a bench—it was warm—and at once I felt so well that I've quite changed since." In all difficult times, he said, he commended himself to the Virgin Mary. "Faith is something very private to me. My relaxation. When I sigh a little, I don't fear heart failure. Perhaps it is like yoga for other people."

Much earlier, describing the abortive revolution of 1848 in Vienna, Trotsky wrote that the Viennese handed the "'dictatorship' of the street" over to students, who, Trotsky continued, practiced "a classically clear form of benevolent revolutionary dictatorship *over* the proletariat." The expression is noteworthy: "benevolent revolutionary dictatorship" over the masses is precisely what all grandmasters of the revolution, from Robespierre to Castro, exercised; at a certain point, just as Trotsky claims, the masses always hand over the "dictatorship of the street" to someone. In the fall of 1980, Solidarity (if not Wałesa personally) suddenly found itself in possession of the "dictatorship of the street," which had been simply handed over to it.

Lenin had formulated a workable revolutionary mantra: the revolutionary party (led by a small group of determined individuals) should be able to recognize the revolutionary situation when it sees one and strike precisely at that time. "No government," he sensibly argued, "would fall, unless dropped." In October 1917, while other people in the leadership (including Trotsky) procrastinated, Lenin ordered the Red Guard into the streets with the famous instruction to capture "the post office, the telegraph and all the bridges." Thirty-six hours later, the government fell.

And was this the moment in Poland? In the fall of 1980, the Polish regime was paralyzed, but, certainly, First Party Secretary Kania was not going to call Wałesa and say, "We concede." The government did not do anything to either crush the revolution or reform itself, as if it had lost its legitimacy internally and knew its time was up. Dual power wasn't an effort at reform or a deliberate compromise, but merely the state of affairs that had developed and that, certainly, couldn't be permanent or even lasting. The government seemed to be whispering, "Why not drop us *now*?"—but the whisper was not registered by Solidarity. The problem was that it didn't have a plan. Wałesa was good at jumping walls in the riskiest situation of all, and now the whole of Poland depended upon his instinct, not wisdom. When the KOR people tried getting Wałesa to read books on sociology and economics, he brushed them off, saying that he was not interested in theory.

The primate, the legendary Wyszyński, was not wild about Solidarity and even less so about Wałesa. He summoned the Great National Hero to Warsaw for a sit-down and said, "It's not a question of wanting to change the leaders, it's they who must change. We must make sure—and I make this comparison quite deliberately—that one gang of robbers doesn't steal the keys of the state treasury from another similar gang. What is at stake is the rebirth of man himself."

Both clusters—the Church and KOR—were not unlike socialists in Russia in March 1917, shocked by the sudden outburst of a mass movement they had been predicting and cultivating for years, wanting to ride it *now*, but not knowing exactly *how*. The Church was even divided into Mensheviks (Wyszyński) and Bolsheviks (the pope). Interestingly, Wałesa and the pope did not connect directly, though Wałesa desperately wanted to. The pope withheld his endorsement, obviously not sure whether Wałesa was the right person to take Poland through the historic change.

On December 7, Carter's national security advisor, Zbigniew Brzezinski, called the pope in the Vatican to tell him that for the past three days Warsaw Pact troops had been standing in full combat order along the Polish borders. At this time, Brzezinski stood for a lame-duck outgoing administration, the president-elect, Ronald Reagan, to be sworn in in about six weeks. Yet President Carter shared his concerns and called the Kremlin, threatening more sanctions against the USSR if the Soviets invaded.

The pope wrote a letter to Brezhnev asking for mercy. Poland was "the first victim of an aggression" in 1939 and went through "the terrible period of occupation." "The destructive fury of the conflict cost Poland the loss of nearly six million of its sons: that is to say, a fifth of its population before the war." He also reminded Brezhnev, a World War II veteran himself, that "the Poles remained side-by-side with their allies" during the entire conflict. "I am confident," the pope said, "that you will do everything you can in order to dispel the actual tension, in order that political public opinion may be reassured about such a delicate and urgent problem."

In 1980, the USSR still looked formidable, its ultimate decay, hastened by the war in Afghanistan, overlooked by most people, including old Russia hands like Brzezinski. Outraged and frightened by the revolution unfolding in Poland, the Kremlin still relied on the Polish Communists to deal with the crisis. Yet, disbelieving the Kremlin's public (but this time true) stand that Solidarity was a domestic Polish political issue and that the USSR would not interfere, the pope decided to reinforce the Poles' will to fight. He *would* see Wałesa.

Technically, Wałesa's January 1981 visit to Rome was sponsored by the three trade unions led, respectively, by Christians, Socialists, and Communists, and at the meetings, the "Bandera Rossa" and the "Internationale" mixed with religious hymns. In Italy and in the West in general, no one knew yet what to make of Wałesa or Solidarity.

Wałesa and his family stayed at the Polish Pilgrim's House in the suburbs; from there they took a bus to the Vatican to meet with the pope. Wałesa dressed up for the occasion. The suit did not look right on him, but he wore a Marian password: the Black Madonna badge.

The meeting was brief but crucial. The pope had officially recognized Solidarity. More international recognition was to follow. Wałesa went to Sweden to pick up a minor peace prize (not a Nobel yet), then to Japan. There, something very meaningful happened. Annoyed by what he called the "railway timetable" of the visit—planned down to every minute—and the pronounced Japanese love for Chopin's music and Wajda's films, which he found affected, Walesa struck back. He said that the Japanese mind-set was "misconceived" and that their rights were being "trampled by progress" and the "invasion of the home by computers." They lived in a "relentless rat race," he concluded. At a reception given by the largest trade union, he took a pair of scissors and cut off the tie of the union's secretary general. The press left with the impression that the Polish bear was not much different from the Russian one: not nice.

In Japan, Walesa heard the news about the attempt on the pope's life. He was in a hotel room in Nagasaki, and the first reports proclaimed that the pope was dead. "I was overcome by a feeling of immense loneliness," he wrote; "the whole world seemed to have turned upside down; with our lodestar gone, some of us were wandering in a wilderness without hope."

The Japanese "reacted promptly, strengthening the measures for our protection, which were already rigorous. I was given an additional bodyguard and we moved now only as a group." When the next day he visited the museum commemorating the victims of the atomic bomb, he wrote in the visitors' book: "Man, how could you do this?"

The details of the May 13 attack, the most televised since the assassination of John F. Kennedy, are well known: the pope's jeep circumnavigating St. Peter's Square; the smiling John Paul standing in the back, Stanisław Dziwisz next to him; the crowds cheering; the assassin firing a shot, the pigeons taking off, the pope lying in Dziwisz's arms like Christ in Mary's, evoking Michelangelo's *Pietà* across the square. The patient's progress is equally well documented: the abdomen wound healing satisfactorily; a sudden attack of cytomegalovirus (a sloppy blood transfusion); the near-death experience; the pope's famous Marian remark about a "motherly hand which guided the bullet's path." What is still unknown is whether it was a contract killing or the act of a Steppenwolf.

At various points during the extensive investigation in Italy, Mehmet Ali Ağca was pronounced a lunatic, a Muslim terrorist, and a Soviet hand. Tracing Ağca's contacts and movements, the investigation first picked up a Bulgarian trail, suggesting that Andropov had asked Bulgarians to act as his proxy, then dropped it due to the very circumstantial nature of the evidence. There was no smoking gun incriminating Bulgaria or any other Eastern bloc country, or, for that matter, the Soviet Union, but the pope was certain the attempt on his life had been ordered by Moscow. Here is what his secretary had to say later: "Ali Ağca was a perfect killer. Sent by someone who thought the Pope was dangerous and inconvenient. By someone who was afraid of John Paul II. By someone who'd been frightened, seriously frightened, as soon as they'd heard that a Polish Pope had been elected. And so it's natural to look to the Communist world, to suspect, at least hypothetically, that the KGB was behind whoever made the immediate decision."

Brezhnev sent the pope a dry message: "I am deeply indignant at the attempt on your life. I wish you a rapid and complete recovery." With Poland in crisis and the pope its living saint, only a madman in the Kremlin could have ordered the killing, many people thought. But a similar argument could have been made two years earlier, when Andropov had insisted on sending ground troops into Afghanistan—generating a crisis that would eventually bring down the system he swore to defend.

The angry, tie-shredding Wałesa traveled Europe. Overall, he was hardly a free-market convert. One thing that disturbed him about capitalism was that the proletariat in countries such as Italy, France, and Japan was still the underdog. Another thing that upset him about the West was consumerism. In a way, the Communist education had worked: a man who rejected communism as a governing principle still shared Marx's values.

He said on French television: "Of course you live better than we do, you possess more things, but are you happier?" At Charles de Gaulle Airport he bumped into a group of American businessmen on their way to Poland. What had become of the credits Western banks had given Poland, they asked. Only reform could guarantee positive changes, Walesa responded evasively, upset by the moneygrubbing Westerners.

Domestically, he had several crises on his hands and became what people called "Lech the Fireman," running all over the country "putting out the strike 'fires,'" a "middleman between Solidarity and the government." On February 9, 1981, *Time* magazine wrote:

> Not since the tumultuous days of last August had so many protests erupted across Poland. From one end of the country to the other last week, hundreds of thousands of workers walked off the job. Farmers laid down their tools. Students staged sit-ins at scores of university campuses.
>
> This time the walkouts were a challenge not only to Poland's Communist government, but to Solidarity, the independent labor union forged during last summer's unrest. The wildcat protests threatened to destroy Solidarity's hard-won unity and shatter the delicate detente between the union and the state. "We must stop all the strikes so that the government can say that Solidarity has the situation under control," warned Union Leader Lech Walesa. "We must concentrate on basic issues. There is a fire in the country."

On February 11, Walesa confronted a new force in the government: a general who had helped suppress the Prague Spring, and who also had survived Soviet captivity during World War II, forgiven the Soviets the death of his father and the loss of the ancestral manor, and enthusiastically joined the Communist movement—a native Pole, Wojciech Jaruzelski, Poland's minister of defense since 1968, now became prime minister.

———

"All that was known about him," Walesa wrote, "was that he came from a large family of landowners and that in 1939 he had been deported with them to the depths of Russia, where he had lost his father . . . Living through Stalin's great terror seemed to have turned him to stone for life." The general spoke "faultless," "lively" Polish, which was probably due to his privileged background; his face was "expressionless," "partly hidden by dark glasses," his figure "stiff."

Now he was the strongman of a regime in dire crisis: one million Communist Party members also belonged to Solidarity. But Jaruzelski was resourceful and optimistic (after all, reversing the previous statistics in *his* favor, one could've said that one million Solidarity members still carried their party cards). He appealed for three months' hard work in calm. And indeed one week after his inauguration, strikes ended. Jaruzelski's pragmatism made sense to the Polish street. Many were relieved. In August 1980, Poland had an imperfect but working economy; six months of strikes left it devastated, and proceeding with revolution would empty the store shelves even more. The return to order was something Wyszyński, no doubt, approved of ("live heroically" instead of "dying heroically," the motto he had pushed twenty-five years earlier, during the 1956 riots).

The weeks of calm didn't last. Jaruzelski's argument, about the need to resume work if people expected the economy to recover, stood, but revolutions do not run on schedule. In a month, the wildcat protests started again. While the Solidarity leadership tried to figure out how an independent trade union could coexist with the Communist Party and what would be the limits of its influence over the government, Polish workers had immediate concerns on a community level: here and there, local authorities hindered the union's activities and had its members sacked, or law enforcement officers overreacted, or factory management turned a deaf ear to the employees' complaints. Truly local, conflicts like that got a massive response. Several hundred thousand workers could go on strike to have five people reinstated in their jobs. In a situation like that, every confrontation could escalate and potentially lead to a bloodbath. Jaruzelski decided he needed a dialogue with Wałesa.

On March 10, Wałesa walked into a meeting room in a government building in Warsaw. However, the person he saw there was not Jaruzelski, but an army colonel who almost twenty years ago, when Wałesa was in the army, was his commanding officer. "I admire people who can organize things in advance, foresee everything down to the smallest detail," Wałesa wrote in his memoir. "It was in just such a way that this incredible meeting must have been arranged. The General must have gone through my file and noted how I had spent my military service; he must have wanted to refresh my memory of a time when I, too, was in the army."

Jaruzelski succeeded. When he saw Wałesa a few minutes later, the Solidarity leader fell under the general's stony and stiff charm. Wałesa acknowledges that there was a "current of understanding" flowing between the two of them and admits to feeling a "certain respect for Jaruzelski, which wasn't exclusively connected with the uniform he was wearing." "We were talking about responsibility," Wałesa concluded significantly.

More meetings would follow. The two leaders found they could work with each other. Their agenda was piecemeal—reaching an eleventh-hour compromise for daily upheavals. Wałesa put it in simple words: "Let's talk before any fires spread." At the rallies, he kept repeating: "We don't want to overthrow the Communist Party. We only want to get rid of the people who are putting the brakes on Poland's renewal."

Within Solidarity, different people wanted different things for a renewed Poland. If Wałesa was looking for some sort of power sharing in defining and maintaining the social contract, radicals wanted the end of communism and the role of the Soviet Union. Jaruzelski believed in communism and alliance with the Soviet Union. Despite his patient collaboration with Solidarity, it was clear that he had guts, and soon people started talking about an imminent declaration of martial law.

Of course, the government's dialogue with the Kremlin took place secretly, unknown to most Poles. On March 4, in Moscow, Brezhnev, Andropov, Gromyko, and Ustinov scolded Kania and Jaruzelski for their "rotten" policy of compromise. Minister of Defense Dmitri Ustinov led the assault. Stalin hadn't appointed him people's commissar of armaments at the age of thirty-three, at the peak of World War II, for nothing. Now the man, fiercely loyal to the dictator's legacy, which obviously included a sphere of influence in Eastern Europe, lost his temper and even shouted something to the effect of the Poles having just two weeks to restore order in the country. In late March, a group of Polish generals sent a letter to Ustinov saying that if Kania and Jaruzelski wouldn't dare to impose martial law, they would. Cornered, Kania and Jaruzelski asked for an urgent meeting with the Soviets.

A month after the first dressing-down, on April 4, Andropov and Ustinov met Kania and Jaruzelski in a railway car outside the town of Brest, on the Soviet side of the border. The venue was a stroke of genius—in twentieth-century Europe, the railway car parked on a siding was a place where kings abdicated and countries surrendered.

Andropov dictated the terms: martial law *now*. No need to pass it through the parliament. Just order the men in uniform (four hundred thousand troops, three hundred thousand reservists, and one hundred thousand police) to take over. Yes, we understand, Kania and Jaruzelski said. We will do it. Within a week. By April 11.

April 11: No martial law. The Soviet leadership was enraged but let Jaruzelski and Kania be.

May 13: Assassination attempt on John Paul II's life.

May 28: Wyszyński died of cancer. The pope had sent Stanisław Dziwisz to Warsaw, and the dying man gave him a letter for the pope. (The pope mentioned the existence of the communication seventeen years later, but it's still unknown what the letter said.) Wyszyński suggested a successor—*his* former secretary, Józef Glemp. Hesitating for almost six weeks, as Glemp was of the Wyszyński school, on July 7 the pope finally agreed.

July 14–20: The Polish Party Extraordinary Congress. Delegates to the convention were elected democratically. With inner party democracy established for the first time in the history of the Polish Communist movement, the congress voted out the traditionalists, and the new Central Committee now consisted of Jaruzelski's supporters *and* proponents of socialism with a human face. There was still no declaration of martial law.

August 3: Erich Honecker of East Germany to Brezhnev:

As the analysis shows, the forces of the right have consolidated their positions in the Central Committee, Politburo, and Central Committee Secretariat. More than 40% of the members and candidates of the Central Committee belong to "Solidarity," three are members of "KOR." Things have gone so far that an advisor to "KOR" (H. Kubiak) has been elected to the Politburo and the Secretariat of the Central Committee.

Every day the counterrevolution under the leadership of "Solidarity" undertakes new campaigns for the subversion, destruction, and seizing of the state's power, for which they exploit the economic difficulties. Among these are the so-called "hunger marches" organized recently in Kutno, Lódz (with the participation of 10,000 women and children) and in other locations, which were held under anti-socialist slogans. Our citizens may see all of this on Western television.

The opportunity at the Party Congress to label "Solidarity" as the true culprit for the economic misery of Poland was not utilized. Instead the members of the former leadership exclusively were blamed for it. With that, the path to capitulation was justified and continued ... The revisionist forces speak openly of a new Polish model of socialism that will have an international impact. We must not underestimate the possibility that the Polish disease will spread.

September 5: In the so-called Solidarity congress, KOR announced self-dissolution—its mission, awakening the working class, accomplished. Wałesa, now branded a moderate, won the Solidarity presidency with just 55 percent of the vote. The Soviet reaction: Ustinov personally commanded Warsaw Pact maneuvers in Ukraine, Byelorussia, and Lithuania along the Polish border. Codename: West-81.

September 14: The pope gave a theoretical response to Solidarity—an encyclical called *Laborem Exercens*, a document that would earn him the unwelcome tag of a social democratic pope. Work is good, the text says, as it follows God's order to "be fruitful, and multiply, fill the earth and subdue it." It goes on to explain that all people are equal, but workers are more virtuous than their employers according to "the principle of the priority of labor over capital." Private property is fine but should be used for the common good.

It was not a prop for Solidarity's legitimacy or a critique of communism but, rather, an attack on a different "ism." What the pope was basically saying was that a *just* order was coming from the *East*, an order that transcended both communism and capitalism, an order in which a laborer operated in a free-market economy but ultimately worked for the public good: the legendary, promised, found, and repeatedly lost third way. Ironically, it took a pope from behind the Iron Curtain to relate to the laborer.

The Soviets missed the point completely. Instead of hailing John Paul II as a Marxist pope, they stupidly kept calling him a reactionary.

But the Poles missed the point, too—though they could be hardly blamed for that. With the shelves in their stores empty, they didn't find the principle of the priority of labor over capital relevant.

On October 18, Kania stepped down—under pressure from Moscow, many believed. Now Jaruzelski was first secretary, premier, and minister of defense. The Kremlin, Solidarity, the Polish Church, and the Vatican expected different kinds of things from the general, but all knew that now he was the force of gravity that held the nation together.

Nothing went well for Wałesa at that point. With Glemp at the helm, the Church continued to say that Solidarity did "excessive politicizing," as if the fight for daily bread could have been waged without it. The Solidarity leadership was up in arms, claiming that Wałesa was unfit to represent the opposition, as if anyone had a better course of action to propose. At a Solidarity conference, the radicals accused him of being soft on the government and introduced a motion "for broader union representation." Wałesa jumped up. "Tears rolled down his cheeks as he yelled: 'But then you go and explain your vote to the nation.'"

In the absence of consistent leadership, protests and strikes grew progressively more violent; on several occasions, revolutionary mobs attempted lynching law enforcement officers. Clashes between the rebels and the loyalists foretold civil war.

Jaruzelski, Wałesa, and Glemp were now called the "Big Three," but it looked like Wałesa was the lame duck of the trio. He didn't take it well, getting into petty disputes over questions like whether he should take Glemp's car to a meeting or use his own. Eventually arriving at Jaruzelski's in the primate's limo, he looked furious. The general noticed, and the man of stone smiled.

On December 10, the Soviet Politburo met to discuss the "Polish disease." Finally, Jaruzelski was ready to go ahead and declare martial law, demanded so angrily from him by Andropov and Ustinov seven months earlier. In a conversation with Soviet envoys, the general had declared that Poland needed "a military dictatorship, of the sort that existed under Piłsudski." But the general attached a price tag to what was called Operation X: $1.5 billion worth of Soviet economic aid.

With the economy brought to a halt by strikes and riots, Poland was in very bad shape. Soon, it would have to pay for its loans from the West, and the government was considering defaulting on foreign debt. Knowing that in case of a default all Polish property abroad would be confiscated, it had already ordered all vessels out of foreign ports and into neutral waters.

The $1.5 billion worth of additional supplies demanded by Jaruzelski included grain and meat but also iron ore, nonferrous metal, fertilizer, oil, and tires. Prior to that, between July 1980 and July 1981, Moscow had already given Warsaw loans in the amount of $4.5 billion. So far, the Polish revolution had cost the Soviets almost as much as the Afghan War.

The head of the Central Planning Committee, Nikolai Baibakov, freshly returned from Warsaw, indignantly reported that the Polish population "is not going hungry. Urban dwellers ride out to the markets and buy up all the products they need. And there are ample supplies of them."

"And are we able to give this much now?" Brezhnev asked.

"Only by drawing on state reserves or at the expense of deliveries to the internal market," Baibakov responded.

The Politburo knew that it was on the hook. A few days earlier, the Warsaw Pact commander in chief, Marshal Viktor Kulikov, in Warsaw on a reconnaissance mission, had done a very stupid thing: he had told Jaruzelski that the Soviets and, probably, other members of the Eastern bloc would be happy to use their armed forces to crush Solidarity if the Polish forces were "unable to cope with the resistance."

Very happy that Kulikov had walked straight into a trap, Jaruzelski immediately invited the Soviets in. He knew they couldn't do it. The Afghan War had hit the home front badly. Every day huge military transport aircraft, painted black and dubbed Black Tulips, brought zinc coffins back from Afghanistan. Some of these coffins had a small window that allowed the parents to see the face of their dead son—swollen, bruised, covered with posthumous stubble. Having been denied any credible explanation by their leaders, the Soviet people saw only that their sons were being sent off to fight a meaningless war in a backward country of no economic or geopolitical value to the people of the Soviet Union. High school students drank insecticides to get medical exemptions from military service; the most desperate ones swallowed metal scraps for the same purpose. Angry parents whose sons had been killed in Afghanistan assaulted the military representatives assigned to attend the funerals.

Now Kulikov's unwarranted ultimatum would cost Moscow. Very angry, the Politburo started venting. "Jaruzelski is apparently trying to pull the wool over our eyes" (Konstantin Rusakov, head of the Central Committee Socialist Countries Department). "Jaruzelski is displaying a certain degree of slyness" (the party ideologue Mikhail Suslov). "What is the connection between the success of 'Operation X' and the delivery of fertilizer and certain other goods?" (Andropov).

But finger-pointing was not relevant any longer. A decision had to be made, and no matter how much the Politburo hated the idea of being blackmailed, it had to pay the price set by Jaruzelski for doing things on his own.

Foreign Minister Gromyko summed it all up: "There cannot be any introduction of troops into Poland." Andropov's conclusive remarks were astonishing: "If the capitalist countries pounce on the Soviet Union, and you know they have already reached agreement on a variety of economic and political sanctions, that will be very burdensome for us. We must be concerned above all with our own country and about the strengthening of the Soviet Union . . . I don't know how things will turn out in Poland, but even if Poland falls under the control of 'Solidarity,' that's the way it will be."

On the next day, Ustinov informed the Soviet representatives in Poland, "the Poles themselves must resolve the Polish question." "We are not preparing to send troops onto the territory of Poland," the communication stated.

Unsure how violent the first night of martial law might turn out, the Soviet embassy in Warsaw prepared an aircraft to evacuate families to Brest, stocked groceries, brought in physicians, and secured field kitchens to feed the embassy guards.

Shortly before midnight, on December 12, in a meeting in Gdansk, Wałesa got a cable reporting, "All communications by telephone and telex have been cut." As he remembered, "Five minutes later, the room was deserted. Snow was falling, gleaming in the yellowish glare from the lights along the path to the shipyard gate. On the way home the snow began to fall heavily. Everything was silent."

At one a.m., the Polish ambassador to Italy informed the pope that in six hours General Jaruzelski would formally announce the imposition of martial law.

5. The Revolution Winters: 1982–88

Operation X proceeded smoothly, with seven thousand Solidarity activists arrested, opposition media silenced, casualties running in the acceptable double digits. Had Jaruzelski caved in under Moscow's pressure seven months earlier and introduced martial law in April, civil war would have been likely, but by the end of 1981 a feeling of overall exhaustion gripped the public, and hunger (if not famine) became a real concern for a nation destroying its economy in the process of fighting for a better one. Some oppositionists escaped arrest, but the resulting underground network, TKK, the Provisional Coordinating Commission, was very loose. When its transmitters sent out a call for a nationwide strike, people did not really respond. Communists did start leaving the party ranks, and it shrank from 3,158,000 (September 1980) to 2,488,000 (June 1982), but the numbers were still good enough for the general.

Like many detainees, Wałesa was not jailed but interned—for the "longest vacation" of his life, as he put it. First it was a villa in the Warsaw suburbs, then Gomułka's villa in the woods, and then a hunting lodge on the Soviet border. The stone-faced general's choices were a private joke at Wałesa's expense, as each location inspired a painfully acute response in the prisoner. The Warsaw suburbs suggested that the general might send for him at any time. Gomułka had lived in the villa in forced retirement and then made a triumphal comeback. The Soviet border sounded sinister, Wałesa thought, though had he been placed on the East German or Czechoslovak border, Soviet garrisons would've been just a few miles away, too.

His family was allowed to join him, and the children got private tutoring. Now and then Jaruzelski's emissaries came. Wałesa refused to cooperate. The bond that the two had forged last spring and summer had been an uneasy one, yet Wałesa felt betrayed. After the family moved back to Gdansk, his wife gave birth to a daughter, talked to every Western correspondent willing to listen (there were many), and met with diplomats and Church people. When she visited, she smuggled in tapes and reading materials without any difficulty.

On the Soviet border, the general's pressure started working. Wałesa's internment was nearing the end of its first year, no TKK rescue squad was in sight, and Wałesa got the impression that the TKK in general was quite comfortable with him locked up. On November 8, 1982, he wrote a letter to Jaruzelski suggesting they meet and "reach some kind of understanding." The letter was addressed to "General Wojciech Jaruzelski" and signed "Corporal Lech Walesa." The signature would later haunt Wałesa.

The next day, he was released. Within a few days, Brezhnev died, and the Politburo elected Yuri Andropov as general secretary of the Communist Party of the Soviet Union.

For Andropov, the vote was a bitter victory. Brezhnev's decline had lasted for too long, and now Andropov himself was dying from a kidney condition. But he set out to make an impact.

He was the first Soviet leader since Stalin to publish a theoretical argument—an article called "The Teaching of Karl Marx and Certain Issues of Building Socialism in the USSR." By the standards of Marx, the argument was flimsy, but it did make an essential point: Marxism *had* to be developed to accommodate late-twentieth-century realities. Knowing that he wouldn't have time to really develop Marx's ideas, Andropov addressed reality in a quick, KGB-inspired way.

A person who has a maximum of two years to live has to have a focus. For Andropov, it was the economy. Forget about structural changes (those would be up to his successor to fix), but what about the moonshine-on-top-of-a-crane attitude that incapacitates the system?

By his lights, the people had lost faith in authority and become incredibly lazy. The solution to the first problem was an anticorruption campaign: firings (top culprit, the minister of interior); suicides (top victim, the minister of the interior's wife); show trials for lesser personages. The solution to the second problem: enforcement. The only sector of the economy that *was* working was the military-industrial complex, and that, in Andropov's eyes, was because "military representatives," *milreps* in Newspeak, monitored research and production. Seeking to replicate this model, he sent state representatives to all major enterprises, calling this "state approval," or *gospriemka*. Another measure was limited largely to Moscow. Instead of hunting down dissidents—a futile, largely paranoid activity, as none had any serious impact on the street—the KGB started raiding supermarkets, barbershops, and saunas during regular working hours, when most people should've been at work. ("May I see your ID? And may I ask why are you having a haircut when you are supposed to be at work?")

But people just laughed. An Andropov joke: "Esteemed members of the Central Committee of the Communist Party of the Soviet Union! Those of you who have voted for Comrade Andropov may put your hands down and back off the wall."

Soon, Andropov moved into a hospital. His absence from public life did not go unnoticed. President Ronald Reagan was particularly hopeful.

Winning the 1980 election, Ronald Reagan, probably unbeknownst to himself, got a multimillion-person shadow constituency—the dissenters of the Eastern bloc, from East Berlin to Vladivostok; throughout the 1980s, people who worshipped Marlon Brando, Sean Connery, and blue jeans kept saying: "Our *last* hope? Ronald Reagan."

In hindsight, this sounds ironic, as Reagan's vision of their societies was hideously dated. As late as the spring of 1981, Reagan thought that the Soviets "were more dedicated than ever to achieving Lenin's goal of a Communist world. Under the so-called Brezhnev Doctrine, they claimed the right to support 'wars of national liberation' and to suppress, through armed intervention, any challenge to Communist governments anywhere in the world." In fact, in 1981 the Brezhnev Doctrine existed largely in the minds of Western observers and antagonists, and, with the Soviet army firmly stuck in the Afghan morass, no further expansion was remotely possible.

Reagan's view of Poland (or of any other Eastern European country, for that matter) was at best simplistic: "brave shipyard workers" versus the "puppet government." But that didn't really matter. As the person who advised him on Eastern European matters, Jack Matlock, writes, Reagan "assumed that there could be changes for the better and that he could influence them."

With Operation X in progress, Reagan wrote in his diary: "We can't let this revolution against Communism fail without our offering a hand. We may never have an opportunity like this in our lifetime." He sent a very strong protest to the Kremlin and announced that the United States was imposing sanctions against Poland and the Soviet Union, suspending negotiations on a new long-term grain-sale agreement, banning the Soviet airline, Aeroflot, from flying to the USA, canceling several exchange programs, and imposing an embargo on shipment to the Soviet Union of pipe-laying equipment needed for a trans-Siberian gas pipeline.

Within the next few days, U.S. Secretary of State Alexander Haig informed the president that the Polish ambassador to Washington, Romuald Spasowski, "wanted to defect immediately." On December 22, Reagan saw Spasowski and his wife in the Oval Office. "It was an emotional meeting for all of us and left me with more disgust than ever for the evil men in the Kremlin who believed they had the right to hold an entire nation in captivity," Reagan wrote.

Of course, to Reagan, Andropov was *the* evil man in the Kremlin. Andropov's letters, Reagan remarked, were "stiff and as cold as a Siberian winter." Returning the favor, the Kremlin publicly called the U.S. president the "Nuclear Cowboy." Relations between the two countries plummeted to a level unseen since the early 1950s. Since the establishment of diplomatic relations fifty years earlier, Reagan was the only U.S. president not to have a summit with the Soviets.

Frankly, this was not Reagan's fault but Andropov's. By sending Soviet troops into Afghanistan, Andropov had turned his country into an international pariah. Even Jimmy Carter, giving Brezhnev a kiss just several months earlier, introduced sanctions against the Soviet Union, including the boycott of the 1980 Moscow Olympics. Now, by all means, it was the Kremlin's turn to make a conciliatory gesture, but one could hardly expect one during Andropov's tenure.

Reagan did nothing to lessen the tension, and many argued that he made it worse. In his memoirs, the president modestly wrote: "I also tried to send out a signal that the United States intended to support people fighting for their freedom against Communism wherever they were—a policy some writers later described as the 'Reagan Doctrine.'" The signal was received loud and clear by Moscow. On a more practical level, Reagan created a crisis in Europe: "When the Russians wouldn't agree to remove the SS-20 missiles that they had aimed at European cities, we said we were going to proceed with NATO's plans for us to deploy Pershing II and cruise missiles in Europe in the fall of 1983 to counter the threat of the SS-20s."

In his memoirs, Reagan noted, "The great dynamic success of capitalism had given us a powerful weapon in our battle against Communism—*money*. The Russians could never win the arms race; we could outspend them forever." On March 23, 1983, he revealed his dream for the Strategic Defense Initiative: "What if free people could live secure in the knowledge that their security did not rest upon the threat of instant U.S. retaliation to deter a Soviet attack, that we could intercept and destroy strategic ballistic missiles before they reached our own soil or that of our allies?"

Later that year, tensions escalated when the Soviets shot down a South Korean Boeing 747 over the North Pacific. The plane had strayed into Soviet airspace and Moscow deemed it a spy mission on behalf of the U.S. government. Reagan was flabbergasted. "We knew from the intercepted communications that the Soviet pilots flew near the 747 for two and a half hours under a bright half-moon and it seemed impossible that, based on its size and insignia, they did not realize they were tracking a jumbo-jet commercial airliner"—still they shot it down with 269 passengers onboard, "including a U.S. congressman and sixty other Americans."

A few weeks later, Reagan watched *The Day After*, a movie "in which Lawrence, Kansas, is wiped out in a nuclear war with Russia. It is powerfully done, all $7 million worth. It's very effective and left me greatly depressed. So far they haven't sold any of the 25 ads scheduled and I can see why . . . My own reaction: we have to do all we can to have a deterrent and to see there is never a nuclear war." Somewhat soon after that, Reagan demanded a briefing "on our complete plan in the event of a nuclear attack"; that was "a most sobering experience." He concluded: "In several ways, the sequence of events described in the briefings paralleled those in the ABC movie. Yet there were still some people at the Pentagon who claimed a nuclear war was 'winnable.' I thought they were crazy."

———

Resuming his activism in the first weeks of Andropov's tenure, Wałesa set up opposition headquarters in his own apartment, trying to reclaim influence over the Solidarity power base. It wasn't working too well. In the eyes of the people, he was still a symbol of resistance and hope, but, as a worker said to a foreign correspondent, "he must lead. We are waiting for him to tell us what to do." Easier said than done.

He lived in sort of a legal limbo. He returned to the shipyard to work as a celebrity electrician. "On my first day back," he writes, "it took me at least two hours to get home. In the square, in front of the second entrance, across from the monument to the 1970 shipyard workers, I had to shake thousands of hands and sign hundreds of autographs." He made statements calling for "effective" protests against martial law, which Jaruzelski tolerated, though technically, with Solidarity banned, Wałesa was in no position to be a public figure. He wasn't allowed to travel abroad, and police agents shadowed him constantly.

But the whole of Poland was in limbo. When he was in detention, the underground had come up with a slogan, "The winter is yours, the spring will be ours," and since then had been setting up random rallies and protests, at which thousands of people showed up. Each time Jaruzelski sent out riot police. At the same time, the general felt confident enough to allow the pope to visit merely a year and a half after the introduction of martial law, with protests flaring up constantly.

People close to the pope insisted that the "de facto Primate of Poland" was in Rome, but this was simply not true: Polish bishops led by Primate Józef Glemp followed the Wyszyński model—the Church asked the people to work for the common good, and it didn't really take sides politically. John Paul was very angry with Glemp, regretting terribly the appointment made two years earlier honoring Wyszyński's wish.

Some individual priests rebelled against Glemp. The exemplar was Jerzy Popieluszko, a "youthful-looking" priest wearing "jeans and a white polo shirt, with a pack of Marlboros sticking out of his breast pocket." Father Popieluszko invited martyrdom: "As Christ says in the Gospel, fear not, fear not those who kill the body, they can do no more than that." Thousands gathered in the streets outside his church in Warsaw, listening on loudspeakers to his polarizing questions: "Which side will you take? The side of good or the side of evil?"

In June, the pope came. According to his secretary, "he made known his intention to back Solidarity as soon as he got off the plane. He kissed the ground—though he had already done that on his first visit—and explained that he felt as if he were kissing a mother bowed down by new afflictions. He added that he was coming for everyone, including those who were in prison. Then, at Cardinal Wyszynski's tomb in the cathedral, he thanked Providence for sparing him the painful events of December 13, 1981."

At an official dinner in Kraków, hearing the students outside, the pope left the table and stayed at the window for a quarter of an hour. Cardinal Casaroli exclaimed in despair: "What does he want? Does he want bloodshed? Does he want war? Does he want to overthrow the government?" It looked like that was indeed what he wanted, feeling that his compatriots lacked determination. His potentially inflammatory behavior had a reason unknown to almost everyone: John Paul II thought he had received a clear sign.

Recovering after the May 13, 1981, assassination attempt, the pope analyzed his near-death experience from every possible perspective. The possible KGB role in the plot did not interest him much. Divine intercession was another matter. The most famed Marian apparition of the twentieth century had been reported in Fátima, Portugal, in 1917, when the Virgin revealed herself to three peasant girls. Two Fátima prophecies (Heaven was real; Russia had to be converted to Catholicism) had been announced back then; the third, known as the "Third Secret," had not been. Here is how the closest person to the pope, Stanisław Dziwisz, described John Paul II's thinking:

> Truth be told, John Paul II didn't think about Fatima at all in the days immediately following the assassination attempt. It was only later, after he had recovered and was getting back some of his old strength, that he started reflecting on what was, to say the least, an extraordinary coincidence. Two thirteenths of May! One in 1917, when the Virgin of Fatima appeared for the first time, and one in 1981, when they tried to kill him.
>
> After pondering it for a while, the Pope finally requested to see the Third Secret. The Third Secret, which Mary had revealed to the three children when she appeared at Fatima, was kept in the archives of the Congregation for the Doctrine of the Faith. And on July 18, if I'm not mistaken, the then prefect, Cardinal Franjo Seper, delivered two envelopes—one with Sister Lucia's original Portuguese text, and the other with the Italian translation . . . This was during the second hospitalization. It was there, in the hospital, that the Holy Father read the "secret." When he was finished, all his remaining doubts were gone. In Sister Lucia's vision, he recognized his own destiny. He became convinced that his life had been saved—no, given back to him anew—thanks to Our Lady's intervention and protection.
>
> It's true, of course, that the "bishop dressed in white" is killed in Sister's Lucia's vision, whereas John Paul II escaped an almost certain death. So? Couldn't that have been the real point of the vision? Couldn't it have been trying to tell us that the paths of history, of human existence, are not necessarily fixed in advance? And that there is a Providence, a "motherly hand," which can intervene and cause a shooter, who is certain of hitting his target, to miss?
>
> "One hand shot, and another guided the bullet" was how the Holy Father put it.

When he went to see the would-be assassin, Mehmet Ali Ağca, the man asked him: "I know I was aiming right. I know that the bullet was a killer. So why aren't you dead?"

Now, in Poland, he attended "a Marian celebration, with Mass and the crowning of four images of the Virgin from four different shrines. There was an incredible crowd of two million people, and in his homily John Paul II expressly stated that Poland should be sovereign and that sovereignty is based on the liberties of the citizenry."

He met Jaruzelski a few times. "In the private interview," Dziwisz writes, "he essentially told the general that, while he might even understand the decision to introduce martial law, he absolutely couldn't understand the abolition of Solidarity, because it was an expression of the soul of Poland . . . In the Holy Father's eyes . . . the general was an intelligent and cultured man, who, in his own way, was even something of a patriot. The problem was that politically he looked eastward, not westward."

The pope saw Wałesa in a cabin in the Tatra Mountains, a setting chosen by the general personally, giving the meeting a conspiratorial color and suggesting that Wałesa was still being persecuted by the regime—which, in reality, he was not. Also, thanks to the resourceful general, the pope visited Wałesa, not the other way around, as it should have been.

Stanisław Dziwisz: "The important thing at that point wasn't what the Pope and Wałesa might say, but the fact of their meeting itself." What Wałesa took away from the meeting was "the atmosphere of openness and simplicity" and also an observation about the pope's feet: "One curious thing struck me during that meeting. I suddenly noticed the Pope's large feet, and I watched how he walked. Surprisingly, his steps were steady, measured, and confident. They seemed to give me back my strength."

A month later, on July 21, Jaruzelski lifted the state of emergency. For the general, John Paul's visit had been a test. Despite the emotional outpouring and gigantic rallies, Poles had not gotten out of line.

———

During the cold war years, for liberals worldwide, *1984* was what the Revelation was for the Christian faithful: a doomsday prophecy that could come true any day. Dreamed up by George Orwell on the secluded Isle of Jura in Scotland in 1948, when Stalin was still in the Kremlin, "1984" had finally arrived.

It proved unremarkable. In the U.S. presidential elections, Ronald Reagan easily defeated Walter Mondale. Europe celebrated the fortieth anniversary of D-day. The Soviets boycotted the Los Angeles Olympics, retaliating for the 1980 Western boycott of the Moscow Olympics (which had been meant as punishment for the Afghan invasion). And Eastern Europeans garnered a great deal of cultural recognition: Miloš Forman received an Oscar for *Amadeus*, Jaroslav Seifert of Czechoslovakia a Nobel Prize for Literature, and Milan Kundera published *The Unbearable Lightness of Being*. In Poland, Father Jerzy Popieluszko disappeared on the night of October 19, while driving to Warsaw from Bydgoszcz; his body was found in the Vistula later, dumped there by the secret police after a severe beating. Glemp presided over the funeral, looking somewhat content.

In the Vatican, John Paul II remained optimistic. He saw Solidarity as a clear result of divine intervention and was positive there was a connection between the crumbling of communism and the Marian apparition in Fátima. In his memoir, Stanisław Dziwisz reminds us that in 1917 the Virgin "asked the Church and the Pope" to consecrate the world—"especially Russia"—to her.

> In the second Secret, she said: "If my requests are heeded, Russia will be converted and there will be peace; if not, she will spread her errors throughout the world . . ."
>
> And so on March 25, 1984, in Saint Peter's Square, John Paul II, spiritually united with all the world's bishops, made the act of consecration to Mary before a statue of Our Lady that had been brought from Fatima for that purpose. He didn't name Russia explicitly, but he alluded clearly to the nations that "particularly need to be thus entrusted and consecrated."

The year of Orwell's prophecy came and went. Eastern European intellectuals discovered that the Apocalypse would not occur, or at least had been put on hold. And the Communist regimes were growing softer. One of the few people in the West who noticed this was Ronald Reagan.

Reagan was defiantly unmodern. He didn't know how to use chopsticks—at one Chinese meal, having difficulty "identifying several items" on his plate, he "stirred them around in hopes of camouflaging [his] reluctance to eat them." But clumsiness with chopsticks and distrust of foreign cuisine were not the only unmodern things about the U.S. president. Unlike Margaret Thatcher or François Mitterrand, Reagan had a dream. If Lenin had sworn by world revolution, Reagan was committed to the global counterrevolution.

"During that beautiful spring [of 1984]," he thought, "events were occurring in China and Poland that were heralding the demise of Communism." His broadcast to the Chinese people was edited, but during his stay the government announced the news about a Chinese family that "had just been able to buy a personal car"; he visited a "sample" free market and a private home and spoke to students at a Shanghai university, "where about half of the faculty members had attended school in America."

What Reagan found so encouraging was not just the budding state capitalism in China or the hibernating but already sturdy freedoms of Poland, but also the Moscow funeral cascade. The KGB Marxist, Yuri Andropov, died in February 1984, after barely fourteen months in office. His successor, Konstantin Chernenko, lasted thirteen. When on March 11, 1985, Reagan was awakened at four a.m. "to be told Chernenko is dead," he turned to Nancy and deadpanned: "How am I supposed to get anyplace with the Russians if they keep dying on me?"

———

Mikhail Sergeyevich Gorbachev stole the show. He ultimately outshone the two Poles—Wojtyla and Wałesa—who set in motion the transformation of Eastern Europe, not to mention the anonymous Gdansk strikers and those who lit candles for them; newscasters of every anti-Communist radio network in the world, from Radio Free Europe to the Voice of the Andes; authors such as Orwell, Kafka, Camus, Hemingway, Pasternak, Brodsky, Bulgakov, Solzhenitsyn, Havel, Hesse, and Kundera; and moviemakers, theater directors, actors, artists, and their grateful audiences. What we remember is Gorbachev's charisma, wisdom, and leadership.

This was not inevitable. Had Andropov not suffered from a kidney condition, and therefore had he not needed to go to Kislovodsk, the health resort in the foothills of the Caucasus, at least once a year, Gorbachev wouldn't have ever had a chance to become a familiar face to the grumpy, untrusting powerhouse. Kislovodsk was in Stavropol province, Gorbachev the Stavropol party czar, and so it was his duty to make sure that any Politburo member staying at the resort could relax, sit back, and enjoy the vacation.

There were long walks in Kislovodsk, Andropov talking about socialist labor ethics, foreign enemies, and the reform of Marxism, and Gorbachev enthusiastically nodding. In film footage, Gorbachev is not unlike a lapdog leaping around a mastiff. Much later, the hagiographic biographies of Gorbachev would make it sound different. They suggest Andropov traveled to Kislovodsk to *see* Gorbachev; the party czar of Georgia, Eduard Shevardnadze, joins them there—not because this is his duty as another neighboring viceroy seeking favors from the KGB chairman, but because he is there for an underground conference of enlightened despots, the Kremlin Young Turks.

The mastiff sniffing out the lapdog: "You are saying you can do tricks? How about fixing agriculture? You have *two* degrees, one in agriculture, correct?" "Correct," the lapdog responds.

He *did* have two degrees, that was correct, but the problem was that he got the first one, in law, during Stalin's era, when the study of law was somewhat oxymoronic, and the second one, in agriculture, in Stavropol, when he was already a local party boss.

Andropov brought Gorbachev to Moscow. He became a Central Committee secretary (agriculture), a candidate member of the Politburo, and soon a full member. In 1984, he visited Britain. The visit was official, as he headed a "parliamentary" delegation, and it was a huge success.

The British found him "self-confident" and "easygoing," a "politician rather than a dictator." He and his wife, Raisa, did not look like a stereotypical Kremlin couple, and what impressed the hosts and the media most was their manner and style. "Natty Gorbachevs Take London—and Its Iron Lady," a headline in *The Washington Post* said. Prime Minister Thatcher was enchanted. In her memoirs, she wrote about the couple's visit to Chequers: "[Raisa] was dressed in a smart western style outfit, a well-tailored grey suit with a white stripe—just the sort I could have worn myself, I thought."

Raisa was the first Kremlin wife to shop in expensive London stores, and the media claimed that she paid with an American Express card. The *Daily Mail* called the couple "the new Gucci comrades." Characteristically, a new English friend, the influential political scientist Archie Brown, who advised Thatcher on the Gorbachevs' visit, indignantly pronounced the allegations not true, saying "she chose earrings, costing several hundred pounds, that were paid for IN CASH by the person accompanying her from the Soviet Embassy."

The sympathetic media quickly forgot that the main purpose of Gorbachev's visit to London had been to warn Thatcher against supporting Reagan's "Star Wars." Right after Gorbachev's visit, Thatcher flew to Washington, where she and Reagan agreed that "no 'Star Wars' antimissile defense system would be deployed without future negotiations with the Soviets."

The West fell in with Gorbachev—not with the man, but with a symbol of hope. The great powers were gridlocked, and the public seemed to be saying, "Give us some hope." None came from the wise men of the West; in 1983, the American astrophysicist Carl Sagan published a book called *The Nuclear Winter*; its thesis, based on a recent study, was that humankind was unlikely to survive even a limited nuclear conflict because of the extreme climate change it would cause.

A Russian proverb suggests, "They meet you by your clothes but they judge you by your wit." In Gorbachev's case, the clothes won.

In April 1985, Gorbachev, recently appointed general secretary, held his first Central Committee plenum, where he announced that reform was necessary. The indignity of three state funerals in a matter of twenty-eight months gave him automatic credit for being young. (A joke: "Do you have a ticket for this coming Red Square funeral?" "No, I have a pass.") The springtime setting for the speech supplied writers all over the Eastern bloc with an infinite number of cheerful metaphors for Gorbachev's new policies. But how new were these policies?

Perestroika, originally, was *not* democratization. It was originally formulated as a package—*perestroika i uskoreniye*—"restructuring and speeding up," or even "catching up." Gorbachev's mentor, Andropov, had sent the KGB to barbershops; along the same lines, the new leader started an anti-alcohol campaign. It was a failed prohibition (wine and beer lost, moonshine won), and before Gorbachev beat a retreat, thousands of alcoholics had died after drinking antifreeze and glue. An economist, William Moskoff, writes: "Noble as Gorbachev's aims were, they led to disastrous results. Not only was the policy deeply resented by the public, it also had unintended economic side effects. Although alcohol production fell during the 1985–1987 period by 37 billion rubles, which was roughly equal to 25 percent of food sales, there was no compensatory production of other goods on which people could spend the money that formerly went to alcohol; and this placed even more pressure on price levels." The British ambassador to Moscow, Bryan Cartledge, summed up the irony neatly in a report to Margaret Thatcher: "Jam tomorrow and, meanwhile, no vodka today."

Glasnost, or "transparency," or limited freedom of speech and information, had its maiden ball at a party congress on February 25, 1986. It was a term borrowed from the paradigm of an earlier reformer—not Khrushchev, as one might think, but Tsar Alexander II. Basically, it was the public's right to be informed. Two months later, Chernobyl happened.

The radioactive cloud was released from the reactor at 1:30 a.m., April 26; the people didn't know until sixty-seven hours later, the evening of the twenty-eighth, and the reports did not reveal the extent of the real hazard until *much* later. (Gorbachev on the Chernobyl catastrophe, circa 1995: "I absolutely reject the accusation that the Soviet leadership intentionally held back the truth about Chernobyl. We simply did not know the whole truth yet.")

In principle, after Chernobyl, Gorbachev's case should have been closed, the person dismissed as a heartless liar responsible for a cover-up of the worst nuclear accident in history and the postponement of evacuation and resettlement of three hundred thousand people, resulting in about nine thousand deaths over the next twenty years. But it wasn't.

Here is the kind of glasnost he promoted: radioactive fallout and Afghan War casualties were excluded, while Margaret Thatcher was given free rein. She went on Soviet TV uncensored. She "literally demolished a group of Soviet journalists interviewing her, who had tried to mumble some ideological bromides that other Westerners used to leave unchallenged. Shown in full on television, the interview was one of the first signs of glasnost," Pavel Palazchenko, who was Gorbachev's English interpreter, writes.

Thatcher was the first leader to bond with Gorbachev, and then every Western leader had to take him seriously. Reagan met with him four times. Already in November 1985, in Geneva, at the famous "fireplace summit," he found Gorbachev "likable," and, unlike other senior Soviet officials, there was "warmth in his face and his style." Very impressed, Reagan continued: "Gorbachev was tough and convinced Communism was superior to capitalism, but after almost five years I'd finally met a Soviet leader I could talk to." There was hope. After Reagan communicated his confidence to a joint session of Congress, the enthusiasm of the lawmakers was so obvious that the president wrote in his diary: "I haven't gotten such a reception since I was shot."

———————

Now Gorbachev was destined to preside over the six other leaders of the Eastern bloc, who were senior not just in age but, more important, in skills and experience. All Gorbachev had to show was relative youth and two good-for-nothing degrees; the Eastern European leaders could point to time in jail, conversations with Stalin, and years on the front line fighting against the Nazis. The six were a vigorous example of leadership, hardly puppets of Moscow.

János Kádár of Hungary led in nicknames: an "iron fist in a velvet glove," a "quisling," a "renegade," a "reformer," and a "troublemaker," he probably had deserved them all. A Comintern-school prewar Communist, he later did time in the Hungarian Gulag, sentenced to life for nonexistent espionage, and was rehabilitated. For a short while, he sided with the reform movement of Imre Nagy, but when the reform grew into a counterrevolution, he fled to the USSR and returned to Budapest in a Soviet armored car. He soon helped the Soviets to trick Nagy into leaving the Yugoslav embassy and, breaching his promise of safe passage, turned Nagy over to the Soviets, who would have him shot. Ordering two thousand Hungarian rebels executed and twenty-five thousand imprisoned, he froze the country for twelve years and then launched the greatest economic reform in the "socialist camp," driving Hungary into the gray area between socialism and capitalism. Keeping heavy industry under state control, he allowed private property where people needed it most, in food and retail. Fifty years after Lenin and Trotsky abolished private property in Russia and at the time when Mao Zedong was engineering the greatest leftist coup of all, the Cultural Revolution, Hungary beat a retreat.

The reform did not stop at store counters. In 1981, 5.5 million Hungarians went abroad, 477,000 of them to capitalist countries and not necessarily on organized tours. This meant that every second person in Hungary traveled abroad that year—and that every twentieth saw a Vienna or New York or London. Two million Westerners visited Hungary as tourists annually; 117,000 Americans came in 1985 alone.

Consequently, Hungary had no angry political dissent or labor unrest. "Most dissidents faced only sporadic repression but also minimal public response," a Library of Congress study of Hungary reported. In the fifth edition of his *Communist Regimes in Eastern Europe*, published in 1988, Richard F. Staar called Hungary the "bloc's showplace of liberalism and tranquility."

The calm in Hungary was a disappointment to the pope. The Catholic Church in Hungary, according to his hagiographic biography, "had increasingly accommodated itself to the regime, and the results had been disastrous. While some sixty percent of the country's population was baptized Catholic, only a quarter of those Catholics, at best, were active members of the Church, and only one third of those 'active members' attended Mass regularly." "In December 1978, shortly after his election," the account continues, "John Paul tried to light a fire under the Hungarian bishops with a personal letter." That didn't work. He summoned the primate, László Cardinal Lékai, to Rome, but the cardinal politely refused to share the pope's aggressive anti-Communist position. A few years later, when asked when he would visit Hungary, John Paul angrily responded: "The Pope will visit Hungary when the cardinal has learned to bang his fist on the table." The pope didn't seem to understand that the majority of Hungarians didn't want the racket of banging fists.

The Soviet party line on Kádár's reforms was ambiguous. Clearly a revision of the Soviet economic model, they did not get much media coverage, and traditionalists in the party thought they were right-wing deviationism, but few Eastern European leaders had proved their loyalty as strongly as Kádár had. Andropov, Soviet ambassador to Hungary in 1956, respected Kádár a lot and was very interested in "goulash communism."

The West approved of Kádár. In 1984, Margaret Thatcher chose Hungary for her first official visit to an Eastern bloc country, as she hoped to "gain a clearer picture from Mr Kádár of the situation in the USSR." (Kádár was ready to oblige. "As he put it," Thatcher remembered, "'the Russians are individuals too.'") Reagan's advisor on Soviet affairs, Jack Matlock, was quoted as saying that the "American government was satisfied with political conditions under Kádár" and did not want Radio Free Europe to emphasize the presence of Soviet troops on Hungarian territory. Radio Free Europe was based in Munich, and from there, allegedly, the chief of its Hungarian service discreetly met with Kádár's envoys in neutral locations such as Rome and Vienna, getting exclusive Hungarian domestic news in exchange for the support of Kádár's cause. When asked publicly what he thought about Radio Free Europe, Kádár wryly said that the station "played good music."

Kádár's southern neighbor, Nicolae Ceauşescu, had the chief of the RFE Romanian Service killed. The only true dictator in Eastern Europe had ordered all typewriters in the country registered with the police and typeface samples filed. The Romanian secret police, the Securitate, was by far the most brutal in the Eastern bloc, and dissent was not possible even for Politburo members. Trusting his family more than he trusted his party, Ceauşescu put his relatives on about sixty important government posts. Elena, the dictator's wife, was a member of every governing body in the country. The party daily called her "a providential personality whose birthday was a crucial date in Romanian history." Maniacal projects, including moving farmers to "agro-towns," had exhausted the Romanian economy, and Ceauşescu put the people on rations.

Yet Ceauşescu had had his finest hour in 1968, when he stood up to the Soviet invasion of Czechoslovakia. Summoning a rally in downtown Bucharest, he called the Soviet move "a grave danger to peace in

Europe"—to the heartfelt cheers of the crowds. Hinting that Romania might be next, he invited workers to join the militia, and about half a million volunteered immediately. Ceaușescu also refused to sever ties with China, condemned the Soviet invasion of Afghanistan, and, defying Moscow's stance, sent his athletes to the 1984 Los Angeles Olympics. Occasionally, he would even hint that Romania and the Soviet Union had an unresolved territorial issue—Bessarabia, annexed by Stalin in 1940.

His courageous and defiant stance in 1968 won Ceaușescu twenty years on the red carpet in Western capitals. Romania was the first Communist country visited by a U.S. president (Nixon in 1969). Romania received Most Favored Nation status from the USA, membership in the International Monetary Fund and the World Bank, and generous loans from the West. The fine rifle Ceaușescu used for hunting was a present from Queen Elizabeth, who bestowed a knighthood on him. As late as 1983, George Bush, the then vice president of the United States, called him "the good communist."

Given the existence of the "Bulgarian trace" in the attempt on John Paul II's life, in Western eyes Todor Zhivkov was a bad Communist. As for himself, he thought he was living up to the nickname given to him by Bulgarian masscult: Uncle Tosho—not a strict father, but a benevolent family patriarch, forgiving what a father wouldn't have. According to a Bulgarian author who knew him quite well, he looked like a small-town person, "the local postmaster, or the teacher in the preparatory school, or perhaps one of the council clerks or the local agricultural expert."

Uncle Tosho had survived eight conspiracies to overthrow him, successfully uprooted the Turkish ethnic minority, and maintained a very capable secret service. More of a tribal chief than a conventional politician, he was the only leader in the Eastern bloc who believed in talking to the dead and allowed a seer, an old woman from the town of Petrich, Baba Vanga, blinded by a storm of 1923, to grow into a living goddess. His provincialism was a cause of amusement for the three sophisticated leaders of the East—János Kádár, Erich Honecker, and Gustáv Husák.

Husák shared a good deal with Kádár. Like Kádár, he was purged in the postwar putsch; Husák spent nine years in prison. Like Kádár's country, Husák's Czechoslovakia was scarred by a recent Soviet intervention. Like Kádár, Husák was a man of painful contradictions. According to a historian of the Prague Spring, Kieran Williams, "the first clarion call for democratization in 1968" was issued not by Dubček, but by Husák. After the August 1968 invasion, "Husák was initially hostile to the Soviets," and emerged as a "reasonable negotiator" only a few months later, when Dubček failed to stabilize the country and another Soviet crackdown became likely. He didn't grant Czechoslovakia nearly as much free market and freedom as Kádár had granted the Hungarians, but that was possibly explained by the precarious nature of the nation: Czechoslovakia was composed of two ethnic groups, and Husák, a Slovak himself, was very much aware of the explosive power of secessionism, which a big "thaw" could have provoked.

Like Kádár and Husák, Erich Honecker knew what it felt like to be an inmate, but his confinement had been longer and his persecutors different. Arrested by the Nazis at the age of twenty-three, Honecker spent ten years behind bars, until the Red Army reached Germany and liberated him in 1945.

No one could say that he embezzled or was nepotistic. Dry and precise himself, he ran East Germany as a factory, with the secret police, the Stasi, keeping files on six million citizens in a country with a population of sixteen million, and the Wall, the embodiment of the cold war, which he inherited from his predecessor, Walter Ulbricht.

Honecker was not bashful about the fortification that cut Berlin in two in order to prevent East Germans from fleeing to the West. A true believer, he was proud to be at the frontier between East and hostile West, and as for locking his citizens up, this served a higher purpose— the utopia that they were still not fully able to appreciate. Angry and disappointed by their lack of self-restraint, Honecker thought that if he was strong enough to live with the idea of two Germanies, so should they be: his hometown, Wiebelskirchen, where he still had family, was in West Germany.

Though proud of the Wall, Honecker didn't like the fact that it was the face of his country in the Western world. Living standards in East Germany were among the highest in the Eastern bloc. After General Augusto Pinochet's right-wing coup d'état in Chile in 1973, Honecker opened the country's doors to Chilean political refugees. His head of foreign intelligence, Markus Wolf, later wrote:

We set in train one of the most complicated rescue missions we had ever conducted. A team of our best officers was dispatched at top speed from East Berlin to check out the permeability of border controls at Chilean airports, at the port of Valparaiso, and at the road crossings to Argentina. From Argentina, we improvised a remarkable operation. The prisoners were smuggled out of the country in cars with hiding places constructed in much the same way that escapees from the GDR were secreted in cars to get past the Wall. When the controls suddenly tightened and this became too risky, we diverted our cargo ships to Valparaiso and smuggled some of the prisoners aboard in jute sacks with the cargos of fruit and canned fish.

Honecker was also proud of how well he had integrated East Germany into the Eastern bloc. It had taken many state visits to clear the Communist Germany of responsibility for World War II. Now Eastern European and Soviet anger focused on the Federal Republic of Germany, not the GDR. Though all the lands given to Poland as territorial compensation in 1945 came from "his" Germany, he maintained friendly relations with Warsaw.

As for the Polish leader, Wojciech Jaruzelski, his accomplishments were obvious. Practically single-handedly, he had frozen the Polish revolution in 1981. Thanks to him, in 1985, life was still good for Honecker, Husák, Zhivkov, Kádár, Ceaușescu, and yes, Gorbachev.

———

It is pointless to ask what Gorbachev's initial plan for Eastern Europe was. He didn't have one. The seven leaders met regularly, as they had under Brezhnev, but now the setting was formal, reflecting new tensions and an overall sense of distrust. Moscow had never been a puppet master, but in 1985 its influence in Eastern Europe was at its lowest. The Kremlin's resignation during the Polish crisis of 1980–81 had made it clear that the Soviet Union was no longer strong enough to send its troops abroad, no matter how dire the crisis. The USSR's economic growth, 4.8 percent in 1970, fell to 1.7 percent in the mid-1980s. The decrease of oil prices had slashed the flow of the petrodollars the USSR relied upon, and from then on Moscow was "steadily reducing" the amount of oil it exported to Eastern Europe at below-market prices, Markus Wolf wrote in his memoirs.

The misconceived anti-alcohol campaign not only weakened the economy, it also provided a huge stimulus for a shadow economy that began as a network of underground breweries and smugglers of alcohol, spreading into the economy as a whole. As any poor country, the Soviet Union had always had high crime rates, but there was little space for organized crime in a dictatorship. Gorbachev's prohibition pushed the criminal world out of its niche, and when the Soviet and international media started talking about a ·"Mafia" or "mafias" within the Soviet Union, it was not an exaggeration. The criminalization of the economy naturally led to more corruption of police and local authorities. Before, the government had provided order without law. Now it could deliver neither.

Unrest in the "republics," as the Soviets called the non-Russian parts of the country, started with Central Asia. In December 1986, Gorbachev replaced the first secretary of the Communist Party of Kazakhstan, a Kazakh, Dinmukhamed Kunaev, with a Russian, Gennadi Kolbin. Prompted by the intention to fight corruption (Kunaev was a notorious embezzler), the choice violated an unwritten rule of the Soviet Union, according to which each republic's party boss had to be a local. Possibly instigated by the outgoing leader, sixty thousand Kazakhs went into the streets of the capital, Almaty, to protest the appointment of a Russian. Kolbin ordered a crackdown that resulted in casualties. Gorbachev dismissed the riots as a nationalistic plot, but the Soviet Union lost domestic peace. A year later, in the Caucasus, Armenia and Azerbaijan clashed over a disputed piece of land, Nagorno-Karabakh. Obviously, none of the republics had an army, so all the fighting was done by spontaneous paramilitary units—and that gave rise to warlords.

To Eastern European leaders, the nosedive of the Soviet Union was of momentous significance. There was not a single economic indicator that would promise a return to the days of subsidized oil and low-interest loans. The growing interethnic violence in the USSR demonstrated that Moscow was no longer capable of controlling the "republics." In a situation like this, it was laughable to think that it would be able to interfere militarily in case of an uprising in any country of the Eastern bloc. Suddenly, after forty years spent under the Soviet economic and military umbrella, the leaders of Eastern Europe found themselves on their own. "We will have to rely on ourselves," Erich Honecker started saying—in the words of his chief of intelligence, "refusing to acknowledge that East Germany had neither the wealth nor the power to act alone."

Gorbachev was hostile to most of the Eastern European leaders; fond of Jaruzelski and Kádár, he barely tolerated Husák, felt harassed by Honecker, called Zhivkov "the Bogdykhan" (an archaic title for the emperor of China in Russian), and as for his nickname for Ceauşescu, it was "the Romanian Führer."

When he and Raisa visited Bucharest, public events were grandiose and full of camaraderie, yet when Gorbachev tried hobnobbing with the people in the street, he decided they looked scared. A new supermarket built and filled with food to impress the visitor was crowded with Romanians hurrying to loot the Potemkin village. Ugly totalitarian buildings were going up everywhere, and Gorbachev viciously told the press: "I hope the historical architecture will be preserved. We failed to do that in some places in Moscow and now we are regretting it." When Gorbachev arrived at the first televised meeting, he discovered that he was to see Ceauşescu in front of a fireplace, as the Romanian wanted to outdo the famous Reagan-Gorbachev image. The day was hot and sitting in front of the fireplace was unbearable; Gorbachev wanted to take his jacket off and couldn't.

At the dinner that night, possessive and protective of her husband as ever and feeling that he remained unappreciated by the host, Raisa told Ceauşescu that Gorbachev was getting three thousand to four thousand letters a day from all over the Soviet Union. "If I were a Soviet citizen," Ceauşescu snorted, "I would have written a letter to him too and asked to slow down on foreign policy and pay attention to the domestic issues." Gorbachev exploded: "You keep the whole country in fear, shut off from the rest of the world." The shouting match that Raisa's remark had ignited was becoming so intense that the security detail felt compelled to violate the secrecy of the negotiations room and open the doors to check on the trio's well-being.

Despite these personal tensions, the Warsaw Pact's huge bureaucratic machine ran virtually on its own, with various committees convening and adjoining without much regard for changing circumstances— meetings of deputy foreign ministers, foreign ministers, experts, and defense ministers assembling regularly and fruitlessly. The Soviet brass was paying little attention, as they had a more pressing issue on their hands: Afghanistan.

In Geneva, pressed by Reagan on the Afghan War, Gorbachev said he "had known nothing about it personally until he heard a radio broadcast." That was one of the Soviet leader's habitual lies. Of course, in 1979 when the decision to send the troops in was taken, he was only a candidate member of the Politburo, having no say in foreign policy matters, but he was already part of the Kremlin inner circle and very close to the father of the Afghan war folly, Yuri Andropov. From 1980, when he got full Politburo membership, and on, Gorbachev participated in many Politburo meetings debating the war.

A year after the Geneva summit and twenty months since becoming general secretary, on November 13, 1986, Gorbachev finally called a Politburo meeting to confront the issue. These twenty months of hesitation had cost the Afghan people about one hundred thousand lives and the Soviet troops at least fifteen hundred. As for the general status of the war, as military professionals warned on the eve of the invasion, it had turned into a quagmire. Fully aware of the dimensions of the crisis, Gorbachev was still not ready for anything but finger pointing and opened the session by angrily berating the army for its ineffectiveness. "We have been fighting in Afghanistan already for six years," he said. "If the approach is not changed, we will continue to fight for another twenty [to] thirty years . . . Our military should be told that they are learning badly from this war."

The logical choice to answer this accusation was the sole representative of the military at the meeting, Chief of the General Staff Marshal Sergei Akhromeyev, but he knew that frankness had cost his predecessor, Marshal Ogarkov, his job, and so he swallowed the insult silently. But someone else did come forward—the foreign minister to five party leaders starting with Khrushchev, Andrei Gromyko. His thin lips twisted in a trademark grimace of squeamish displeasure, he unceremoniously interrupted Gorbachev's diatribe by saying, "It is necessary to establish a strategic target. Too long ago we spoke about the fact that it is necessary to close off the borders of Afghanistan with Pakistan and Iran. Experience has shown that we were unable to do this in view of the difficult terrain of the area and the existence of hundreds of passes in the mountains. Today it is necessary to make clear that the only viable strategic assignment is the one that is directed toward bringing the war to an end."

Despite the fact that Gromyko's statement contradicted what he had just said, Gorbachev mumbled his agreement. Without acknowledging Gorbachev's concurrence, Gromyko impassively continued: "It should be concluded so that Afghanistan becomes a neutral country. Apparently, on our part there was an underestimation of the difficulties, when we agreed with the Afghan government to give them our military support. The social conditions in Afghanistan made the resolution of the problem in a short amount of time impossible. We did not receive domestic support there. In the Afghan army the number of conscripts equals the number of deserters."

Had this come from the military leader Akhromeyev, Gorbachev could have and likely would have dismissed it as whining by an inept strategist. But it was hard to argue with Gromyko, who carried with him the respect due to a man who had risen to power under Stalin and survived every change in Soviet leadership since that time untouched. When one Politburo member with a reputation as a yes-man gilded the lily, suggesting that it would be good to end the war by the seventieth anniversary of the Bolshevik revolution the following year, Gromyko retorted icily, "It is difficult to talk about such a period of time."

The message was clear. The war had drained the Soviet Union not only emotionally, but financially as well, and had to be brought to an end. The unspoken words were "even without victory." The leadership had finally caught up to the Soviet people on the futility of pressing the war in Afghanistan. Inflation, practically unknown before, became a new and unwelcome fact of life. In 1985–86, the budget deficit had more than doubled, and so had the foreign debt. Gorbachev's positive rating stood at 35 percent. The Soviet Union was out of time, out of patience, and out of money.

The only person to voice dissent was the KGB chairman, Viktor Chebrikov. This was not surprising. The Afghan War was, after all, a child of the secret service. But Chebrikov's attempt to reverse the consensus building around Gromyko's position had no traction at all.

All that was left was for the army to put on record that it had done its job on the battlefield. The problem was political. "There is no single piece of land in that country that has not been occupied by a Soviet soldier," Marshal Akhromeyev said gravely. What they didn't win was "the battle for the Afghan people."

Negotiations with the Afghan opposition, made public in 1987, caused mirth in Eastern Europe. The Soviet Union had cried uncle.

A planned economy works as long as people at every level listen to the plan. They listen, as they are afraid of repercussions. Now, though Gorbachev hadn't formally annulled anything—the leading role of the party inscribed in the constitution, the laws punishing anti-Soviet activities and social parasitism, the KGB presence in every factory, college, and research center—the fear was gone. The apparatus that was supposed to enforce it—from local party committees to the KGB—found itself paralyzed by the overwhelming political uncertainty. Clearly, they would have stepped in had a person started pulling down a Lenin statue or distributing "Death to Communism" leaflets, but the Soviet public hadn't rebelled yet. All they were doing was quietly opting out of the system. The KGB couldn't step in when a person refused to go to a collective farm to harvest potatoes.

The Soviet agriculture system had functioned only because each fall millions of urbanites, from workers to academics, obediently spent weeks in the fields, ordered there by the party (in the mid-1980s, seven hundred thousand a day on average). Circa 1988, they refused to go. Agriculture collapsed, lines to buy food grew. The hoarding of goods began. William Moskoff writes:

> The hoarding of goods is a rational response by a citizenry that has lost faith in the capacity of its leaders to guarantee the supply of essential commodities and that has expectations of future inflation. Although the old Soviet system of centralized supply had many well-known failings, the population was sufficiently secure with it not to feel the need to resort to hoarding on a large-scale basis. There had always been shortages, but people had felt that a minimum supply would be available; there had been few fears that the system would not consistently provide at least the minimum ... Hoarding began as early as 1987

when, according to one estimate, as much as a quarter of the population, fueled by rumors, was already stockpiling goods, especially food. Panic buying of food never stopped after that.

A perestroika joke: There is a long line in front of a grocery store. A man freaks out—"I've had it. I am going to the Kremlin to shoot Gorbachev." When he is back, people ask: "So?" "I couldn't! There is a line there, too."

With glasnost, shortages were discussed in the media. The new activism was not necessarily anti-Communist, but it was often antigovernment. Predictably, the society was polarized by these new public criticisms. The media was equally split, and by 1987 the only centrist outlets were those directly controlled by the Communist Party Central Committee—such as the infamous *Pravda*.

For the media, acquiring freedom of speech was a chaotic process achieved through insubordination. Here is how the Soviet media worked: when considering a potentially explosive piece, the editor in chief of a newspaper had to call the newspaper division of the Central Committee. The head of the newspaper division weighed all the pros and cons and then either approved the piece or vetoed it. If the watchdog was in doubt, he called his superior—the secretary of the Central Committee in charge of ideology. The latter's verdict was final. But here is what happened in September 1987 with a glasnost milestone, the obituary of the writer Viktor Nekrasov.

In the light of the ideological battles that followed thereafter, the case looks shockingly insignificant. Forty years earlier, right after the war, Nekrasov received the Stalin Prize for a patriotic novel, *In the Trenches of Stalingrad*. In 1974, he emigrated to Paris, where he lived until his death in 1987. As Nekrasov was not nearly as controversial a figure as Solzhenitsyn, when he died, a liberal weekly, the *Moscow News*, decided to publish an obituary. The editor in chief called the newspaper division of the Central Committee. The Nekrasov case was borderline, so, unsure what to do, the division contacted the Central Committee secretary, who promptly vetoed the obituary. The *Moscow News* still published it.

What followed was typical of glasnost. Gorbachev, on vacation at the time, went ballistic (as his colleague recalled, "We never touched on the artistic side of the writer's work, and dealt only with his political position as an émigré"). At Gorbachev's insistence, the party ideologues thrashed the *Moscow News* at a meeting of newspaper editors the next day. Instead of standing up to the ideological pressure, the *Moscow News* editor simply lied, saying "he had not received any instructions from the Central Committee." "This led to a brouhaha," Gorbachev's colleague continues—meaning finger-pointing within the Central Committee.

The insignificance of the initial cause of all the trouble (the "political position" of a second-tier émigré author) does not make the Nekrasov obituary case less emblematic of the Gorbachev years, when the media acquired freedom in a piecemeal way—and the party lost its power in a similar manner.

More important, the party itself was going through a schism. In 1987, a few weeks after the Nekrasov "brouhaha," Gorbachev was confronted with his own Wałesa: Boris Yeltsin. The comparison is not as far-fetched as it might seem. Yeltsin had climbed the party hierarchy to the very top, but he also grew up on a farm, never pretended to be anything but a person with working-class tastes, and, like Wałesa, was prone to jumping fences. At a party plenum in 1987, Yeltsin did an unimaginable thing: he stood up to the general secretary, accusing the leader of moving too slowly and not being democratic with colleagues. Angry beyond words (Yeltsin had also hinted that Gorbachev was under Raisa's heel), Gorbachev got him fired, unintentionally making Yeltsin into a martyr. As Yeltsin disappeared from the public eye, Moscow cab drivers started saying that he had shot himself and was lying "frozen" in the Kremlin mortuary.

Yeltsin soon reappeared, surrounded by cultured freethinkers, but, just like Wałesa in Poland, very quickly shook them off. Highbrows praising Western democracy (of which they knew little) and capitalism (of which they knew even less) won newspapers subscribers; Yeltsin won the street, as he was exactly the kind of person the Russian public was willing to support: down-to-earth, inarticulate, boorish, angry.

For the antigovernment forces, Yeltsin was a godsend. The awakening of the Russian core of the Soviet Union resulted in the emergence of three major opposition camps, each built around a media outlet. Liberals, who closed ranks around the *Moscow News*, focused on a free market, free elections, and westernization. Reactionaries, mobilized by *Nash*

Sovremennik, swore by the nineteenth-century Slavophile legacy built around Russian nationalism and fundamentalist Russian Orthodox Christianity. Neo-Stalinists, with *Sovetskaya Rossiya* their mouthpiece, argued that any reform was lethal for communism and aspired to fight the counterrevolution that, they said, came from Gorbachev, the liberals, *and* the reactionaries. Yeltsin could not appeal to the neo-Stalinists. The fact that liberals rallied around him was well known. However, many of the reactionary nationalists accepted him, too, because Russian national pride had been high on his agenda from the start.

While battles in Moscow remained largely ideological, the non-Russian parts of the Soviet Union saw tensions boil over into violence. Armenia formally "annexed" Nagorno-Karabakh, and Azerbaijan answered with anti-Armenian pogroms. Every republic of the union had a secessionist movement, and in Estonia, Lithuania, Latvia, Georgia, and Ukraine those movements grew into influential parties. All the republics started withholding revenues from the federal government.

The neo-Stalinists were the only political camp that wanted to restore Moscow's rule in the provinces. Liberals believed in nations' right to self-determination, nationalists said that the republics had bled Russia white, and if the ungrateful entities wanted to secede now, that would be good riddance. The temporary alliance between liberals and reactionaries made possible by the emergence of Boris Yeltsin as a Russian antigovernment leader meant that the Russian core of the USSR wanted to secede from the union, too—on par with Estonia and Georgia.

That left Gorbachev and his circle without a power base. As the Yeltsin-led alliance strengthened, Gorbachev was turning into the mayor of the Kremlin. With the Russian Main Street willing to let the republics go without a fight, it couldn't care less about preserving its sphere of influence in Eastern Europe. Before Gorbachev had a chance to figure out the Eastern Europe dilemma—to stay or to evacuate—Main Street had made the choice for him.

One is tempted to say that Gorbachev repeated the path of Alexander Dubček, who gave the Czechoslovak street too much too quickly—but, emphatically, this was not the case. In 1968, Dubček ushered in freedom of the press and freedom of foreign travel within five months, while in 1985–89 Gorbachev introduced no significant *legal* changes to the USSR's social contract. Glasnost was not a set of new laws, but rather an approach. In Gorbachev's case, a halfhearted reform from above led to a full-fledged revolution from below.

It's little wonder that the pope thought Gorbachev was a "providential man." The pope's official biographer, George Weigel, explains: "Gorbachev seems more likely to appear as the instrument of a Providence he never understood than as the conscious servant of a higher design."

On June 10, 1987, Ronald Reagan delivered his famous speech at the Brandenburg Gate in West Berlin: "Standing before the Brandenburg Gate, every man is a German, separated from his fellow men. Every man is a Berliner, forced to look upon a scar." And then the bold demand: "General Secretary Gorbachev, if you seek peace, if you seek prosperity for the Soviet Union and Eastern Europe, if you seek liberalization: Come here to this gate! Mr. Gorbachev, open this gate! *Mr. Gorbachev, tear down this wall!*"

The speech, immediately recognized in the West as one of the most important ever delivered by a politician, did not cause much of a stir in the Soviet Union because the country had been rattled by another German-related event: twelve days before Reagan addressed the Berliners, on May 28, a plane bearing a German flag had landed on Red Square in Moscow.

The German pilot, nineteen-year-old Mathias Rust, had rented a Cessna in Finland and flew all the way south over the most sensitive Soviet strategic facilities. After he landed, it took the Moscow police about an hour to arrive at the scene. Rust was sentenced to four years in labor camps (commuted to fourteen months in prison), Gorbachev was livid, and heads rolled in the Ministry of Defense, but the real fallout of the adventure was that the empire lost face. In Western studies this is a quaint footnote to the end of the cold war, but for the Soviets, Rust's flight was a historic cataclysm.

If Gorbachev did not have a plan for Eastern Europe, maybe Eastern Europe had a plan for him? In 1985, even the distrusting rebel intellectual Adam Michnik, a former leader of KOR, sounded sufficiently excited about Gorbachev: "The Soviet state has a new leader; he is a symbol of transition from one generation to the next within the Soviet elite. This change may offer an opportunity, since Mikhail Gorbachev has not yet become a prisoner of his own decisions. No one can rule out the possibility that an impulse for reform will spring from the top of the hierarchy of power. This is exactly what happened in the time of Alexander II and, a hundred years later, under Khrushchev. Reform is always possible, even in the face of resistance by the old apparatus."

In less than three years he came to a different conclusion, and in early 1988 articulated his views in an interview for the *Times Literary Supplement*: "All the changes taking place from above in the Soviet Union are designed to maintain or modernize its empire. Gorbachev is not a man fighting for freedom. He instead wishes to make the Soviet Union more powerful." Michnik explained that the Soviet leader "wants to defend the system by reforming it." Wałesa seconded the argument in not so many words: "One privately owned café in Moscow," he said to journalists, "does not constitute reform—particularly when it is frequented mainly by the KGB!" (The café in question, on Ostozhenka Street, was indeed frequented by foreigners and KGB operatives.)

Michnik's sibling in Czechoslovakia, Václav Havel, was, for some reason, able to look at the "Gorbachev factor" with more irony and sympathy. When Gorbachev visited Czechoslovakia in April 1987 to deliver a public speech on the "common European home," Havel responded with an essay entitled "Meeting Gorbachev." According to the essay, Havel took his dog out for a walk and, "unable to resist," headed toward a crowd of compatriots greeting the Soviet leader in downtown Prague. Initially, Havel was skeptical: Gorbachev was just the "Glasnost Czar" and Havel felt "sad" because Czechs and Slovaks put too much faith in him and didn't realize that liberation couldn't come from "some external force." But Gorbachev "is walking just a few yards away from me, waving and smiling his friendly smile—and suddenly he seems to be waving and smiling at *me*." Havel "shyly" raises his arm and waves back. "It is, after all, one thing to respond to his smile, but something else again to try and excuse my own reaction by blaming him for smiling in the first place."

Havel was the biggest dissident celebrity in Eastern Europe and he was very special. He wrote powerfully about freedom and existential choice; his essay "The Power of the Powerless" was a samizdat bestseller in Poland, Hungary, and, of course, Czechoslovakia. Inspired by KOR, he founded the high-profile human rights group Charter 77 (after the year when its manifesto was published), and was imprisoned for his role. But Havel, above all, was a playwright, his best-known work being *The Memorandum*, brought to the United States and awarded the 1967–68 Obie Award for Best Foreign Play (it was about a synthetic language called Ptydepe, "built on a strictly scientific basis," requiring a "steadfast faith" in its truth, and sounding like "Ra ko hutu d dekotu ely trebomu emusohe"). His open letter to the party leader, Gustáv Husák, used word combinations such as "quaking like aspen leaves," "existential pressure," and "entropic regime." If KOR was a revolutionary underground, Charter 77 was an in-your-face Voltaire.

Though officially KOR self-dissolved back in 1981, its founders were very willing to share their expertise with other dissidents in the Eastern bloc. Havel's collaborator Jan Urban remembers: "From the end of 1987, we Czech dissidents had concluded that it wasn't enough to make links with groups in the West, welcome as that was. We had to develop a broader context, and even co-operation, with dissidents in other parts of Eastern Europe." They began to meet with former KOR leaders such as Adam Michnik and Jacek Kuroń in the mountains on the Polish border, filming one picnic and sending it to the Western media; the prompt broadcast of the event sent a mischievous message to the secret services of the East: Catch us if you can. "They" couldn't any longer, because secret services need shade to operate in, and Eastern Europe was becoming more and more transparent. Encouraged, Urban founded the Eastern European Information Agency. "From now on, whatever happened in Eastern Europe, we consulted with our friends in the neighboring countries and were able with them to publish joint comments on events."

On the twentieth anniversary of the Soviet invasion of Czechoslovakia, Urban remembers, "suddenly, the streets of Prague were streaming with demonstrations. I remember the panic at the police station where they were holding me . . . All of us, policemen, politicians, dissidents, had simply forgotten that twenty years is enough time for a new generation to grow up."

Yet, despite epiphanies like this, in 1988 no one actually expected communism to fall within a year. The authoritative American cold war historian, John Lewis Gaddis, wrote later: "As I was pondering this problem, I suddenly found myself thinking about a declining dinosaur. From the outside, as rivals contemplated its sheer size, tough skin, bristling armament, and aggressive posturing, the beast looked sufficiently formidable that none dared tangle with it. Appearance deceived, though, for within its digestive, circulatory, and respiratory systems were slowly clogging up, and then shutting down."

Stanisław Cardinal Dziwisz, the most authoritative source on Pope John Paul II, wrote almost twenty years later: "John Paul II wasn't expecting it. Yes, he did think that the system was doomed to collapse sooner or later because it was so socially unjust and economically inefficient. But the Soviet Union was still a geopolitical, military, and nuclear power." In Poland, the mother of the Eastern European revolution, no decisive battle was in sight. Or had it already happened, the final push gone unnoticed?

Despite allegations to the contrary, Jaruzelski had no intention of restoring the pre-Solidarity order, as he was an intelligent man and knew that it was not possible. His favorite word was *normalization*, but, unfortunately, "normalization" couldn't do much for the main national issue, the economy. Like his predecessors, the general had to borrow heavily from the West, but since the declaration of martial law, economic sanctions against his government had been in place. How could he prove to the West that the thaw was real? The simplest thing was to release political prisoners. He announced that "those internees who desist from activities 'contrary to the law' will be released." Many of the internees complied. There was, however, a hard-core group of intellectuals, such as Michnik, who refused a "few strokes of the pen on the loyalty declaration." The general tempted them with an offer to leave the country, but they cleverly declined.

Michnik was particularly unforgiving: "This is an undeclared war. On that Saturday night in December [1981], agents of the security service banged on our doors; then—after breaking them open with crowbars, beating us severely, and attacking us with tear gas—they drove us away to prisons and called us internees." Now did the general have to use tear gas *again*—this time, to make Michnik leave his prison cell?

Jaruzelski wanted desperately to be admitted to the IMF and the World Bank, so in 1986 he announced amnesty for all political prisoners and put the murderers of Father Popieluszko on trial. Of course, this was about appearances, as Michnik correctly noted, but is there a clear boundary between "appearances" and "performance"?

Realizing that the leaders of the dissolved KOR, more radical than Wałesa, were still a formidable political force, the general divided the opposition quietly and successfully. It was not all that difficult to play Wałesa against Michnik. In interviews and writings, Michnik referred to the early Marxist Rosa Luxemburg, the theory and practices of Jacobinism, the existentialism of Karl Jaspers, and the dialectical philosophy of Hegel. Wałesa declared that social gatherings—not studies—were "a kind of barometer for the political climate and the social mood." Michnik's favorite star was Daniel Cohn-Bendit, the legendary Paris revolutionary of 1968; for Wałesa, it was Elton John ("very nice and affable, with his big smile and his big glasses . . . he gave me his hat as a gift"). A *Times Literary Supplement* correspondent asked Michnik: "What if some strange turn of events confronted Poland with the possibility of replacing General Jaruzelski with a General Pinochet?" Michnik: "If forced to choose between General Jaruzelski and General Pinochet, I would choose Marlene Dietrich."

In one of his first postprison interviews, Michnik said, "a process of social detotalitarianization has been taking place during the past ten years. It has had many phases of varying intensity, but there is no denying that this group of about fifteen people—the KOR founders—has come to represent a certain model of collective behavior. Simply put, that behavior is the combination of a relentless struggle for human rights and a refusal of violence."

De-to-tal-i-ta-ria-ni-za-tion? "A certain model of collective behavior"? How about Elton John giving you a hat—a crown of mass recognition, practically? Intellectual revolutionaries lost, but they bowed out graciously. Criticizing Wałesa for the politics of compromise, many KOR founders, like Michnik, made a responsible choice to support him.

In 1986, Wałesa, the general's favorite, created the Solidarity Provisional Coordinating Board and got Solidarity admitted to the International Confederation of Free Trade Unions and the World Confederation of Labor. Meanwhile, on paper, Solidarity remained banned in Poland. Grateful to the general for looking the other way, Wałesa called on the United States to lift economic sanctions against Poland.

In his thousand-page biography of the pope, George Weigel devotes just one page to the end of communism in Poland, sandwiching it between Gorbachev's recognition of the Russian Orthodox Church and the religious revival in Czechoslovakia. The name of the section is telling: "History on Fast-Forward." Both the uncharacteristic brevity and the title make total sense to the student of Eastern European history. No matter how detailed the narrative, no episode can ever explain why in 1988–89 Polish communism dissolved so quickly, painlessly, and smoothly.

The true sphinx was Jaruzelski. Have we mentioned that the dark glasses he wore at all times were a health necessity, as he had partially lost his vision while doing slave labor in the Soviet coal mines forty-five years earlier? He let Wałesa see foreign dignitaries such as Prime Minister Thatcher and Vice President Bush in a vague capacity. The general traveled to the Vatican to have a private moment with the pope, and several months later Wojtyla descended on Poland, scolding Jaruzelski publicly, ordaining new priests, beatifying a "young peasant girl killed while resisting rape by a Russian soldier in 1914," and celebrating mass for one million in Gdansk. But the sphinx had the last word. He said to the departing pope in public: "You will take with you, in your heart, its image, but you will not take with you the homeland's real problems." Brazen, to put it mildly: "Render unto Caesar that which is Caesar's"—and this in the most Catholic country in Europe, one that had put the Virgin Mary on the barricades only seven years earlier. Speaking out loud, Jaruzelski subjugated spirituality to materialism ("heart" versus "real problems") and pronounced the pope a mere visitor to Poland. The remark did not cause riots, for the general getting away with a salvo like that meant that there *was* normalization in Poland.

In February 1988, responding to a deepening budget shortfall, Jaruzelski announced price hikes, "the steepest since 1982." Spontaneous strikes lasted into May. Wałesa called it "the first avalanche." In July, Gorbachev visited and encouraged the Poles to "learn from Lenin"—advice sounding unbelievably untimely, but sadly typical for a leader who was unable to interpret his own country. After the "second avalanche" of strikes, Wałesa and the general started negotiating the Round Table, a forum that would lead to democracy or, strictly speaking, a free vote in Poland. The call for open elections was rooted in the economic hardship. Despite the fact that Wałesa and Solidarity didn't really have a detailed economic program, the Polish street was convinced that any aggressive free-market reform would bring better results than the stagnant Communist system.

The situation didn't look real. Technically, Solidarity was not yet legal and Wałesa was still not allowed to travel internationally, so the general was negotiating with a phantom political movement whose leader's civil rights had been suspended. But it was clear that Jaruzelski was gradually transferring power to the banned movement and its persecuted leader.

Mid-October: The Round Table *table*, custom-made and twenty-eight feet in diameter, was delivered to the Jabłonna Palace in the suburbs of Warsaw.

Mid-November: Negotiations collapsed. The Round Table *table* was dismantled and returned to the manufacturer.

December: President François Mitterrand invited Wałesa to Paris to commemorate the fortieth anniversary of the Universal Declaration of the Rights of Man. The general let the corporal go.

New Year's Eve: Sipping champagne, Wałesa "reflected on what the old year had brought us." It was practically all good: "True, we weren't yet legal; but it seemed only a matter of time now."

Unbeknownst to Wałesa, this cautious optimism was an understatement. Just three weeks later, on January 21, 1989, the Soviet Politburo decided to start pulling out five hundred thousand troops from Eastern Europe. The argument Gorbachev used at the meeting was frightening: the government, he said, needed them back home for "the maintenance of internal stability." The remark underscored that the reformer was close to despair and was considering using force in Armenia, Azerbaijan, and other rebellious regions within the Soviet Union. As for Eastern Europe, he acknowledged bitterly that it was all but gone already. If the Soviet Union pulled the leash a bit harder, he admitted, "the leash will break."

Part Three

1989

6. The "Polish Disease" Spreads: June–September

On July 9, *Air Force One* was over the Atlantic, heading east. The wait-and-see president was on his way to Eastern Europe, to deliver help to anti-Communist rebels. He wasn't carrying cash or weapons, or even food; the help in transit was himself, George H. W. Bush. Not unlike the pope, the president of the United States had supernatural clout.

The forty-first president of the United States was among the shyest in history—most agreed that Bush had grown repressed by eight years in the White House in the shadow of Ronald Reagan. He spent his first months in office worrying about doing the wrong thing and then worrying about worrying. In foreign policy, everyone's biggest concern was the fate of Gorbachev's perestroika, but Bush, in his sixth month in the White House, had not yet made any plans to meet the Soviet leader. Gorbachev was enraged, and Bush got some very bad press.

This July mission was going to make Gorbachev even angrier: the president was flying to the two breakaway "socialist countries," Poland and Hungary, and then attending a summit in Paris to which Gorbachev wasn't invited.

The inexorable and totally unexpected acceleration of the Eastern European revolution was precisely what compelled Bush to travel to Eastern Europe. The Polish bug had become a pandemic, and even the most cautious person in the world couldn't have failed to see in events a huge opportunity for the United States, one prayed for throughout the past forty years.

Recognizing Poland as the mother of the Eastern European revolution, Bush bypassed Hungary for now and set down in Warsaw.

As 1989 began, despite all the preparations for the Round Table, Solidarity was still not legal. In January, Jaruzelski struggled at the Polish party plenum, defending his suggestion to legalize it and provoking such a violent response that the general called for a vote of personal confidence, which he won, thus forcing the party to take a "historic step" (says Wałesa). Stretching the metaphor only a bit, one could say that the general was living the Polish myth, seeing himself as a mere caretaker for the absent king and now preparing the stage for the king to return.

On February 6, fifty-seven people finally sat down at the Round Table. Wałesa: "Why was it twenty-eight feet wide? The joke going through the corridors had it that it was because the world's record spitting distance is only twenty-five feet!" "The Round Table completed its mission on the evening of the sixtieth day, April 5, 1989," Wałesa wrote. The pope, in a weekly general audience, said, "Today I wish to thank You, Holy Mother, for all the good that has emerged out of these trying times." Poland would have free elections, but this was going to be "the thirty-five percent democracy," in Wałesa's words, as the party reserved 65 percent of the slots for itself and its "look-alikes."

The bizarre arrangement was not accidental by any means. This was the kind of free vote Gorbachev had given the Soviets a few weeks earlier. The new Soviet supreme legislative body, the Congress of People's Deputies, had 2,250 seats, of which 750 were reserved for "public organizations," not the general population, to fill. Gorbachev allocated the party a modest 100 seats, but almost all other "public organizations" remained the party's franchises. Still, in the first free parliamentary election in the Eastern bloc, on March 26, all the notable members of the opposition, such as Yeltsin and Sakharov, were voted in. This historic development did not, however, prevent the Soviet army and local Georgian police from massacring rioters in Tbilisi on April 9.

Following the Round Table agreement, Wałesa flew to Rome. Before seeing the pope, he talked to professors and students at the University of Sacro Cuore, part of which was the Gemelli Clinic, where the pope had been taken after the assassination attempt: "We came here to thank you for saving Solidarity. Yes! It was you who saved the Holy Father after the assassination attempt in May 1981. And it's hard to imagine that Solidarity would have survived without him." On April 20, the pope received Wałesa. In contrast to previous visits, he treated him as a head of state, with red carpets and ceremonial clashes of halberds.

The month of May promised gigantic changes. On May 25, the Congress of People's Deputies opened in Moscow; the event was televised live, and the opposition courted controversy, asking for the article in the constitution fixing the party's "leading" role to be removed, the Tbilisi massacre to be fully investigated, and a multiparty system to be introduced. In China, students occupied the local Red Square: Tiananmen. On a prearranged schedule, Gorbachev paid an awkward visit to Beijing, accompanied by a flock of international media, who all but forgot about the historic Sino-Soviet "normalization" and started covering the tumultuous Chinese youth instead. The unrest hit other cities, and by the end of the month every university campus had hundreds of *dazibao*—handwritten opinion pieces or news bulletins glued to walls, lampposts, and revolutionary monuments. In Tiananmen, students put up a statue of liberty. At one point, misinterpreting the movement of government limos, Western media reported that the government had fled to Nanjing.

On June 4, Poland went to the polls. Solidarity claimed victory, winning practically all the contested seats, but the general wasn't totally unhappy either, as the turnout was just 62 percent, which he read as a sign of exhaustion and apathy; though not without considerable hesitation, he planned to run for president, so this was very good news. The low turnout seemed to suggest that free elections were not actually what the Polish Main Street needed at that point. Definitely free from fear, now the Poles aspired to be free from want, and as no party in the June elections suggested a clear path to this end, casting ballots lost its liberating appeal.

The same day, the Chinese military occupied Tiananmen Square, leaving anywhere between four hundred and three thousand young men and women dead. From then on, the specter of the Tiananmen massacre would haunt Eastern European revolutionaries and reformers everywhere except Poland. Its new social contract unwritten, its economic future dim, Poland had achieved civil peace. By the summer of 1989, the Poles had understood that free elections were just the means, not the end. Nine years earlier, Solidarity, young and boisterous then, came up with the slogan "There is no bread without freedom." Now, after a heroic journey, the Poles knew that there is also no freedom without bread.

Bush was not bringing much. America's "resources had shrunk," Brent Scowcroft admitted, and "a new Marshall Plan was not possible." The Bush administration wanted "to spread the burden of economic response to East European needs"—in other words, make Europe foot the bill. The package included rescheduling Poland's $39 billion foreign debt, "a request to the World Bank for $325 million in new loans," and $100 million in "US funds." In that year Egypt received $968 million in American foreign aid. With the Soviet Union toothless, Eastern Europe could be liberated on the cheap.

According to Scowcroft, the president's motorcade was "sparsely attended by the citizens of Warsaw," and the visitors felt disappointed "with the absence of masses of enthusiastic Poles cheering the President." With a certain sadness, Scowcroft, who had witnessed Richard Nixon's 1972 triumphal ride into town, admitted that now the crowds were "simply 'normal.'"

The president liked Jaruzelski even better than in 1987. According to Bush, "Jaruzelski opened his heart and asked me what role I thought he should now play. He told me of his reluctance to run for president and his desire to avoid a political tug-of-war that Poland did not need. He did not think Solidarity would provide enough support for his election, and he worried about the humiliation of being defeated. I told him his refusal to run might inadvertently lead to serious instability and I urged him to reconsider. It was ironic: Here was an American president trying to persuade a senior Communist leader to run for office. But I felt that Jaruzelski's experience was the best hope for a smooth transition in Poland."

Jaruzelski complained that if in the United States organized labor controlled 20 percent of the workforce, in Poland it was 80 percent. "Solidarity was demanding that farmers get three times more for dairy products than the store price." "Solidarity must realize all this must change." Bush nodded. Jaruzelski continued: "It is important that you remind Polish workers to keep their feet on the ground and to work hard. It is not enough to simply admire American riches."

Jaruzelski was "very special," "particularly complex, and yet clear-headed." At a luncheon at the residence of the U.S. ambassador, where, under Bush's benevolent smile, "some forty Communist, Solidarity, and Catholic leaders . . . had sat down together at a social gathering—the jailers and the jailed at the same time," Bush suggested "we remove our coats, an idea greeted with enthusiasm. When Jaruzelski arrived, he hesitated to take off his coat, but after vanishing into another room he reappeared without it. During the toasts he confessed to me that he had removed his suspenders as well and was afraid to give too long a speech for fear his trousers would fall down."

Wałesa was also a familiar face from the 1987 visit. His requests struck the president as "a bit uncertain and unrealistic," and Bush wondered "whether he understood all of the details of what he was showing," such as a plan to put all enterprises on the auction block—even farms, which he thought U.S. farmers might want to buy. "It was an ambitious plan," Bush recalled tongue-in-cheek. Wałesa hoped Jaruzelski wouldn't run. It was clear where Bush's sympathies lay.

To abuse Tolstoy, each miserable country is miserable in its own way, and what passed for misery in Hungary would have been heaven for Soviets, Bulgarians, East Germans, and Romanians.

With Bush's visit in the works, in March the Hungarian foreign minister told Secretary of State James Baker: "When perestroika began, we were ready to go and we were pursuing ideas more radical than those being pursued by the Soviets." That was not an overstatement: when Gorbachev came to power, Hungarian communism had already been reformed, and those efforts had made Hungarian living standards the highest in the Eastern bloc. When the first private restaurant in Moscow opened with much fanfare in 1986—"One privately owned café . . . does not constitute reform"—Hungary had about thirty thousand private businesses.

János Kádár's "goulash communism" had deregulated prices, and now the state fixed roughly one thousand goods' prices, leaving the remaining one million for enterprises to value, thus creating a market if not a market economy. Instead of begging ministries and departments for more resources, now enterprises could get raw materials and labor themselves. Though officially private farms were scarce, agricultural cooperatives received surprising autonomy, and household plots—all but private except in name and title—numbered six hundred thousand. Hungary became self-sufficient in food, the only nation in the Eastern bloc exporting wheat and corn steadily.

Thanks to Kádár, Hungary became the paragon of consumerism in the Eastern bloc—and that bought him the loyalty of the people. According to Kádár's minister of the interior, every year only about ten Hungarians tried to cross to the West illegally—"drunks, children with bad school reports and husbands sneaking away from their wives"; he also insisted that Hungarian dissidents were either spoiled nomenklatura children or experimenting Communists. Both statements were exaggerations but not complete lies.

Interestingly enough, the empire understood. Not approving of Kádár's reforms and privately calling them revisionism of Marxism-Leninism, Brezhnev's Kremlin trusted and respected Kádár: no matter how different goulash communism was from the Soviet model, Kádár had secured Hungary after the bloodbath of 1956.

Kádár's reforms made the economy work but they also had to be supported by loans. According to Gorbachev, Kádár "had to go to the Soviet leadership about once every ten years for substantial financial assistance, and hundreds of millions of dollars were apportioned to Hungary." Around 1983, the Soviet Union's own economic crisis made it impossible to subsidize its allies freely. Unabashed, Kádár switched to Western banks.

Soviets loans were often interest-free; borrowing from the West thoughtlessly and living beyond its means, Hungary got caught in a basic debt trap, when one has to give away almost all one earns in interest payments. By 1987, Hungary had accumulated $18 billion in foreign debt. Its obligation to sell its products to the Eastern bloc at subsidized prices didn't help the situation either. Domestic prices and inflation soared. The Hungarian Politburo asked Kádár to retire. Surprised and hurt, the man who had led Hungary for thirty years stepped down obediently.

Presided over by Károly Grósz, the new leadership consisted of the party radical Imre Pozsgay, the long-time Kádár economic advisor Rezsö Nyers, and the forty-year-old Miklós Németh. The group created a basic stock market, reduced taxes on businesses, and allowed full foreign ownership of businesses in Hungary. Hungarians responded with civic engagement, or, one should rather say, *some* engagement. New political groups ranged from the "historical," pre-1949, parties to totally new entities, such as the Alliance of Young Democrats, and from anti-Communist to reformist Communist to neo-Stalinist; independent publications skyrocketed—but despite political rallies and demonstrations the Hungarian street remained not overly interested, and the parties failed to become a decisive factor in politics. None of the oppositionists—"historical" or otherwise—was a Wałesa or a Yeltsin.

Yet, in the first weeks of 1989, without any critical popular pressure, the government passed laws on associations, freedom of assembly, and the right to strike—basically creating a civil society in Hungary. Though the country had no dissident underground in waiting, ready for the right moment to strike at the regime (the material comforts of goulash communism explained that), it became the second Eastern European country to dismantle communism.

That clearly was a revolution from above. If in 1989 Gorbachev was still a captive of Communist dogma, the Hungarian reformers didn't seem to have much faith in any form of communism. They clearly aimed at a Western European social democracy. Were they motivated by the "Polish disease"? Absolutely. They acknowledged that it had already spread to Hungary and knew that half measures would bring only temporary calm. The reformers were also sure that they didn't have to worry about Soviet intervention: the Soviet Union was clearly at the nadir of its power.

The Soviets still had troops in Hungary distributed across 170 bases, but their withdrawal was already under way, kept secret at Gorbachev's insistence. The Politburo had already chosen to move troops back home to help "maintain domestic stability"—in other words, to deploy against the Soviet people, if necessary—but Gorbachev thought a public announcement would mean a loss of face.

Both sides knew that communism was dead in Hungary, yet both kept pretending. Talking to Németh on March 3, Gorbachev started lamenting the lack of inner party democracy under Stalin, as if that mattered any longer, with Stalin dead for thirty-six years and the Hungarian leadership making a political U-turn. Németh immediately affirmed the point by saying that things had been much better "when Lenin was at the helm" (which, incidentally, had been thirty years before he was born). Concluding this absurd conversation, Gorbachev came up with a quote from Lenin: "We Bolsheviks have conquered Russia, so now we have to learn how to govern it."

On March 22, random liberal-minded groups founded the Opposition Round Table, openly imitating the mother of the Eastern European revolution, but skipping strikes, mass protests, hot debates, clashes, deaths, and martyrs, and rallying around a single point of agreement—a corpse. Everyone thought that the remains of the 1956 reformer, Imre Nagy, had to be exhumed and given a state funeral.

Indeed, the majority of the Hungarian Politburo shared the sentiment. At a meeting, Rezsö Nyers asked a rhetorical question: "Where the hell do we find counterrevolutionary ideas with Imre Nagy?" His own answer was brilliant: "If he was still among us now unchanged, he would be more of a Stalinist."

A saint to the street, Nagy was scheduled for reburial on June 16. The Hungarian secret police worked hard so that the "extremists" "from both sides"—in other words, liberals and Stalinists—did not turn the funeral into a Tiananmen. The method it chose was not arrests or detentions but rather persuasion and misinformation. Hungarian diplomats and spies were to hold "friendly conversations" with Western colleagues and émigré Hungarian activists informing them that if the opposition turned the funeral into a demonstration this would only strengthen "the forces urging restoration" (the wording exquisite, so Habsburg in its inflection). A double agent was to send a dispatch to the CIA, saying verbatim: "Certain extremist groups are planning to exploit the funeral of Imre Nagy for anti-government disruption. In such a case, the authorities are expected to act harshly." A similar message had to be given by another operative to West German intelligence.

The funeral turned emotional but not violent. The Hungarian Round Table opened three days before—a peacefully grandiose event, involving one thousand people. The assembly included representatives of the Communist Party, state agencies, newborn opposition parties, and trade unions. From the start, it was agreed that Hungary would have free elections, so negotiations focused on the practicalities of the electoral system. Gradually, the Communists gave up the privileges ob tained during their forty-year rule—like the right to have party cells in the workplace, a basic principle of every Communist regime originating in Lenin's system.

On July 6, János Kádár died. In a poll taken that day, 75 percent of the respondents agreed that "with his passing Hungarian political life has lost one of its greatest figures." Still in America, President Bush made a public statement expressing his respect for the good Communist. Yet Kádár's funeral was postponed until after the visit of the leader of the free world.

A summer thunderstorm delayed *Air Force One's* arrival in Budapest, and the president was late for a downtown rally. "The people were drenched," Scowcroft says, "but their enthusiasm was undampened." When after a lengthy and formal introduction by the hosts Bush "stepped up to the microphone, waved off the umbrella, and proceeded to tear up his speech . . . the crowd went wild." He gave an old lady a raincoat loaned to him by a Secret Service agent, and shook many hands. "The empathy between him and the crowd was total," Scowcroft writes.

In Scowcroft's words, the "difference in mood between Poland and Hungary, to outward appearances, was dramatic." Poland had struck the Americans as depressed; Hungary, to the contrary, boiled with enthusiasm. In more practical terms, Scowcroft thought, Budapest "could manage the hard transition ahead . . . determined to make drastic change as calmly and orderly as possible." The Americans were also positive that Hungary "was in much better economic shape than Poland."

The thirty years of Kádár's "iron hand in a velvet glove" had paid off. Like every Eastern European nation, Hungary *was* divided—but the mixed economy, with its private businesses ensuring a comfortable level of materialism, prevented bitterness and anger and, subsequently, political confrontation. If Hungary had a "revolution," one may argue that it had been started by Kádár twenty years earlier.

The president didn't come empty-handed but he didn't pose as Santa Claus either. Hungary would get modest U.S. financial aid, exchange programs, a culture center, Peace Corps volunteers, and—if the parliament passed a law on the freedom of emigration—Most Favored Nation status. Bush didn't particularly care for Grósz, but the radical reformers captivated him. Prime Minister Miklós Németh (the person who discussed Stalin and Lenin with Gorbachev) gave him a plaque with a piece of barbed wire from the border fence between Hungary and Austria—a prototype of the souvenir item that would later become iconic and very popular with tourists.

Addressing an audience at Karl Marx University, Bush praised the new Hungarian saint lavishly: "A generation waited to honor Imre Nagy's courage; may a hundred generations remember it." Meanwhile, on the day of Nagy's reburial, June 16, the KGB chairman, Vladimir Kryuchkov, sent a report to the Soviet Party Central Committee claiming that during the Great Terror of the 1930s Nagy, then a political refugee in the USSR, voluntarily offered his services to Stalin's secret police. To quote Kryuchkov, the person who "acquired the halo of a martyr, of an exceptionally honest and principled person," had denounced dozens of his fellow exiles as being "anti-communist," "terrorist," and "counter-revolutionary." "A part of these were shot, a part were sentenced to various terms in prison and exile." Kryuchkov ended the memo with the advice to inform the Hungarian Communists "about the documents that we have and advise them about their possible use."

After the inspired Imre Nagy speech, in the U.S. embassy Bush met with the opposition, but the Americans were not really impressed: for some reason, the embassy had invited not the new, vocal generation of heterodox thinkers but the pre-Communist has-beens. Scowcroft says: "I was struck by the contrast between these aging leaders, some of whom had held the same position in their parties when they had been banned in 1947–48, and the progressive thinkers in the ranks of Communists.

A number of these men were setting forth the same tired old positions which had made it so easy for the Communists to set them aside when they took power at the beginning of the Cold War."

From Budapest, *Air Force One* flew to Paris for a G7 summit. That year, the choice of the locale was very deliberate: François Mitterrand was throwing a party to celebrate the French republic's bicentennial. No U.S. administration had ever been on easy terms with Paris, and the Bastille Day military festivities on July 14 looked to the Americans "like a Soviet May Day parade." Mitterrand was as difficult as ever; the parade over, he left in his motorcade quite royally, leaving the twenty-five heads of state in the reviewing stand to their own devices. In an interesting breach of both etiquette and security, the French had supplied the foreign staffs with no order of departure, hinting at a deliberate snub, and now the twenty-five convoys carrying the most powerful men and women of the Western world were stuck in an undignified stampede. Years later, Scowcroft, still unforgiving, commented: "It was chaos at its best."

The summit was equally chaotic. In 1989, no conference could stick to its agenda. The G7 quickly dismissed the environmental issues it was meant to discuss and proceeded to deal with Eastern Europe and China. Unwilling to foot the bill himself, Bush made the Europeans relax "Poland's payment schedule on its foreign debt" and create a "conference to develop and coordinate Western aid to Poland and Hungary." As for China, the Europeans wanted exemplary punishment, but Bush urged them to be prudent in their response, as "the US-Chinese relationship was too important to world peace," and China got away with a slap on the wrist.

Gorbachev, though not invited, *was* a presence at the conference, sending a letter to Mitterrand asking for cooperation on global economic issues. "Although it was not specifically a request to join the Economic Summits," Bush writes, "there was no mistaking the intent." "In my view," Bush continued, "Soviet reforms were not far enough along or sweeping enough to include the USSR as a full partner. All the G-7 leaders agreed that the reply should be positive but noncommittal."

In Hungary, Bush had felt like the president of presidents—as his son would visiting Albania eighteen years later—but here, on the snobbish French terrain, "there was some press grousing that, unlike his predecessors, the President had not dominated the discussions, but had accepted ideas from his colleagues," and, Scowcroft continued, some reporters "seemed to thrive on flamboyance and fireworks, rather than on friendly persuasion and cooperation."

On July 16, sitting on the steps of the terrace in the U.S. embassy garden with Scowcroft and Baker and feeling dejected, Bush suddenly said that he would like to meet with Gorbachev. Neither of the advisors "remonstrated with him," in Scowcroft's words.

On January 18, 1989, just two days before the inauguration of George H. W. Bush as president of the United States, Gorbachev had a private meeting with a most interesting visitor, a former U.S. government official who had been at the very pinnacle of power in the Richard Nixon and Gerald Ford administrations. The only others present were a Soviet interpreter and Anatoli Dobrynin, ambassador to the United States for twenty-three years. A written summary of the meeting referred to the visitor only as "Kitty," but those who were given access to the summary knew precisely who Kitty was.

The visitor was there to deliver a letter from the incoming president to Gorbachev, but availed himself of the opportunity to make a stunning proposal of his own, that the two superpowers undertake a cooperative effort on a quite grand scale: a Soviet-U.S. condominium over Europe. "Let us make an agreement," Kitty is quoted saying, "so that the Europeans do not misbehave."

From the perspective of Realpolitik, the United States should indeed have been worried about the disintegration of the Soviet empire in Europe. There was not a single Eastern European nation that didn't have territorial issues with its neighbors. If the "Polish bug" spread to East Germany, the number-one demand of the people there would be reunification, and a united Germany wasn't exactly what the Realpolitik school of thought in the United States would want to see.

Whatever Kitty's purpose in making the proposal, Gorbachev took from it a glimmer of hope that with the help of a new U.S. president, the Soviets might yet hang on to what Ronald Reagan had described as an "Evil Empire."

This was not the first attempt by George Bush to reach out to

Gorbachev. Just a year earlier, when Gorbachev was in Washington to meet with Reagan, Bush, then vice president, had gone out of his way to advise Gorbachev to treat as campaign rhetoric any anti-Soviet statements he might make during the upcoming election campaign. Gorbachev took Bush at his word and during the campaign made no attempt to reply in kind.

But when Kitty finally delivered the first written communication from the new president, Gorbachev was confused. The letter contained nothing more than the standard diplomatic pleasantries exchanged between heads of state on such occasions, with no reference directly stated or implied about the possibility of a Soviet-U.S. condominium in Europe. What was he to make of two messages so different in tone and content delivered to him on the very same day? Had George Bush been unaware of the proposal Kitty would make? Had Kitty been unaware of the contents of the letter he delivered? The latter seemed unlikely, for the Americans had chosen a highly powerful individual to act as messenger, a man whose feline cunning the Russians respected: the Russian word for "pretty kitty" is *kisa*.

Bush may have served under Reagan, even observed him in action from a front-row seat, but he was not Reagan. In a moment of interregnum euphoria, he had agreed to Henry Kissinger's mission to Moscow, with its verbal proposal, persuaded by the sweet-talking Kitty that if a tone of cooperation between the two leaders could be established early, history might enshrine Bush as the president "who ended the Cold War." But soon afterward, Bush decided not to rush into any such grand scheme. Instead, he summoned a group of Soviet experts to a conference in Kennebunkport, Maine. Tasked with making up the list of those who would be invited was a thirty-four-year-old White House staffer named Condoleezza Rice.

By 1989, U.S. Soviet experts were divided into two distinct camps. One advocated strong support for Gorbachev (Jack Matlock, now U.S. ambassador to Moscow, made the case eloquently in his memos to Washington). The other group either did not trust Gorbachev or expected him to lose power very soon, and so were cautious about investing too much U.S. credibility in him. Rice was a member of this second group, and so the Kennebunkport guest list she composed turned out to be clearly stacked in favor of those who shared Rice's political philosophy.

As a consequence, Bush did not have an opportunity to hear opposition views as they might have been advanced by that side's most effective advocates. Reassured that the situation in Eastern Europe called for the value he cherished most, prudence, he proclaimed the Kennebunkport retreat "one of the best such sessions" he had ever had, and he put Gorbachev on hold. As for Kissinger's bold plan, it was dumped.

Now, six months later, with events outpacing them, the two leaders were, finally, to meet.

On board *Air Force One*, Bush penned a letter to Gorbachev. "I am writing this letter to you on my way back from Europe to the United States," the first line of the epistle said. "My mind is full of fascinating conversations that I had with people in Hungary and Poland and with the many world leaders gathered in Paris for France's bicentennial.

"Let me go quickly to the point of this letter. I would like very much to sit down soon and talk to you, if you are agreeable to the idea . . . Perhaps it was my visit to Poland and Hungary or perhaps it is what I heard about your recent visits to France and Germany—whatever the cause—I just want to reduce the chances there could be misunderstandings between us. I want to get our relationship on a more personal basis."

The letter opened in this promising way, but quickly Bush's cautious approach took over: "I want to do it," the text went on, "without thousands of assistants hovering over our shoulders, without the ever-present briefing papers and certainly without the press yelling at us every 5 minutes about 'who's winning,' 'what agreements have been reached,' or 'has our meeting succeeded or failed.'" Bush wanted a "no agenda" meeting. "In my view," he continued, "it would be preferable to avoid the word 'summit' which is, at best, overworked and, at worst, a word whose connotation is one of a momentous happening." He suggested a visit in late September, when the United Nations General Assembly would be in session: "The General Assembly seems to me to provide the ideal cover needed for a 'spontaneous' invitation to an unstructured, informal meeting." Gorbachev could come either to Camp David or to his seaside house in Maine, where Gorbachev would get "a glimpse of our Atlantic seacoast. It would also give me a chance to take you for a ride in my speed boat and maybe catch a fish."

The letter was not intended to be insulting, but nevertheless it was. A "cover" for a "no agenda" meeting at which Gorbachev might "catch a fish"? And this ambivalent invitation at a time when the Soviet leader was struggling? On July 22, Moscow finally confirmed the existence of the 1939 Molotov-Ribbentrop secret protocols, making the USSR officially responsible for the dismemberment of Poland; on July 26, the mujahideen fired rockets on the Soviet embassy in Kabul; on July 27, the government reported that 200,000 Soviets had emigrated from the country in the past eighteen months; on July 29, 250 radical parliamentarians formed the Interregional Group—to all intents and purposes, an umbrella opposition bloc. Five cabinet ministers flew to Great Britain and spent $165 million on consumer goods, including fifty million pairs of pantyhose. In his economic history of perestroika, William Moskoff writes: "The frustration of the whole population was turning ugly, and violence was erupting in a number of places. In Vologda, over a four month period, twenty-nine store workers were reported injured in clashes with consumers. In Irkutsk, angry customers broke store windows, damaged counters, verbally abused and even frisked clerks to look for hidden goods. In Khabarovsk, when a local clothing store sold all its merchandise, the angry customers who had gathered outside broke through barriers and destroyed windows and doors. And in Tula Oblast, a twenty-three-year-old liquor store clerk was killed after he refused to sell vodka after hours."

With Gorbachev's homeland descending into chaos, Bush was inviting the Soviet leader out on a cheap date.

To make things worse, Bush gave the letter not to the Soviet ambassador to Washington but to Gorbachev's arms control advisor, Marshal Sergei Akhromeyev, who was then visiting the United States. Bush and Scowcroft thought he would be "a foolproof way to ensure absolute secrecy for a most sensitive communication, although some at the State Department were upset over bypassing normal channels." Akhromeyev was a hawk, but Bush liked him as an "honorable and honest professional soldier," cultivating a presumed World War II camaraderie. Deeply disliking Shevardnadze, Akhromeyev gladly kept him in the dark, igniting the foreign minister's fury.

Gorbachev hadn't been happy when Bush went to Eastern Europe.

Ambassador Jack Matlock: "Gorbachev's anxiety grew when Bush announced a trip to Hungary and Poland and began to talk of the need to remove Soviet troops from Eastern Europe. This was indeed a worthy and essential goal, but making a public issue of it when Gorbachev was under pressure from so many forces at home was likely to do more harm than good." In early July, Gorbachev said to Matlock: "Tell the president to please be a little more considerate. What he says has an effect here." "While Bush was in Eastern Europe," Matlock writes, "his comments about the Soviet role were so circumspect that Shevardnadze made a point of sending word that they had been pleased with Bush's 'responsible behavior' during his trip."

But now Gorbachev was going ballistic about the "no-summit" summit. He soon responded that a visit to the USA was not acceptable: he wanted somewhere neutral. Bush suggested a shipboard meeting in Malta. His brother William H. T. "Bucky" Bush had recently vacationed on the island and liked the place; also, Baker writes in his memoirs, Bush loved the sea and was fascinated with FDR's "practice of meeting foreign leaders on ships." Now Bucky's favorite vacation spot invited an unwelcome phrase, "From Yalta to Malta"—particularly since on the eve of Yalta, in February 1945, FDR had a shipboard summit with Churchill in Malta.

But the public was not yet to know. "The most vital secrets of U.S. weaponry," Matlock writes, "were given less protection than the information that Bush and Gorbachev were planning a meeting later in the year." Matlock himself had announced to the embassy staff with quiet sarcasm: "Our marching orders are clear. Don't just do something—stand there."

Meanwhile, Washington received a Russian visitor who had zero respect for privacy, secrecy, or prudence.

On September 10, Bush dictated to his diary: "The question came up whether to see Boris Yeltsin. The Ambassador recommends that he be received in the White House, but not necessarily by me. I think it's a good thing to do. Yeltsin is over here and seems to be blasting Gorbachev . . . State is goosey about my seeing him, but I don't quite see why we shouldn't see him . . . The Soviets receive all kinds of people running for President who are against me and trying to get my job, so they've got to be understanding about our willingness to see their people, especially those who want to see perestroika succeed. It's not like we're seeing some curmudgeon who was trying to throw Gorbachev totally out of office . . ."

Contrary to Bush's assessment, Yeltsin was trying to do precisely that, and a visit to the White House would be an important step in his crusade. Not only was Russia parting ways with the "republics," such as Ukraine and Uzbekistan, it was also parting ways with the Soviet Union. Outraged by economic hardships hitting the ethnic and political core of the empire just as badly as anyone else in the Soviet Union, the Russians were considering seceding from the union. Unlike the secession of Estonia or even Ukraine, that would have meant the death of the existing state.

Yeltsin was pushing for a breakup. He had already won the loyalty of the Russian street and was now looking for endorsements. In 1989, a visit to the Oval Office was *the* endorsement. Scowcroft, however, wanted the date to be brief and quiet. "The President and I," he writes, "had worked out a sliding scale of importance for receiving visitors at the White House. At the top was a scheduled visit with the President himself. Next was a visit with me, as a part of which I would take the visitor down the hall to 'drop in' briefly on the President. Slightly less prestigious was one with me, during which the President would 'drop by' to greet the visitor, giving him total control over how long he spent with the guest. The lowest rung, other than not getting into the White House at all, was simply a meeting with me . . . Yeltsin was not an easy call."

"I wanted to see Yeltsin," Bush picks up. "He supported the kinds of fundamental change in the Soviet Union we hoped for . . . In the end, I decided on a 'drop-by' in Brent's office."

To say that Yeltsin was not an easy call did not even begin to describe the problem. James Baker, who didn't want the meeting to happen in the first place, reluctantly received the guest at the State Department. He found himself in front of a "large, physically intimidating man who reminded me more of a NFL tackle than a legislator . . . His axlike hands cut the air, and he was extraordinarily ebullient . . . this was a man of action who would rather break china than sip tea from it."

Running half an hour late, on September 12 Yeltsin arrived at the

West Basement entrance, the lowest portal of all, to be met by Condoleezza Rice. The guest plainly refused to leave the car "unless he was assured that he would be seeing the President." Rice told him that he was to meet with Scowcroft. The Russian bear started arguing. Rice said that "if he did not plan to keep his appointment . . . he might as well go back to his hotel."

In Scowcroft's office, Yeltsin sourly embarked on an aggressive diatribe about the changes the Soviet Union needed. Never a good speaker, now, with his mind fixated on the perceived insult, he rambled. When Bush dropped by, Yeltsin "brightened visibly." Bush stayed for just a few minutes and then Dan Quayle showed up for a photo op, but that was all Yeltsin needed.

According to Scowcroft, the administration "had brought Yeltsin into the West Basement entrance to avoid encounters with the press," but on his drive out Yeltsin spotted a number of reporters on the lawn, ordered the car to stop, and launched a press conference. Rice took this personally. In all likelihood, she was the White House aide who anonymously trashed the Russian visitor to the press.

Yeltsin "left a bad impression at the White House," Matlock writes. A few days later, Italy's *La Repubblica* reported heavy drinking in New York—to Gorbachev's delight. Communist Party media outlets picked up on the image of the drunken elephant in a china shop. The problem was that the Russian street didn't mind.

The reformist leaders of Hungary sandwiched Bush's trip between two events: a session of the Political Consultative Committee of the Warsaw Pact in Bucharest on July 7–8 and a trip to Moscow on July 24–25. In Bucharest, the Hungarian delegation was reported to have "caused difficulties" by "exaggerated pretensions . . . with regard to human rights" and attacking the host, Ceauşescu, for violating the rights of the Hungarian minority in Transylvania. In Moscow, President Nyers asked that the withdrawal of Soviet troops from Hungary be made public. Gorbachev consented. Nyers also asked for assistance in locating the graves of Hungarian soldiers who had died on the battlefields and in the Gulag as POWs. Gorbachev said the Soviets were ready to assist. The irony of the latter request was stunning: a nation allied with Hitler and defeated by the Soviets during the war and still technically occupied by Soviet armed forces was asking for something very close to the exoneration of its anti-Soviet fighters.

Nyers promised Gorbachev "democratic socialism" in Hungary, but in fact the party was negotiating surrender, now yielding, now fighting on issues such as party property, depoliticization of the armed forces, and withdrawal of party organizations from the workplace. Provoking short-lived tempests, these zigzags were meaningless. Readying themselves for the elections and hoping to be propelled into power, the opposition started preparing the Soviets for the coming shock. Representatives of the opposition met with the Soviet ambassador to Budapest, Boris Stukalin, to brief him on their stand. According to a witness, Stukalin, formerly employed in the propaganda business, listened to them "with a poker face." Meanwhile, somewhat unexpectedly, Hungary transmitted the "Polish disease" to a neighbor. It all started with the demolition of the barbed wire fence on the Hungarian-Austrian border that supplied President Bush's gift.

The Hungarian minister of the interior at the time, István Horváth, said the barbed wire electrified with a low-tension current on the Hungarian-Austrian border was a "very imperfect Russian mechanism. Setting it off, a rabbit or a roebuck would start the guards running in that direction. The whole system was due to be renovated in 1995 at a cost of hundreds of millions of forints, and in 1988 I concluded that we had better deal with this problem right away. It was no longer in our interests to incur these costs for such results. This proposition was accepted, and in the following spring we began to dismantle the signaling system, proceeding faster than expected, so that the job was completed within a few months."

The demolition project set off a powerful reply in another Eastern European country: East Germany. In the summer of 1989, the GDR had no strong underground dissident and few public protests—but this is not to say that the "Polish disease" hadn't touched it. It had. However, the inspiration led to a very idiosyncratic rebellion: many East Germans decided to leave their country. Fearing that the GDR might remain politically unchanged like Cuba or China (Honecker, by the way, had praised the Tiananmen massacre enthusiastically), its citizens opted for escape. Unlike Poles or Hungarians, they had another homeland—capitalist and as free as a nation can be in the real world.

The Berlin Wall and the equally impenetrable border with West Germany were a death trap, but if a citizen of the GDR took a long detour through the Eastern bloc, he could attempt crossing into Austria from Hungary and Czechoslovakia. As soon as Western radio broadcasts made the demolition of the security system on the Hungarian-Austrian border public, thousands of East Germans headed to Budapest.

That was not the first time East Germans had used Hungary as an escape route. Even under Kádár, the Hungarian-Austrian border was not a Great Wall of China. Horváth again: "At the beginning of that summer I put a stop to the earlier practice, whereby if we captured a German trying to cross the border we transferred him back there. This was a minor technical question. But of course the Germans noticed, first that we were no longer transferring them back, and secondly that we had got rid of the signaling system. They began to settle down here. By the end of July we calculated that there were already over 20,000 . . . But what would happen to them by the autumn?" The refugee camps were overflowing, and soon it became "clear that we would be compelled to let them go."

Secretary of State James Baker: "By the end of the summer, thousands of East Germans who had traveled to Hungary began to demand that they be allowed to cross into the West. On August 24, Chancellor Kohl met with Hungary's Prime Minister Németh and Foreign Minister Horn, and they made a dramatic decision: They agreed to open Hungary's border with Austria, which, in effect, opened a back door around the Berlin Wall."

The former Hungarian minister of justice Kálmán Kulcsár insists that the Soviets hadn't been informed. When asked why they did it, Kulcsár came up with an interesting answer: "Poland and Hungary were then the only two countries on the road to reform and it was by no means excluded that others in the Warsaw Pact would try something against us. We were pretty sure that if hundreds of thousands of East

Germans went to the West, the East German regime would fall, and in that case Czechoslovakia was also out . . . We took the step for our own sakes." Rezsö Nyers offers more evidence, claiming that when the party leader Károly Grósz went to Czechoslovakia to go shooting with his counterpart, Miloš Jakeš, the latter offered military help.

Meanwhile, Radio Free Europe and other radio outlets covered the crisis extensively. Scowcroft thought that this "posed an exquisite dilemma for East Germany" and that it "revealed and widened the gulf within the Warsaw Pact between the liberalizing countries and the entrenched hard-line regimes." Baker wrote to his president: "The East German population hemorrhage has acutely embarrassed the GDR regime." "Our reaction was one of guarded optimism," Scowcroft says.

On September 10, the foreign minister of Hungary announced that if the refugees chose to simply cross into Austria, the Hungarian border guards would just let them through "without any further ado and I as sume the Austrians will let them in." He proved right on both accounts. Within three days, twenty-two thousand East Germans walked from Hungary into Austria.

Not every East German who aspired to leave could go to Hungary. Many went only as far as Czechoslovakia. That was an act of despair, as in the summer of 1989 Prague remained conservative. Yet it worked. It is understandable why Hungary, a country trying to score as many points as possible with the West, accommodated East German refugees, but it is not entirely clear why the hard-line Czechoslovak government had let them in. In any case, their obvious plight and solemn determination to get to their eventual destination now changed the mood in Prague. The refugees streamed to the West German embassy, their cars abandoned on the streets, some of them with the ignition keys left in. "They walked with fixed intent, those East German refugees, quite uninterested in the beauties of Prague . . . They were climbing over the walls of the Embassy gardens, handing up their children to others above. Many people cried in the streets."

Sharing a border with Austria, just as Hungary did, Czechoslovakia still wouldn't open it. The reformist leaders of Hungary couldn't care less about East Germany's reaction, but the leadership of Czechoslovakia still felt bound by its Warsaw Pact commitments. Without

Honecker's imprimatur, nothing could be done. The seventy-seven-year-old Honecker, meanwhile, was in a hospital undergoing emergency gallbladder surgery. He resumed his duties only on September 25.

In the last week of September, at the UN General Assembly, Baker asked West Germany's foreign minister, Hans-Dietrich Genscher, "What can I do for you?" The German suggested talking to the Hungarians and the Czechs. In his memoir, Baker wrote that "meeting with the Hungarians was straightforward." Budapest "was already doing quite a bit to help." Prague, Baker noted, remained "reactionary."

Frederick Taylor writes in *The Berlin Wall*: "With America acting as broker, a deal was done between the Czechs, the Hungarians, and the GDR. On 30 September, the West German Foreign Minister flew to Prague. He announced to the masses waiting stubbornly in the grounds of the embassy that they would be allowed to leave." Honecker was eager to resolve the crisis before the October 7 celebrations of the GDR's fortieth anniversary and said the refugees could go to West Germany—as long as they departed from the GDR, not some third country. This was totally surreal: the arrangement meant that the refugees would be put on trains and taken back to the GDR and only then would they be allowed into the Promised Land.

Surprisingly, Honecker kept his word, and instead of being arrested, defectors started arriving in West Germany in the first week of October. All in all, twelve thousand East Germans took this unlikely escape route.

7. The Wall Opens Up; the Magic Theater Raises
the Curtain: October—November

Learning that the Hungarians had opened their border, the last German Marxist hissed: "We trusted them, but they betrayed us!"

While Poles fought for a better life but stayed, East Germans had been fleeing to the West, to the other Germany. In Berlin, only the Wall separated the two, and at night from their apartments East Germans could see the lights of capitalism just a hundred yards away. The fact that dissent was focused on leaving, not rallying, originated in the East Germans' unique situation: the Germany they wanted already existed, and before the Wall went up walking straight into utopia had been easy.

The Wall was, actually, not simply a wall, but rather a fortification that evolved over decades. The ninety-six miles of this barrier went through four stages of transformation between 1961 and 1980. The final result was not just a wall that prevented movement between the two Berlins but a psychic front line: two concrete barriers framing one hundred yards of open space easily covered by snipers in watchtowers—the Death Strip, as it was in fact called. The Wall had eight gates or, as they were known, border crossings, but their existence seemed only to emphasize the Wall's imposing presence.

Contrary to the enduring myth, the Wall had been the creation of the native East German regime, not Moscow. By 1960, the revolutionary generation to which the founders of the German Democratic Republic belonged had clashed with the generation of reformist apparatchiks in the Soviet Union. In 1929, when Khrushchev was doing office work for the Ukrainian branch of the party, Walter Ulbricht was a member of the Reichstag (where he advocated the creation of a Soviet republic in Germany) and the party leader of Berlin.

At the peak of World War II, in 1943, Ulbricht, in the USSR at that time, together with a bunch of other German Communists, created the National Committee for a Free Germany, a cell that would grow into a new German government. In 1945, Stalin dispatched him to Berlin with the task of dismantling the Nazi legacy and establishing a transitional regime. Stalin's instructions were explicit: socialism in Germany was out of the question, as the Allies wouldn't approve.

The Soviet dictator never, actually, had a consistent long-term plan for postwar Germany. Building communism in the country where Karl Marx had been born meant everything to people like Ulbricht; the only thing that mattered to Stalin was Germany's strategic location between his sphere of influence and the West. To Ulbricht's dismay, the GDR was created only in October 1949, as a response to the creation of the Federal Republic of Germany four months earlier. As late as 1952, Stalin still advised Ulbricht and his colleagues "not to shout about socialism at this point" because he feared it would disrupt his bigger plans: he had approached the United States, Britain, and France proposing a deal—a reunited and neutral Germany. It is not entirely clear why Stalin would even propose that. The most likely explanation is that he wanted a buffer zone between his empire and NATO—and with Germany reunited, that zone would have been four hundred miles wide. The West German chancellor, Konrad Adenauer, rejected the idea energetically. Understandably, a notion of "neutrality" coming from Stalin sounded problematic. Second, the left in East Germany would have been a difficult partner to deal with in the reunified state. Third, two thirds of West Germans in 1952 refused to recognize the new borders in the east—the lands lost to Poland, the USSR, and Czechoslovakia.

For Ulbricht, Stalin's death was not so much a loss as a chance to radicalize his regime—specifically, by closing the border with West Germany and West Berlin. As soon as he approached Moscow for permission, the Kremlin angrily called his plan "politically unacceptable and grossly simplistic." Furthermore, Moscow advised Ulbricht to stop forced collectivization, encourage small private businesses, and ease his grip on intellectuals and the Church.

Unaware of the debate but also expecting change after Stalin's death, the workers of East Berlin took to the streets on June 16, 1953. Starting as protests against poor pay, in a matter of hours the unrest turned political, the workers demanding Ulbricht's removal and the reunification of Germany. The Soviets took over, sending troops into the city and sealing off the border with West Berlin; approximately one hundred thousand rioters held out for two days before dispersing, losing two hundred comrades.

Ironically, the uprising saved Ulbricht. Moscow wearily kept urging him to liberalize—as Hope Harrison writes in *Driving the Soviets up the Wall*, "the Soviets favored, when possible, a focus on the legitimacy of the regime in the eyes of the people, and Ulbricht favored the control of the regime over the people"—but after June 1953 his harshness seemed legitimate, if not fully justified.

Every month, fifteen thousand to twenty thousand East Germans crossed the border never to come back. Ulbricht decided the only solution was to lock them in.

Khrushchev wasn't totally persuaded. Though acknowledging that "ideological issues are decided by the stomach" and "the attraction of one or the other system" by "the shop windows," he suspected that a move to seal the border would mean a major crisis in world affairs.

In the summer of 1961, he agreed to pay a secret visit to West Berlin to see for himself whether the city was as alluring as Ulbricht was claiming. Of that visit, Khrushchev wrote, "I never got out of the car but I made a full tour and saw what the city was like." Presumably, the man who two years earlier had lost the Kitchen Debate to Richard Nixon was sufficiently impressed by capitalist Berlin because shortly thereafter he sent Ulbricht a "yes."

Ulbricht had had everything lined up. The West Berlin perimeter would be fortified with 2,100 concrete pillars and 303 tons of barbed wire; subway and commuter trains, buses and boats connecting the two halves of the city would be terminated. Khrushchev asked what would happen to the houses on the border. Ulbricht had his answer ready: "In those homes which have an exit to West Berlin, we will brick up the exit."

The Wall stopped many but not everyone. In the first five weeks, 417 more East Germans escaped. Enraged, Ulbricht issued a "shoot-to-kill" order. Over the years, approximately 5,000 East Germans still made it across the Death Strip, at least 125 were killed trying, and once an eighteen-year-old was left dying in the no-man's-land in full view, to teach both East and West Berlin a lesson. The last deadly shot was fired as late as February 6, 1989.

The twenty-eight years separating 1961 from 1989 seemed to solidify the concept of two Germanies, particularly since the cold war division of two other countries—China and Korea—looked permanent. In 1972, the two Germanies signed the Basic Treaty recognizing each other's existence, and, twenty-seven years after the war, West Germany signed peace treaties with the USSR, Poland, and Czechoslovakia, acknowledging the 1945 territorial transfers. That was already on Erich Honecker's watch; in 1971, the founder of the GDR, Walter Ulbricht, stepped down.

Economically, East Germans were doing far better than Romanians, Bulgarians, or Soviets, partially because Honecker was a conscientious manager, partially due to the famed German work ethic, and partially because the GDR's social contract was defined not solely by the power of the infamous Stasi but also by some social progressivism (measures such as abolishing capital punishment and decriminalizing homosexuality were very liberal for the Eastern bloc). In the 1970s and '80s, even emigration became possible. Honecker began a human trade with West Germany: Bonn could buy freedom for East Germans for hard currency. Monitored by the Stasi, which obviously made a decision on who could be let go and who couldn't, and negotiated by an unscrupulous East Berlin lawyer, Wolfgang Vogel, the release of 33,755 political prisoners and family reunifications for 215,019 people brought in $2.4 billion dollars.

Fifteen years after the fall of the Wall, a former Soviet intelligence officer nostalgically remembered his tenure in Dresden between 1985 and 1990, when he lived in a country "where they had everything" while the homeland had just "lines and shortages." The East German abundance was catastrophic for his waist, as he gained twenty-six pounds in five years.

But what made the young Soviet spy obscenely happy—by the way, his name was Vladimir Putin—made East Germans frown scornfully, as Germans in *another* Germany, behind the Wall, lived better. East German meals—"potatoes with a heavy sauce and a slight admixture of sausage, no salad" and "jars of Bulgarian cherries" for fruit—were "a caricature of a German meal, at a risibly low price." Meanwhile, beyond Germany, farther west, lay the glimmering riches of Paris and London, and if one jumped high enough one could almost see the country with the most riches of all—the United States.

A few years after the Wall fell, John Lewis Gaddis wrote: "The abrupt collapse of that structure and the system it symbolized twenty-eight years later came as an even greater surprise than its creation. Some strange mechanism seems to have been at work in Germany that allowed the bizarre over the years to become unexceptionable, only to reverse the procedure virtually overnight."

The exodus of the summer of 1989, the first serious slap in the face of the regime since 1953, shook East Germany. There *was* an exit from that hermetically sealed world, where even Soviet publications, blasphemously revisionist, were banned. Honecker was adamant about banishing perestroika; Gorbachev's policies had unleashed a storm, and Honecker was intent on sheltering his Germany from it. The East German spymaster, Markus Wolf, testified: "Honecker jutted out his obstinate jaw and said, 'I will never allow here what is happening in the Soviet Union.'"

Honecker hadn't expected the 1989 exodus. Still, he felt fully in control as he insisted on the evacuation of East German refugees in Prague through the GDR (those in Hungary didn't need anyone's permission to cross the border into Austria, so, helpless to stop them, the stubborn old man just chose to ignore their existence). By his lights, that would be a good lesson in humiliation and intimidation as the twelve thousand were put in sealed trains, their citizenship withdrawn. But things did not go as planned. At the Dresden railway station fifteen hundred young people assembled and tried to get aboard. The refugees tore up their IDs and "tossed them out of the train windows, along with the worthless Eastern marks they would not be able to spend once they arrived in the West . . . Fighting broke out. Substantial areas of the concourse were wrecked. One man slipped under the train and was so badly injured that he had to have his legs amputated. After the trains left, demonstrations continued."

The exit strategy the refugees had used seemed unfairly easy to those who stayed. Furious at the embarrassment to the regime, Honecker had closed the border with Czechoslovakia, and those who hadn't been smart enough to slip into the breakaway caravan in August now seemed to be locked up for life. Had that happened ten years earlier, in all likelihood, those who were late wouldn't have opted to protest. In 1989 they poured into the streets carrying signs: "We want out!"

In principle, Honecker could have said, "All right. Those who want to go—go!" But that would have meant a chaotic exodus of the youngest and the brightest, the regime likely collapsing in the process, so the old man did nothing. But when very quickly the wounded pride of the street transformed "We want to go!" into "We are staying!" he knew he had to act.

The epicenter of the unrest was in Leipzig, around the Nikolaikirche. The venue had nothing to do with the Vatican or John Paul II, as, first, the church was Protestant, and, second, its improbably named pastor, Christian Führer, acted on his own. In the early 1980s, amid the diplomatic crisis over NATO cruise missiles in Europe, he had suggested a campaign slogan, "Swords into Ploughshares." The authorities smiled, and in 1982 the pastor started Peace Prayers on Mondays. But the "peace activist" soon started protecting dissidents and the rights of those who openly filed a petition to leave (they were losing jobs and housing in the process). Honecker dismissed those efforts. "They are fools and dreamers. We can deal with people like that."

He had a point. Pastor Führer was not a Wałesa or a Yeltsin. However, the East Germans had the help of one unexpected foreign agent of change: Gorbachev.

Leadership is both a subject and an object: some leaders change the world through their decisions, the accumulation of acts and pronouncements recorded and filed in the appropriate presidential (or dictatorial) archives. Other leaders achieve the same transformative power unwittingly, by virtue of just being there—their image, clout, aura, or charisma objectified by the people as a galvanizing force. That is what the pope meant when he started calling Gorbachev a "providential man."

For Poles, Gorbachev was the Evil Empire; for Soviets, the man who had managed to impoverish even the KGB officers; for East Germans, Gorbachev was the wise man of the east, an inspiration, a model of sorts. The previous and only rebellion in East Germany had occurred in 1953; the country had never had a unified and vigorous dissident movement or an iconoclastic charismatic figure, so an established Communist reformer—Gorbachev—became the East German street's inspiration. Moreover, many expected him to actually influence Honecker or maybe replace the old man with a more lenient person.

As long as the Platonic idea of Gorbachev inspired a rebellion, he *was* helping East German protesters, though he himself didn't realize at the moment that his star power in East Germany would, eventually, contribute to the Wall's fall. Gorbachev was not the man who tore the Wall down (as Reagan had suggested he should and hoped he would), but the man who bumped into it, smashing it to pieces absolutely unintentionally. In fact, it wasn't *his* wall to tear down—he didn't have the key to the gates.

The providential man definitely helped East German protesters in one respect: he kept them out of harm's way for six weeks—again, not because he pleaded their case with Honecker or even cared whether they would be massacred (as his army had massacred protesters in Tbilisi half a year earlier), but because he was scheduled to visit East Germany in the first week of October.

Fuming about the escape route the treacherous Hungarians had provided, Honecker decided to raise the flag and celebrate the fortieth anniversary of the GDR in style. Guests such as Ceaușescu and Zhivkov would have probably applauded a massacre preceding the festivities ("A revolution is worth something only if it can protect itself"—Lenin), but Gorbachev would have definitely canceled, embarrassing the hosts beyond words.

For Honecker, the visit went very badly: in Berlin, mobbed by fans, Gorbachev announced that *they* had to decide what was good for their country. Quite predictably, Honecker reproached him furiously for interfering in somebody else's domestic mess and acidly asked: "Has your population enough food, bread, and butter?" The meeting turned disastrous and, leaving, an exasperated Gorbachev told his advisors that Honecker was a real "asshole." Suspecting just as much, at least two thousand Berliners assembled outside the venue chanting, "Gorby, help us!" "Gorby, come out!"

Gorbachev left, arrests were made. Now Honecker felt free to apply a Tiananmen-style solution—if it had worked in one Communist nation, why shouldn't it in another? Location: Leipzig, where the Nikolaikirche remained packed. Date: October 9, 1989.

Schools and the university closed, the center of the city was blocked by the army and riot squads; tanks allegedly hid behind the closed doors of fire stations. But the streets were still overflowing with protesters.

It's not really clear why no violence occurred that day. Apparently, the city's party leaders ignored Honecker's order to break up demonstrations and signed an agreement with the opposition leaders promising more dialogue. The signees for the opposition were a symphony conductor, a pastor (not Führer), and an actor. In a week, on October 17, the East German Politburo replaced the last German Marxist with a younger opportunist, Egon Krenz.

Receiving Krenz in Moscow, Gorbachev blamed everything on the old man: "He lost his vision. If he had been willing to make the necessary changes in policy on his own initiative two or three years ago, everything would have been different now." He advised Krenz that ties with West Germany "should be kept under control."

This was *not* the man the Berlin protesters saw and talked to. This was a person totally blind to political reality, thinking leadership change would help stem a revolutionary flood unprecedented in his lifetime.

"We have already taken a number of steps," Krenz assured. "First of all, we gave orders to the border troops not to use weapons at the border, except in cases of direct attacks on the soldiers. Second, we adopted a draft of a Law on Foreign Travel at the Politburo."

The conversation took place on November 1. A week later, the Wall fell. The mighty fortification that, according to Honecker, should have easily lasted a century more (he had said that in August) met its end through misinterpretation.

The East German Politburo had indeed passed the Law on Foreign Travel, and now it was up to the minister of propaganda, Günter Schabowski, to present it on state television. Schabowski went on air at 6:53 p.m., November 9. Incidentally, November 9 was a fateful day in twentieth-century German history: on that date in 1918, the Weimar Republic was proclaimed, and in 1938 Kristallnacht had occurred. Schabowski read the official document promising that "travel authorizations" would be "issued within a short period of time" and that "permanent exits" would be possible "via all GDR crossings to the FRG and West Berlin" after the applicant was issued a visa for permanent exit.

The Western press present in the studio got confused by the bureaucratic language (also, likely, made even less comprehensible in the simultaneous translation). Someone asked Schabowski when the new law came into effect. Here Schabowski lost it. Though the law was not supposed to become effective until the next day, he said: "So far as I know, that is, uh, immediate, without delay." In his history of the Wall, Frederick Taylor writes: "At five past seven, Associated Press pulled ahead of the pack and spelled its interpretation out in a simple but sensational sentence: 'According to information supplied by SED Politburo member Günter Schabowski, the GDR is opening its borders.'"

By 9:30 that night, the erroneous announcement had been repeated by every TV station. As soon as the population heard this, thousands stormed the border checkpoints. Immigration officers, fearing for their lives, ceased all controls at 11:30 p.m., November 9. The German Democratic Republic died in a stampede.

⸻

If East Germany had spent the cold war in the eye of the storm, Bulgaria seemed to have been spared by it. Few people in the Soviet Union, and even fewer in the West, paid attention to how Todor Zhivkov, in power since 1954, managed the country.

"Uncle Tosho" was the occupant of numerous residences and the author of many books; he hadn't paid a penny for the villas, and as for the books, they had been written by ghost authors. His native village, Pravets, now had the Zhivkov family museum and a street named after his mother. He had bestowed numerous material benefits on his home-town, and Pravets had fared better than Sofia, the capital. When in January 1987 Gorbachev announced perestroika, the Bulgarian Politburo met three times to discuss the challenge, finally affirming that Bulgaria had begun its own perestroika thirty years earlier, with Zhivkov's ascendance to power. So now there was no real need to change anything: things were good as they were, the circular reasoning went.

In the diary of Communist Bulgaria's founding father, Georgi Dimitrov, Zhivkov's name comes up only once but in a revealing context: "Zhivkov reported on the work of the committee for the purge in the Ministry of Foreign Affairs." This promising start led to a long reign secured by terror. Between 1985 and 1989, 105 people were shot for trying to cross the border. While the Bulgarian secret service's role in the assassination attempt on the pope's life is unclear, Scotland Yard came to the conclusion that it was behind one of the most spectacular assassinations of the cold war—that of the leading Bulgarian dissident, Georgi Markov, in London: approaching him from behind on Waterloo Bridge, the assassin stung his thigh with an umbrella, whispered, "I am sorry," hailed a taxi, and left. Markov died four days later, and Scotland Yard found a metal pellet in his thigh filled with a fatal dose of ricin, a product of castor beans, *Ricinus communis*, the scientific name suggesting an uncanny pun.

Zhivkov's regime censored Soviet art and literature before allowing it into the country. "More Catholic than the Pope, and more Turkish than the Sultan"—that's how Bulgarian intellectuals defined their government. In the Prague Spring year, 1968, a Bulgarian drama critic pronounced, "Comrades, the most dangerous ideological sabotage is coming to us via the Soviet Union!"

No one went to bed hungry in Bulgaria, but food such as quality beef or salami or pasta could not be bought with money alone, and connections or privilege or sheer luck had to be in play. Bulgaria's climate supported pretty much anything a human might have wanted to grow, yet food shortages were endemic. Practically every household had a radio, a TV set, and a refrigerator, but only 42 percent had a telephone and 37 percent had a car. All this came with forced industrialization, the latter with Soviet loans and technological assistance. In the 1980s, Moscow was involved in three hundred industrial projects in Bulgaria, including the nuclear power plant in Kozloduy.

The Russian was a controversial figure in Bulgaria. Deservedly credited with liberating Bulgaria from Turkish rule and creating the modern Bulgarian state in 1878, the Russian spoke a fraternal Slavic language, shared a religion with Bulgarians, assisted them economically, and clearly trusted them. Bulgaria did not have any Soviet troops on its territory. Yet both cultural proximity and pronounced trustworthiness backfired. In the snobbish mind of the Soviets, Bulgaria was the lowest among the socialist countries, the assumed friendliness its major fault. For a Soviet citizen, it was easier to go to Bulgaria as a tourist than to Hungary or Poland: no one, including the KGB, took Sofia seriously. "Chicken is not a real bird, Bulgaria is hardly abroad," Russians said. Bulgarians got firsthand accounts of their second-class status: in 1989 alone approximately forty-five thousand of their compatriots worked or studied in the USSR. Rumor had it that Zhivkov had suggested making Bulgaria a Soviet Socialist Republic within the Soviet Union, on a par with Turkmenistan et al.

Memories last long in the Balkans and national sentiment beats ideology there, so the Communist regime kept a monument in the center of Sofia, to the Russian tsar Alexander II, credited with the liberation of Bulgaria in 1878. As for the Turkish minority, in the eyes of many Bulgarians, it was still a problem. Interestingly, the worst purge of Bulgarian Turks came very late—between December 1984 and March 1985, when the authorities forced nine hundred thousand ethnic Turks to change their names to Slavic ones. According to Zlatko Anguelov,

> Men were called up in the army and placed in a well-guarded military camp. Each Turk was surrounded by Bulgarians and was allowed no contact with anyone from his family or with other Turks for reasons of "military security." He then was called by his commanding officer and informed that the Minister of Defense had directed that all Turks in the army had to assume Bulgarian names. He was warned that if he refused he would be court-martialed . . . If he decided not to accept one of the names, he was threatened, abused, or outright beaten. If he persisted, he was escorted to a prison labor camp and kept there

until he signed a declaration stating that he had "voluntarily" adopted a new name.

If the man's wife refused to accept the change, her paychecks were stopped and so was her health care. If a village resisted collectively, armored personnel carriers and light tanks surrounded it and the commandos "would go from house to house and anything that looked like a traditional Turkish garment was seized, cut up, torn, and trampled in the mud. Also consigned to the mud were books in Turkish (including the Koran)."

One hundred Turks were killed, two hundred and fifty jailed. Circumcision and the washing of the dead were banned, and so was the use of the Turkish language in public; Turkish newspapers and radio stations were closed. The propaganda machine went out of its way to justify the genocide: Turks were Bulgarians who had become confused about their ethnic identity; Turks had a dangerously high birth rate; Turkey might invade Bulgaria like it had invaded Cyprus in 1974 if Turks remained an undisturbed fifth column there.

Bulgarian Muslims started responding to the genocide only in May 1989. It is fair to assume that their inspiration was the rebellion of ethnic minorities in the USSR. Also, no matter how conservative Zhivkov was, Bulgaria did not exist in some kind of vacuum, and a crackdown on the protesters in a time of unprecedented thaw all over the Eastern bloc would have made his regime an international pariah. The demonstrations were generally peaceful—the Turks carried signs reading, "We want our real names," "We want to speak our language," "We want to practice our religion freely." In an imperious way, Zhivkov went on TV and suggested that the discontented leave for Turkey—not much of a concession, as all he granted them was the misery of exile in a poor country. Before Turkey, overwhelmed by the stream of refugees, closed its borders in August, 344,000 Bulgarian Turks had moved—or, rather, fled.

Georgi Markov, the martyred dissident, had written that Zhivkov's "unerring instinct told him that the only people who could seriously disturb his quiet reign were precisely the members of the creative intelligentsia." But in Bulgaria, until very late, the intelligentsia did not in fact challenge Zhivkov. It didn't have too many foreign allies, either. There was no strong Bulgarian diaspora overseas. Western radio broadcasts in Bulgarian had an estimated audience of five million—60 percent of the population—but the Voice of America broadcast just 10.5 hours in Bulgarian a week, versus 119 in Russian and 49 in Polish. The Bush administration simply dismissed Bulgaria as "lagging well behind" other countries of Eastern Europe. The only important foreign influence was the Soviet perestroika.

In February 1989, a party activist, Konstantin Trenchev, started a free trade union, Podkrepa, interestingly enough planned as a body for "intellectuals, artists, writers, and scientists." Earlier, in November 1988, Zhelyu Zhelev and Petko Simeonov created an umbrella organization for the opposition, the Club for the Support of Perestroika. Many were party members (Zhelev was expelled for publishing a book called *Fascism*, which hinted at the similarities between Nazism and Stalinism, following closely the argument of Hannah Arendt's *Origins of Totalitarianism*), and several were philosophers by training. They didn't invoke martyrs, as the Hungarians did with Imre Nagy or the Czechs with Jan Palach or the Poles with the 1970 Gdansk workers; they didn't have a powerful symbol like 1956 or 1968, or the Wall, in the national consciousness to support their demand for freedom. The only cause célèbre Bulgaria had was Markov—hardly a rallying point for the opposition, as before he defected to the West he had been a pet writer of Zhivkov's. The Club for the Support of Perestroika worshipped Gorbachev, who was already perceived as not radical enough in his own country. The organization was not influential or popular and received the most attention not from fellow Bulgarians but from supportive Westerners: when in January 1989 President François Mitterrand visited Bulgaria, he invited Zhelev and a few others for breakfast.

Much more popular was the environmentalist movement. About 60 percent of the agricultural land in Bulgaria was polluted by pesticides, excessive fertilizers, and industrial fallout; the nuclear power plant at Kozloduy was built in an earthquake-prone region, its reactors unsafe; the Yantra River, a tributary of the Danube in central Bulgaria, was classified as the dirtiest river in Europe. But, cautiously, the environmentalists focused on a *foreign* source of pollution—namely, the Romanian town of Giurgiu on the Danube despoiling Ruse across the river in

Bulgaria; because of the Romanian plant, chlorine levels in Ruse almost doubled. Most of the activists were, again, party members, and some belonged to the leadership class, such as the wife of the chairman of the National Assembly, Stanko Todorov.

Truly, the budding revolutionaries in Bulgaria, in early 1989, were insignificant. Zhelev's group got the most mileage from the least effort, lionized by Western diplomats and journalists who thought that if this was Eastern Europe, there should be philosopher-revolutionaries here. Feeling important and aware of the abuse of power in previous democratic revolutions, they took precautions: the Club for the Support of Perestroika created a rotating chairmanship, though they didn't really have anything to chair yet. The Turks had a solid cause for revolt but they spoke for a dispersed and even reviled minority. Environmentalists were real, but one does not bring down a totalitarian regime over the pollution coming from a foreign plant across the river.

The conspiracy against Zhivkov started simmering in the summer of 1989. Three younger leaders plotted it—Foreign Minister Peter Mladenov, Prime Minister Georgi Atanasov, and the Politburo candidate-member Andrei Lukanov. Two party veterans joined them: Stanko Todorov and the minister of defense, General Dobri Dzhurov. Their motives were obvious. The end of Soviet subsidies promised economic collapse. Under Gorbachev, the Soviet economy went into recession—trade deficit, foreign debt, 9.2 percent inflation in 1988—and as a result the USSR had to stop economic aid to its allies. The opposition movement was weak in Bulgaria, but not so in Poland and Czechoslovakia, and the men feared a domino effect.

None of the conspirators was a lamb. The youngest and the closest to Gorbachev, Mladenov and Lukanov, had been engineering Bulgarian support for leftist rogues in the third world, accompanying Zhivkov to meetings with the likes of Hafez al-Assad, the dictator of Syria. All had spent years in the corridors of dictatorial power: Mladenov, twenty; Todorov, fifty. As for their inspiration, it was Gorbachev.

Gorbachev was very angry with Zhivkov. The oldest Communist leader in the world except for Kim Il Sung of North Korea, Zhivkov "kept trying to instruct Gorbachev in both theory and practice." If some Eastern European leaders were somewhat delicate about Soviet subsidies, Zhivkov was not. Successfully exploiting "special" relations between Bulgaria and the Soviet Union, he blatantly demanded a payback. Moscow subsidized Bulgaria's foreign debt ($10.6 billion by 1989) in cash and oil; some of that petroleum Bulgaria stealthily reexported. When the economic crisis in the USSR made cheap energy exports to the allies difficult, Gorbachev shut off the oil flow to Bulgaria with pleasure.

Gorbachev's role in the plotting is still debated. In his memoirs, he admits that Bulgarian leaders bad-mouthed Zhivkov behind the Bulgarian leader's back and kept Gorbachev informed about the secret goings-on in Sofia. There, his revelations stop. Mladenov, meanwhile, has provided a tantalizing account of what happened on July 7 and 8, 1989, when the Political Consultative Committee of the Warsaw Pact met in Bucharest.

"We were each sitting in our delegations," Mladenov said in an interview much later. "Gorbachev was at one end of the hall, and he crossed its whole length to come over to me. He said, I want to talk to you. So we went, the two of us, into a corner where there was nobody. In a totalitarian system it was inconceivable to have the Foreign Minister rather than the First Secretary talking to Gorbachev. I was not authorized to have private discussions with him. Of course we knew what Zhivkov was like and we had to hope that nobody was eavesdropping. If he had known what was going on between Gorbachev and myself, he would have acted preemptively. It was then that I told Gorbachev that we intended to carry out our change in early November. He did not advise me, he made no comment on the time-span, he did not say whether we were being too hasty or should move more slowly. This is entirely your business, he said, you have to sort it out by yourselves."

In the Eastern bloc, it was indeed inconceivable for a foreign minister to meet with a Soviet leader without first clearing the exchange with his own boss. In the Eastern bloc, a Soviet leader crossing the length of a meeting room to talk to any person at all was received as a public message. How did Zhivkov react to what he saw? And how could one possibly expect that Ceauşescu would not have had an important conference room bugged?

During the same summit, apparently after Gorbachev's endorsement, Mladenov had a "final talk" with General Dzhurov. The two most important Bulgarian cabinet ministers "went out into the street where there was no fear of eavesdropping. It was not an easy discussion, as General Dzhurov had to give his final consent. I realized that the outcome could have been very different." If we trust Mladenov's account, the defense minister's acquiescence fully depended on Gorbachev's blessing.

On October 24, Mladenov wrote a letter of resignation to the Politburo. It began with petty grievances: Zhivkov had scolded him rudely for not standing up to the U.S. ambassador the day before, but it was unlikely that over his eighteen-year tenure as Bulgarian foreign minister Mladenov hadn't been exposed to worse humiliations. This was merely an excuse to make a more damning accusation:

> I have come to the conclusion that the real reason for Comrade Zhivkov's irritation and rudeness is that he realizes that he has led our country into a deep economic, financial, and political crisis. He knows that his political agenda, which consists of deviousness and petty intrigues and is intended to keep himself and his family in power at all costs and for as long as possible, has succeeded in isolating Bulgaria from the rest of the world. We have even reached the point where we are estranged from the Soviet Union and we find ourselves entirely on our own, in the same pigs' trough as the rotten dictatorial family regime of Ceaușescu. In a word, with his policies Zhivkov has forced Bulgaria outside the currents of our age.

Indeed, Zhivkov had become an embarrassment to the Kremlin with his anti-Turkish campaign, particularly unwelcome at a time when Moscow had to confront rising Islamic self-consciousness in Central Asia and the Caucasus.

Shortly thereafter, another conspirator, Lukanov, went to Moscow and had Mladenov's letter passed to Gorbachev. Frightened, Zhivkov contacted Moscow and asked for permission to visit and talk, but Gorbachev put him on hold. After visiting China on November 5 and 6, Mladenov made a stopover in Moscow. In all likelihood, there he informed Gorbachev that Zhivkov's days in office were numbered.

In the meantime, détente's toothless child, the Conference on Security and Cooperation in Europe, was holding the World Eco-Forum in Sofia. Like all Eastern European dictators, Zhivkov loved events where Western peaceniks and academics mixed with Eastern propagandists and provocateurs, because happenings like those gave the regime a patina of respectability, but this event, scheduled long beforehand, now looked totally mistimed. Adding to the tension, a Bulgarian group called Eco-Glasnost mobilized four thousand people for a demonstration in central Sofia. On October 26, they put a table in the center of a garden and started collecting signatures for a petition against the diversion of two rivers for hydroelectric purposes. The minister of the interior, Dimitar Stoyanov, sent in the police, arresting twenty people. "They were hit a couple of times, and then driven out into the countryside and dumped there, obliged to walk back to Sofia," an opposition leader recalled.

With the crisis in its second week, on November 7 the Soviet embassy in Sofia held a reception honoring the Soviet national holiday, the Great October Socialist Revolution Day. There, Dzhurov asked Zhivkov for permission to talk with him the next day. In all likelihood, Zhivkov already knew only too well what the talk was going to be about.

By the time the party plenum opened on November 10, the morning papers had drily informed Bulgarians that "nervous crowds had started demolishing the Berlin Wall at several places," but the select audience, of course, already knew.

The plenum voted Zhivkov out and a new strongman, Peter Mladenov, in. A series of conversations with the leaders whom Zhivkov had used to trust blindly made it clear to the old man that every single person had abandoned the sinking ship, so now he just accepted his fate. A party built on the premise of rejecting any notion of a free vote dismissed its chief through an honest Central Committee ballot and had invited the TV crews to shoot the procedure. Mladenov wanted a fresh start.

At the elevator, Mladenov and Zhivkov talked. Zhivkov would get a pension and a residence, would retain his office with all the aides and secretaries, and would be allowed to "sift through" all his files on his own. Both men knew that the last provision was beneficial to everyone in the Bulgarian leadership, old and new.

Had the coup taken place a few months earlier, its leaders wouldn't have had to seek the population's support, but they did in November 1989, when the Wall had fallen. This is the kind of report that reached Sofia:

> What happened in Berlin last week was a combination of the fall of the Bastille and a New Year's Eve blowout, of revolution and celebration. At the stroke of midnight on Nov. 9, a date that not only Germans would remember, thousands who had gathered on both sides of the Wall let out a roar and started going through it, as well as up and over. West Berliners pulled East Berliners to the top of the barrier along which in years past many an East German had been shot while trying to escape; at times the Wall almost disappeared beneath waves of humanity. They tooted trumpets and danced on the top. They brought out hammers and chisels and whacked away at the hated symbol of imprisonment, knocking loose chunks of concrete and waving them triumphantly before television cameras. They spilled out into the streets of West Berlin for a champagne-spraying, horn-honking bash that continued well past dawn, into the following day and then another dawn.

The Bulgarian opposition had played no role in the palace coup, but the fall of the Wall energized it, and dissidents led by Zhelev invited people into the streets. The first rally of the new era occurred on November 18. "A small group of self-proclaimed 'oppositionists' had been promptly formed," a disenchanted activist writes, "and they negotiated the authorization." What he meant was that on November 14 fourteen informal groups merged into the Union of Democratic Forces with Zhelev as their leader. Almost all of them were still party members.

The rally took place on the square in front of the Alexander Nevski Cathedral. "The handful of oppositionists at the rally," the activist continues, "read their ebullient speeches proclaiming communism dead and praising themselves as the harbingers of democracy. We, the populace, were all there, amidst national flags, flowers, and placards written with children's markers at the very last minute. We yelled for the first time in our lives at a rally, angrily shouting 'Down!' after every mention of a prominent communist name, and 'Hooray!' at the slightest suggestion of democratic appeal. The foreign TV crews were filming us. We were unexpectedly reentering the world."

They were reentering the world indeed as the Western mass media announced the fall of communism in Bulgaria, but the opposition's joy and the media's enthusiasm were premature. Power remained in the hands of the refurbished party for six more months, and in December 1989, at yet another rally, looking at the turbulent human sea beneath the podium, Mladenov uttered a sentence that secured him a special place in Bulgarian history: "Better the tanks come." Next summer, his slip of the tongue was leaked to the media, and that brought Mladenov's political career to an end, and Zhelyu Zhelev became the first democratically elected president of Bulgaria.

While the Bulgarians were "reentering the world," a revolution was stirring in Prague. Its leader, Václav Havel, was out of town. Like Lenin in Switzerland in February 1917, Havel almost missed the show.

Unlike Hungary, East Germany, and Bulgaria, Czechoslovakia had an established and influential dissident movement, yet the November revolution there started spontaneously. Interestingly, it is still not fully known what happened on November 17 in Prague. The hard facts are that the authorized demonstration turned antigovernment, that the police attacked, that blood was shed, and that one person, a student called Martin Smid, was reported to have been killed.

Initially, the student unions, inspired by the revolutionary miracle across the border in East Germany, approached the government asking for permission to celebrate the fiftieth anniversary of the death of a medical student, Jan Opletal, shot dead by the Nazis in Prague. The government agreed, duped by the politically correct "antifascist" cover and hoping that a march would let the young people unwind. But the slogans the fifty thousand marchers started chanting on November 17 were "Democracy and Law," "Academic Freedom," "Genuine Perestroika," and "Free Elections."

In a memoir written a few months after the march, the number-two man in the Czech opposition, Jan Urban, explains that Martin Smid's existence would never be "proven for certain." The most popular interpretation was that Martin Smid was a creation of the Czech secret police *and* the KGB. According to this conspiracy theory, Gorbachev wanted Miloš Jakeš out and his friend Zdeněk Mlynář in, and the Martin Smid killing would serve as a reasonable pretext for a palace coup in the Czech Politburo. Another explanation was that the authorities intended to discredit the rebels by producing a live and well Martin Smid later on. On November 19, state television actually showed *two* "Martin Smids." Fourteen years after the events, a Martin Smid, at least a man entitled to the name by a birth certificate, still expressed great frustration that someone had invented the death of a "person with my name and studying in the same year at the same university," as he was just an ordinary person whose only encounter with the police had been "when they once told me off for playing the guitar in a train."

Asked many times about his possible involvement in Prague events, Gorbachev laughed off the inquiries. Not that his testimony can be trusted, of course, but the supposition looks far-fetched indeed. For starters, why would Gorbachev interfere in Czechoslovakia when Poland, Hungary, and East Germany had been already lost? Furthermore, Zdeněk Mlynář would have been the last choice for anyone looking for an alternative to Miloš Jakeš as Czechoslovak party leader. In the early 1950s, Gorbachev and Mlynář were indeed classmates and friends at Moscow State University, but the last time the two had seen each other was in 1967. In 1968, Mlynář, then a young Politburo member of the Czechoslovak Communist Party, became a vocal proponent of the Prague Spring—and, naturally, lost his position and influence when "normalization" began. Later, when he joined Havel's Charter 77, the authorities advised him to leave the country, which he promptly did, moving to Vienna. These misadventures made him popular with Western intellectuals but hardly with anyone else. His adherence to the 1968 concept of socialism with a human face made him insufficiently radical for the Prague street, and his sojourn in Austria was treason in the eyes of the Czechoslovak party and, of course, the Kremlin.

As with many mysteries of 1989, it doesn't really matter whose creation "Martin Smid" was—the news about his death caused a public furor, and on November 18 students of the School for the Dramatic Arts went on strike, shortly followed by "an absolute majority of Czech theaters." A general strike of *theaters* was the engine of revolution? Yes. In one particular theater in Prague, actors and students formed a group called Civic Forum, and Urban telephoned the news to Radio Free Europe and the Voice of America, not suspecting that in a matter of hours Civic Forum would turn into a revolutionary party.

When on November 17 students marched past Václav Havel's house chanting, "Long live Havel!" Havel was at his country retreat, Hradecek, escaping the "Prague merry-go-round." Only when reports about the violence in Prague reached his hideaway did he drive back to the city to find himself in the shoes of a revolutionary predecessor, Lenin, who returned to Russia in 1917 to find an established grassroots power network (in his case, the Councils of Workers' Deputies, the *soviety* in Russian) for him to mobilize.

Havel's revolutionary headquarters were set up in a theater called the Magic Lantern, where "sixty to eighty people were working twenty four hours a day." It's still not entirely clear what they were "working" on, their only proven activity being Havel's publicity machine. When the writer Timothy Garton Ash flew into Prague, he found Havel not in the streets, but rather "in the back-room of his favoured basement pub." Incredibly excited, Ash exclaimed: "In Poland it took ten years, in Hungary ten months, in East Germany ten weeks: perhaps in Czechoslovakia it will take ten days!"

Havel grinned. Ash had just coined the velvet revolution's slogan. He summoned over "a video-camera team . . . who just happened to be waiting in the corner . . . I was politely compelled to repeat my quip to the camera, over a glass of beer," Ash remembers. The line, caught on tape by the crew, who just happened to be waiting in the corner, won over the Czechoslovak newspapers and Western media instantly.

Insightfully, Ash describes Havel as "at once director, playwright, stage-manager and leading actor in this, his greatest play." To get into the Magic Lantern Theater, all one had to do was to get a ticket saying "Please let in and out" in purple ink, "signed by Havel's brother, Ivan, and authenticated by the playwright's rubber stamp."

"Short, with light hair and moustache, and a thick body perched on small feet, he looks younger than his fifty-three years. Even in quieter times, he is a bundle of nervous energy, with hands waving like twin propellers, and a quite distinctive, almost Chaplinesque walk: short steps, slightly stooping, a kind of racing shuffle. He wears jeans, open shirts, perhaps a corduroy jacket, only putting on a suit and tie under extreme duress"—for example, when he "slips away off stage" to receive an international prize, such as the Peace Prize of the German Book Trade (awarded yearly by the organizers of the Frankfurt Book Fair since 1950) and the Olof Palme Prize (in its third year in 1989). Collecting a prize or two during a revolution, he withdrew to the pub to have a beer and a vicious local concoction called *becherovka.* He said he missed his two cats, Yin and Yang, whom he hadn't seen for a week.

Yet Havel was the rallying figure for the opposition in Prague. When Alexander Dubček, the 1968 Prague Spring hero, returned on November 21, he reunited with Havel as a junior partner in the alliance. The atmosphere was jubilant: "the voice of '68," the singer Marta Kubišová, sang "The Times They Are a-Changin'." The crowds chanted: "Dubček! Dubček!" "Dubček-Havel!" "Free elections, free elections!"

The Civic Forum started negotiations with the Communist prime minister, Ladislav Adamec, the day before, November 20. The Czechoslovak leadership was in spectacular disarray. It was clear that the people of Prague had handed over the "dictatorship of the street" to the Civic Forum and its leader, Havel. There was absolutely no evidence of any militancy on the part of the protesters—in other words, there was no pretext for using force against them. Meanwhile, international TV crews had flown into Prague firmly intent on documenting the revolution. In this situation, the government's hands were tied. The party leader, Jakeš, who earlier that year had promised the Hungarian Communists to send Czechoslovak troops to Budapest if necessary, still lived in a bubble and believed that if he sent the army into the streets of Prague, a massacre could save the day. But Jakeš didn't have dictatorial powers, and realists such as Adamec made sure that no force would be used. On November 24, they voted Jakeš out and elected the little-known and gullible Karel Urbánek as secretary general of the party. Their stand was a combination of humanism, common sense, and personal ambition: with the situation so fluid, Adamec, for one, aspired to become a new, reformist leader of Czechoslovakia. As for Gorbachev, it looks like by that time he had washed his hands of the Eastern European revolution and counterrevolution altogether. In the fall of 1989, he had to deal with secessionist movements in all the republics of the

Soviet Union, including Russia. The antigovernment surge had claimed the media. Only two years earlier, *Moscow News* had found it daring to publish an obituary of an émigré author, but in November 1989, it published a story about the government's cover-up of the Chernobyl disaster under the headline "The Big Lie."

Overwhelmed by the escalating crisis at home, Gorbachev didn't have any strength left to address the most important foreign policy issue of all—the reunification of Germany. In principle he was against it, and had he been determined to slow it down, he would have easily found many allies in Europe and America. Every Western publication those days quoted the French writer and Nobel laureate François Mauriac's old quip "I love Germany so much that I am glad there are two of them." An article in *Time* published on November 20 read, "reunification of Germany into a giant that would overwhelm Europe the way it would dominate an Olympic Games is, at least in the immediate future, probably not likely and perhaps not wise." Beleaguered, Gorbachev voiced his concerns but postponed action.

With Gorbachev struggling, the Czechoslovak Communist leadership had to deal with the revolution on its own. The commotion above led to aggressiveness below. The state-run media outlets joined the revolution's bandwagon, 75 percent of the population supported the two-hour general strike announced by the Civic Forum, and on November 26 about eight hundred thousand protesters crowded Prague. That same day, Havel and Adamec for the first time met face-to-face. The sly Adamec suggested an alliance: he would persuade the government to cave in on freedoms such as free elections, and the freedom of speech and travel, if Havel agreed to work with him in a coalition government. This was the easiest solution to the crisis, and Havel agreed—though the rebellious Prague street did not take the compromise well.

The revolution made itself heard. The coalition government led by Adamec lasted for just seven days. The Civic Forum found it was underrepresented (it was: five cabinet ministers stood for the Civic Forum and fifteen for the Communist Party), and another "reformist Communist," Marián Calfa, agreed to chair a cabinet where Communists would be in the minority. After massive protests, on December 29, the Czechoslovak parliament, still overwhelmingly Communist, elected Havel president of the country.

The Americans were sending to Malta the flagship of the Sixth Fleet, the USS *Belknap*, the Soviets, the *Slava* and the cruise ship *Maxim Gorky*. The Bush-Gorbachev summit was to be held on the warships, with the *Maxim Gorky* serving as a hotel for Gorbachev and his entourage.

But now a "no agenda" meeting looked farcical. Between July, when Bush sent a letter to the Soviet leader, and late November, when the preparations were heading into their final stage, the Wall had fallen; East Germany, Czechoslovakia, and Bulgaria had had velvet revolutions; the pope's friend Tadeusz Mazowiecki became prime minister of Poland. Europe was in turmoil because of the prospect of a united Germany, and François Mauriac's quip took on a life of its own (the prime minister of Italy, Giulio Andreotti, was quoted saying, "We love the Germans so much that the more Germanies there are the better"). The idea of a Soviet-American condominium over Europe redefining the superpowers' spheres of influence, suggested by Kissinger and rejected by Bush eleven months ago, now looked plausible—and sensational. Journalists picked up on the possibility enthusiastically, and the phrase they coined—"From Yalta to Malta"—was disturbing. At a White House press briefing, Secretary of State Baker promised "this was not going to be Yalta II." Yet, on November 22, Bush sent Gorbachev another letter with a list of topics for discussion. Eastern Europe, subheaded with an A, sat at the top.

Curious to see the exotic country, Gorbachev arrived in Malta early, flying there from Rome, where he had met John Paul, smiled a lot, and even invited the pope to visit the USSR. But John Paul already looked like a retired revolutionary, as the upheavals under way now could not possibly, at this stage, be influenced by him.

The evening in the capital, Valletta, went well as Gorbachev schmoozed with enthusiastic crowds in the streets. On the next day, things turned sour. According to Baker, the weather was "atrocious," and twenty-foot waves and gale-force winds battered the ships. The *Belknap*'s captain, John F. Sigler, pronounced that in twenty-five years in the navy "he had never experienced such rough seas in harbor." Bush was excited. He managed to "squeeze in some time to fish off the fantail of the ship" and when he went to bed he "could hear the sea lapping at the hull."

The first session was scheduled to start on the *Slava*, which was anchored barely a mile away from the *Belknap*, but Gorbachev refused to travel in a launch in rough seas. The *Maxim Gorky* had berthed at the dock, and so the two leaders met there. The arrangements "had to be made hastily," Gorbachev's interpreter remembered. "Finding a table long enough for the two delegations was . . . difficult, so two tables of somewhat unequal height had to be put together and covered with a green tablecloth."

Gorbachev was determined to stay distrustful. Bush had been procrastinating for too long, and now the Soviet leader was inclined to examine carefully "every sentence, every formula of the new U.S. president," despite the flowery language of the November 22 letter, in which Bush had thanked him for perestroika and exclaimed that "the fate of my own precious grandkids and yours is dependent on perestroika's success."

When the two leaders finally met, Bush praised Gorbachev to the skies, particularly his prudence in dealing with the cascade of events in Eastern Europe, and promised to move ahead with disarmament talks, but also pressed him to sever ties with Castro and with the Sandinistas in Nicaragua. This was precisely what the Kremlin hawks had been saying for years: give Americans an inch and they will take a mile. The Eastern Europe discussion, however, proceeded smoothly. Bush said, "I hope you have noticed that as dynamic change has accelerated in recent months, we have not responded with flamboyance or arrogance that would complicate Soviet relations. What I am saying may be self-serving. I have been called cautious or timid. I *am* cautious but not timid. But I have conducted myself in ways not to complicate your life. That's why I have not jumped up and down on the Berlin Wall."

Gorbachev nodded. "Yes, we have seen that, and appreciate that."

The Soviet leader said he was concerned about Germany. "Mr. Kohl is in too much of a hurry on the German question. That is not good." He suggested the two powers "should let Kohl know that his approach could damage things." Bush responded by saying that Kohl was under enormous emotional pressure but promised that the United States would "do nothing to recklessly try to speed up reunification."

The talks were riddled with misinterpretations, and when Gorbachev, thinking he was building an ideological bridge between socialism and capitalism, suggested that "much property in the West was held collectively: corporations, for instance," Bush and Baker were "struck by how poorly Gorbachev understood market economies."

The evening session had to be canceled altogether because the weather had turned worse. In Brent Scowcroft's words,

The swells, even in the harbor, were enormous and the wind was howling. We had great difficulty getting aboard the ship and made it only because of the great skills of the crew of the Admiral's barge. The swells would take the barge up or down fifteen feet in a second, and transferring to the *Belknap*'s landing platform was quite a trick . . . By nightfall, the ship was rolling like mad. The storm prevented any of our people then ashore from getting to the ship, and we ourselves could not leave, even though we were riding at anchor. Gorbachev could not reach the *Belknap* for dinner that evening, so we ate a marvelous meal meant for him—swordfish, lobster, and so forth. Here were the two superpower leaders only hundreds of yards apart, and they could not dine together. The storm cut us off from the rest of the world.

Bush, nevertheless, was in high spirits: the triple-decker bunks in the sailors' quarters reminded him of the USS *Finback*, the submarine that rescued him after he was shot down in 1944. The sailors posed with him for pictures, "which was fun." One of them warned him "not to stand by one of the bow anchor chains, and pointed out that it had been chocked down. If it snapped it might well take my leg off." Scowcroft, meanwhile, stayed alert. Radio communications with Washington proceeded only with "modest success," and he "said a small prayer that no crisis would explode that night."

As for crises, Gorbachev had been living one for the past four years. Now, with him abroad, leaders of the opposition, led by Yeltsin, called for a two-hour general strike demanding that Article 6 in the Soviet Constitution guaranteeing the party's "leading role" be abolished. Ominously, Yeltsin invited Gorbachev "to learn the lessons of East Germany, where reforms were delayed so long that they were eventually accomplished within a week." The second session of the Soviet parliament, the Congress of People's Deputies, where the opposition controlled about 30 percent of the seats, was scheduled to open in Moscow on December 12.

Gorbachev also had lesser but still annoying concerns. The deputy foreign minister, Aleksandr Bessmertnykh, prodded him to meet Bush on the *Slava* as planned. But the commander in chief of the navy, Admiral Vladimir Chernavin, kept saying that this was too risky. Next morning, the idea of meeting on either warship had to be dumped altogether. Though the storm had eased, "Gorbachev still could not be persuaded to venture out to the *Slava*," Bush wrote with a seasoned sailor's condescension, "so we went back to the *Maxim Gorky*." In their turn, to boost troop morale, the Soviets spread a rumor that Bush was seasick.

Bush still thought they were "on the same wavelength" and, indeed, Gorbachev started the second day of negotiations by saying that "the Soviet Union will under no circumstances start a war" and that "the Soviet Union is ready no longer to regard the United States as an adversary." Bush revisited the German question because he felt he had to. "You are closer" to events, he told Gorbachev, but "we cannot be asked to disapprove of German reunification." None of the leaders was particularly interested in discussing arms control; an issue deemed absolutely crucial only a year earlier was now all but irrelevant.

Throughout the talks, Gorbachev made a few condominium hints, saying, "We accept your role in Europe. It is very important that you be there." But Bush played deaf. Dismissing Kissinger's proposal almost a year earlier, he had done the right thing, actually. Had he reached some "understanding" with Gorbachev on Eastern Europe before the revolutionary cascade, the agreement would have tied him to Gorbachev's sinking ship and limited the United States' role in Warsaw, Prague, and Budapest. Prudence had paid off. As the president's visits had demonstrated, now the United States—and not the Soviet Union—was the most sought-after partner for Poland and Hungary. Washington's involvement in the German refugee crisis in September, engaging East Germany, Hungary, and Czechoslovakia, meant that the United States was welcome to act aggressively on the whole territory of the Eastern bloc. Now there was nothing left for the Soviet leader but to "accept" the United States' poaching. Annoyed, Gorbachev suddenly said he wasn't happy that the administration was talking about "Western values" in speeches and public statements. "Why not call them 'democratic values'?" Baker suggested. "That's fine," Gorbachev said.

Except for the phrase "From Yalta to Malta," the summit had produced very little. Held at a pivotal moment in world history, it was just the first meeting of the two leaders of the formerly antagonistic great powers at which they got to know each other and assured the world of their unwavering goodwill. Bush hadn't expected anything grander. Gorbachev, for whom the reunification of Germany was an awkward domestic issue, as many Soviets remembering World War II only too well watched the fall of the Wall with great concern, had hoped Bush would agree that reunification should be delayed; but the U.S. president refused to cooperate.

Angry and disappointed, Gorbachev had to face another summit, this one totally farcical—a meeting of the Warsaw Pact. Of all the Eastern European leaders, only Nicolae Ceaușescu of Romania spoke for the pre-1989 world. The other five represented nations were in different stages of divorce from the USSR and communism. The prime minister of Poland, Tadeusz Mazowiecki, was certain to report every detail of the Warsaw Pact situation to the Vatican, and from there, if the pope wished, the news would reach every NATO government. Military alliance now looked oxymoronic, and the summit was just a convenient pretext for Gorbachev to hold conversations with the Eastern European leaders. One had been scheduled with Ceauşescu.

Gorbachev had always strongly disliked "the Romanian Führer," and the day he received him in the Kremlin, December 4, he liked what he saw: Ceauşescu looked "strange," his eyes too bright, his behavior both "obsessed" and "hampered." The hypertension did not help his stutter and, getting stuck in the middle of a difficult word, his whole face convulsed. Yet the last Eastern European despot started the conversation with a preemptive strike.

"Do you know what Lenin said in 1903?" he asked.

"No, I do not," Gorbachev responded wearily.

"No matter how few we are, we must raise the flag."

It took Gorbachev only several minutes to retaliate. He knew what would upset Ceauşescu most: a reference to Honecker, now under criminal investigation in East Germany.

"Look at the situation in which our common friend Comrade Honecker is today. We have a great deal of mutual sympathy, but as of late, he did not want to speak with me, and I did not have a chance to speak with him. After all, I told him, Comrade Honecker, it is your job to decide, we will not decide for you, we do not force you to adhere to our decisions. As a matter of fact, I know that both of you have criticized me . . ."

"No, we did not criticize you. On the contrary, we decided that we should meet more quickly and discuss what we could do to work better together."

Paying no attention to the remark, Gorbachev maliciously continued: "Sincerely speaking, I am very uncertain about the future of Comrade Honecker."

The arrow hit the target, as Ceauşescu hurried to say, "I am very sorry about this and that is why I even brought it to the attention of the public. Something must be done, because things cannot continue in this manner. That includes, of course, Comrade Zhivkov."

But Gorbachev had no compassion for either Honecker or Zhivkov, and instead of suggesting a rescue plan, gleefully brought up the name of yet another loser—his "old friend" Miloš Jakeš of Czechoslovakia. "I told him," Gorbachev continued sadistically, "you have a great country, a well-trained population, well educated and well organized. You need to make the necessary changes faster, faster. Otherwise, you'll end up like us, having to solve your problems under the marching of boots. Jakeš listened to me and said: Then we shall wait until others come to power in the Soviet Union. He waited, and this is what happened."

Ceaușescu nervously responded, "Beginning with 1968 we said: We need to develop our economy because no one will help us otherwise. We have taken steps in that direction."

"You have done a lot," Gorbachev agreed.

"Until 1984 we did not import even one liter of gasoline from the Soviet Union."

"You had no need for it. You had your own gasoline. This is already clear now."

"I just wanted to remind you."

"In any case, you have done a lot."

"We have worked on and succeeded in bringing about the development of society and the economy. What you are doing now we have tried in the past. We created then the so-called private-holders, and after a year we saw they were getting rich and we put a stop to the entire situation."

"Is this the future you see for us?"

"If some get rich by playing the market, that is not a future, you know that, I'm sure. We have introduced the idea of economic self-rule, the new economic mechanism, and the leadership councils."

After more of this back-and-forth, Gorbachev suggested with irritation: "Maybe the Romanian government could explain what it expects from the Soviet Union." The explanation didn't take long to come. Ceaușescu wanted to be put back on the financial aid "respirator." In 1989, this meant oil.

The request hit a nerve. Romania was the only serious oil producer in Eastern Europe, and Gorbachev believed that it wouldn't have needed all that Soviet oil had it not been for Ceaușescu's megalomania.

"And how much do you extract from Romania?" Gorbachev asked.

"Only about ten million tons since we no longer have reserves."

"But there was a time when you were extracting about twenty-two million tons."

"It was closer to about fifteen million, but that was some time ago. We no longer have reserves. We thought about going to ten thousand meters depth."

"Our extraction is also falling."

Gorbachev's prime minister, Nikolai Ryzhkov, stepped in to say that Moscow was not ready to cooperate with Romania until it figured out its new foreign-trade policy—namely, how to move from barter to "regular commerce"; in plain language, a move toward market prices and payments in hard currency.

"I do not believe that for the Soviet Union it will be acceptable to move from the ruble to the dollar," Ceauşescu snapped. The Romanian prime minister, Constantin Dăscălescu, added: "For the past few days, something must have happened on your side, because we are receiving seven million cubic meters less a day. We were told that this will only last a few days. Could you please analyze this problem?"

At that point, Gorbachev lost his patience: "This happens every year. Always something more."

Very good at politicking, Gorbachev could be condescending or rude only with the people whose goodwill he didn't need any longer. In December 1989, he regarded the notoriously corrupt and despotic Ceauşescu as baggage.

——

Ceauşescu was indeed a megalomaniac. The razing of downtown Bucharest to make room for totalitarian buildings destroyed twenty-six churches and displaced forty thousand people, and thousands of abandoned dogs roaming the city were a gruesome reminder of the destruction. A highway through the highest mountain range in the country and the Danube–Black Sea Canal drained the treasury dry. The "systematization" campaign announced in 1988 was to reduce the number of villages from thirteen thousand to five thousand; eleven million farmers had to move to bleak "agro-towns."

In 1981, the dictator was forced to introduce rationing. Soon the people were getting two pounds of flour, sugar, and meat, a pound of margarine, and five eggs per month. By 1985, energy consumption per household plummeted to 20 percent of the 1979 level. In 1988, the state banned the use of private cars in wintertime, outlawed vacuum cleaners and refrigerators and street lighting in the villages. The maximum temperature suggested for workplaces was 44 degrees Fahrenheit. While Bulgarians complained about Romanian pollution spilling over the border, a plant at Copşa Mică destroyed practically all vegetation within a radius of four miles in Romania itself.

Worried by declining birthrates, Ceauşescu intruded into the most private of spaces. Some of the measures looked familiar to the Soviets—an unmarried couple could not share a hotel room and the childless had to pay a special tax—but Ceauşescu also made divorce difficult, banned abortions, and ordered random medical examinations of women to catch secret pregnancies.

The regime's power was maintained by the infamous secret police, the Securitate. A conversation with a foreigner had to be reported within twenty-four hours; according to different estimates, between one million and five million of the population were informers, voluntary or otherwise.

The birthplace of the Romanian revolution was unlikely: the town of Timişoara had a population of merely 350,000. It had a significant Hungarian minority, and László Tökés, the pastor of a local Calvinist church, was its spokesman. Though unnoticed by the mainstream Western media, Tökés was popular in Hungary. When in the fall of 1989 Romanian authorities started a court procedure to evict him from the church premises, the Hungarian Foreign Ministry summoned the Romanian ambassador and dressed him down; Hungary contacted the United Nations on Tökés's behalf, and the Hungarian parliament nominated him for the Nobel Peace Prize. The rights of the Hungarian minority in Romania had always been a thorny issue for Budapest, yet Kádár muffled the polemics for the sake of Warsaw Pact stability. Now the new Hungarian leadership was only too happy to take up the issue, as this made it look good in the eyes of the population—as the Hungarian leaders did in July 1989 at the session of the Political Consultative Committee of the Warsaw Pact in Bucharest.

The final eviction decree was not issued until December 7. Tökés asked his parishioners to gather on the fifteenth to witness the disgrace, and in the morning, about forty elderly men and women were at the church. In his book detailing the Romanian revolution, Peter Siani-Davies writes: "the crowded passing trams were to act as a grapevine, spreading news of the events outside the church throughout the city." Passengers waiting at the tram stop "mingled with the members of Tökés's congregation, swelling the size of the crowd so that, in the restricted space, it appeared more numerous, giving heart to the pa rishioners and drawing in the curious." Members of other persecuted congregations in Timișoara—Pentecostals and Baptists—arrived at the scene. By the evening, Siani-Davies continues, "the numbers had grown sufficient to bring traffic to a virtual standstill on the nearby boulevard." When the mayor appeared, he was nearly lynched. At night, the crowds started chanting "Freedom!" When most of the protesters went home, about fifteen people stayed for an overnight vigil.

On the morning of the sixteenth, the crowd swelled again. Advised by the mayor and, apparently, by his own conscience, the pastor asked them to leave to prevent bloodshed. But they didn't. Later Tökés wrote: "The crowd looked to me as a figurehead, in truth I was prisoner of their anger."

By the end of the day, the crowds realized that they had got away with the defense of Tökés and now thought they would get away with more. Looting stores, they headed to the center of town and attempted ransacking party headquarters. They didn't disperse until the Securitate brought in reinforcements.

Tökés was arrested that night and eventually forced to sign an acceptance of his eviction, but his surrender did not matter any longer. On December 17, about two thousand protesters clashed with the Securitate in front of party headquarters. Now they had the familiar slogans: "Free elections, democracy, freedom for all." As in East Germany and Czechoslovakia, observers noted, the national flags carried by the protesters had the Communist symbols torn out.

Accepting casualties, the combatants forced their way into party headquarters and a number of other buildings, capturing five tanks on the way. By the afternoon, revolutionary mobs took control of

Timişoara's downtown. The loyalist forces had reclaimed it by that night, killing more than sixty civilians and arresting about seven hundred.

Ceauşescu focused his attention on the Timişoara crisis on the sixteenth, demanding from the local authorities a "show of strength." On the next day, after the news about the ransacking of Timişoara party headquarters reached Bucharest, he convened the Politburo. There he said that both "East and West"—in other words, Moscow, Washington, and Budapest—stood behind the events. He told the army "to kill hooligans not just beat them." The alternative, he said, was "the liquidation of communism" in Romania. His wife, Elena, added: "You shoot them and throw them in the dungeon. Not even one should see the daylight again!"

This was a civil war, but in the dictator's mind rebels had to have foreign sponsors, and after the unpleasant conversation with Gorbachev earlier in the month, he thought that the USSR, hostile to him since 1968 when he opposed the use of force in Czechoslovakia, was behind the unrest.

On the same day, December 17, Romania started closing its borders. Yugoslavian authorities reported that the defenses on the Romanian border were "fortified by troops along its whole length, including checkpoints. So far the Romanian side authorized only the passing of people with diplomatic and other service passports." Suspecting the Soviets of infiltration, Ceauşescu annulled visa waivers for them. On the morning of the eighteenth, the Soviets began calling the Romanian embassy in Moscow "from border crossings into Romania, implying that there are hundreds of vehicles" stuck at the border. Meanwhile, the Soviet Foreign Ministry remained clueless about what was happening in Romania. If the KGB knew, it did not share the information.

Promising the army, the police, and the Securitate that there would be serious consequences if they failed to stop the uprising, on the morning of December 18 Ceauşescu left for Tehran. Romania and Iran were ready to close a significant deal in which Romanian arms were to be exchanged for Iranian oil and gas, the latter crucial for Ceauşescu's regime's survival, so the trip could not possibly be postponed. Elena was to run the country during his absence.

When Ceauşescu chose to go on with the foreign trip, the situation in Timişoara looked calmer—troops had taken up positions all over the city, outbound roads were blocked, telephone communications cut, mail suspended. But the departure was a mistake. Rumor had it that the dictator had left for good carrying billions in gold with him, and in the Balkans rumors have killed more despots than revolutions have.

On the night of December 19, the bodies of the Timişoara victims were brought to Bucharest in a refrigerator truck, cremated, and the ashes scattered. The secrecy was a mistake. Sixty corpses grew into thousands in the popular imagination; the absence of proper burials fueled the public's rage. On the twentieth, demonstrations flared up in Timişoara again and by the end of the day one third of the city's population was in the downtown streets. The army evacuated the city. A number of top government officials descended on Timişoara, including Prime Minister Dăscălescu. They attempted negotiations with a bunch of random representatives of the rioters, whose demands kept shifting between economic (better housing) and political (Ceauşescu's resignation) concerns.

Meanwhile, returning to the country at three p.m. on December 20, Ceauşescu decided concessions were not working. He dispatched by special trains to Timişoara between ten thousand and twenty thousand workers armed with clubs to enforce proletarian justice. Yet when the trains began arriving in the city on the morning of the twenty-first, the workers proved too confused and wary to act. Most of them never left the railway cars.

Riots began to spread to other towns—and to Bucharest. Three hours after landing, at six p.m., Ceauşescu met with the army and Securitate commanders. At seven p.m., he addressed the nation, accusing Hungary and other unspecified foreign countries of staging the unrest.

The news about the Timişoara massacre reached the world as early as the afternoon of December 17, and Western broadcasts transmitted the story to the rest of Romania, where there was a media blackout of the crisis. Radio Free Europe's Romanian service stayed on the air through the whole night. One commentator writes, "many Romanians would later testify to the great excitement of that night." The broadcasts also described an outpouring of support. East Germany, Poland, and Hungary had protested the massacre officially, and crowds gathered around Romanian embassies all over Eastern Europe.

Meanwhile, Ceaușescu summoned the Soviet chargé d'affaires and declared that the action in Timișoara had been "prepared and organized with the consent of countries [that are] members of the Warsaw Treaty Organization" and "plotted within the framework of the Warsaw Treaty Organization." The accusations were baseless.

In his memoirs, Gorbachev admitted that he was getting "signals" from the opposition in Bucharest but, he insisted, he had refused to "get involved." A Romanian Communist Party dissident, Silviu Brucan, reported a meeting with Gorbachev in November 1988. "From the outset," Brucan claims, "he stated his agreement with a well-conceived scenario to topple Ceausescu, provided it was created and carried out so as to maintain the Communist Party as the main political force in the country . . . But he stated in categorical terms that the Soviets were not going to interfere in any way with the whole process: 'Nonintervention is a sacred principle for us. Don't expect us to help you. It is your business a hundred percent.'" If Brucan's account is accurate, Gorbachev's response to Ceaușescu was similar to what he allegedly told the Bulgarian plotters.

According to Brucan, Gorbachev "promised to take care of my personal safety. Indeed, officials found an ingenious way of doing that by instructing the *Pravda* correspondent in Bucharest, Stanislav Petuhov, to visit with me regularly, thus signaling to the Romanian authorities the Soviet concern for my well-being."

At a certain level, speculation about Gorbachev's involvement in the Timișoara crisis looks absurd—not because Gorbachev articulated noninterference in other countries' domestic affairs, but because in December 1989 he was more King Lear than King Richard. His foreign minister wrote to him on December 20: "On the events in Romania in the last few days we can still only judge on the basis of information that comes from news agencies, primarily Western ones. This information is often contradictory and does not allow one to construct a true picture. Our attempts to obtain the official version via Bucharest produced no results." Of course, in principle, one could maintain that Gorbachev was involved in Romanian matters and had totally bypassed Shevardnadze and the Foreign Ministry in general— but the only tool for that in 1989 would have been the KGB, and by that point Gorbachev in fact had little control over the imperial secret service. Very angry at him for letting the empire disintegrate domestically and lose influence abroad, the KGB had distanced itself from Gorbachev. As for the supposition that the KGB could have interfered in Romania on its own, this doesn't hold water. The maverick of the Eastern bloc, Ceauşescu, was as popular with them as he was with Gorbachev, but the KGB had proved unable to stop the disintegration of the Soviet Union itself. Incidentally, one of the republics constituting the USSR, Moldavia, sat on the border with Romania, was indistinguishable from it in language, culture, and history, and by the fall of 1989 had developed a strong secessionist movement of its own. Powerless to disperse the multithousand anti-Soviet and anti-Russian rallies in the Moldavian Soviet Socialist Republic, the KGB carried even less influence across the border.

In the early afternoon of December 21, in Bucharest, Ceauşescu called for a rally in front of the Central Committee building. There, from the balcony he used for public occasions, as Mussolini did in the Palazzo Venezia, he would address the nation. He had scored many public relations victories before—as in 1968 when he condemned the Soviet invasion of Czechoslovakia—and, confident of his powers of persuasion, he commanded the rally to be broadcast live.

When the dictator, flanked by Elena and court sycophants, approached the microphone, the clocks stood at 12:31 p.m. Millions of Romanians were frozen in front of their televisions. A minute or two into the speech something happened in the square. All the TV audience heard was noise and screams and all they saw was Ceauşescu's wary face, and then the broadcast stopped. The event was on air again a few moments later, but many in Romania insisted that this moment, this dead time on television, and not the riots in Timişoara, was the real start of the Romanian revolution.

It is still not known for sure what the commotion was and why Ceauşescu looked startled. Interpretations vary: a rogue firework, an antigovernment chant, a collapsing streetlamp or a banner, the firing of tear gas grenades in the distance, a short-circuit in the loudspeakers.

Continuing after the almost supernatural interruption, Ceauşescu praised the achievements of the socialist revolution, promised to raise the minimum wage from 2,000 to 2,200 lei and increase children's allowances and pensions, and asked for the people's support against foreign plotters. He got the reaction he wanted—applause—from some, but others catcalled. The rally devolved into chaos. Nicolae and Elena chose not to leave the Central Committee building that afternoon. Shortly, downtown Bucharest saw the first deployment of troops. Student dormitories were placed under watch, a number of dissidents arrested. Meanwhile, spontaneous rallies sprang up in the center of town. The police responded with fire. The people began building barricades.

To the best of our knowledge, those were the only barricades of 1989.

⸻

The Ceauşescus spent the rest of the day and the night in the Central Committee building, protected by army units and the Securitate. Rumor had it that during that fateful night the despot took a final ride through Bucharest.

People chanted "Freedom!" and "Down with Ceauşescu!" There were street fights: "Water cannons and tear gas were finally followed by bullets," and the troops advanced in two lines. The first consisted of "men with riot shields and sticks; among them were unarmed men grabbing and carrying off revolutionaries," and in the second line "were the troops who fired, some of whom were in civilian clothes." A witness remembered: "I believed then that they wanted to kill everybody, but after a couple of hours they disappeared." Another witness adds, "By three in the morning, everybody had gone home." The toll of December 21 in Bucharest was 49 dead, 463 wounded, and 698 arrested.

But the "subway had never stopped running," and the phones kept working, including public phones where the street battles raged. The first thing Jaruzelski had done in Operation X eight years earlier was to cut all telephone communications in Poland.

. . .

On the morning of December 22, the rioters returned to the downtown, paying little attention to the national state of emergency announced at eleven o'clock. Then another announcement followed: the minister of defense, General Vasile Milea, had killed himself. Worse, the dead man was now blamed for cooperating with "the traitors within the country and with the imperialist circles." It was impossible not to think of foul play, and, as a historian writes, the army "almost immediately went over to the revolution."

Today the majority of historians agree that Milea did shoot himself at nine-thirty in the morning right after a conference with Ceauşescu (some insist, though, that he was shot by Ceauşescu's detail or even the dictator's brother). Practically everyone is in accord that the general had quietly sabotaged Ceauşescu's ruthless orders, not wanting the army to massacre the people of Bucharest.

Now army commanders ordered their units to freeze or withdraw. Some units fraternized and occasionally merged with the crowds. People assembled in the square in front of the Central Committee, where Ceauşescu tried to address them from his balcony again, but "the crowd was yelling accusations at him and he withdrew hurriedly" after an aide whispered that the doors had been forced open.

On the rooftop was a waiting helicopter, its engines running. It was noon.

In the square in front of the Central Committee building random speakers berated Nicolae and Elena. Television broadcast them live. Meanwhile, popular intellectuals and party dissidents were arriving at the TV station and taking control of the state-run media. Several figures in different locations claimed to have formed a democratic revolutionary government. Ceauşescu's helicopter took off at noon, and at 2:30 p.m. a TV anchorman introduced to the audience an outstanding "patriot," Ion Iliescu.

A privileged party apparatchik who went to college in Moscow in 1971 at the age of forty-one, Iliescu was viewed as Ceauşescu's heir apparent. Shortly thereafter, falling out with the ruling couple, he started losing influence, ending up in a publishing house dealing with technical books and journals. Practically every author writing about the Romanian revolution calls Iliescu "self-appointed," but of course he was, like all revolutionaries (Robespierre, Lenin) or the people who inherit a revolution (Napoleon, Stalin). Self-appointed he surely was, but authors disagree on whether this was a spontaneous occurrence or the result of a plot by the reformist apparatchiks, the army, and possibly even the Securitate. Iliescu implied that he knew Gorbachev, and is on record saying, on December 22, that the personal connection could help if things went bad and the new government had to ask Moscow for help.

Now, on air at 2:30, Iliescu informed the audience that he had spoken to the acting defense minister and that now all the troops would be sent to the barracks. That was indeed what General Victor Stănculescu, appointed to the post by Ceauşescu a few hours earlier, ordered. "Therefore, comrades, at this moment we have guarantees that the army is with the people." He announced that later in the day a revolutionary government would be created.

From the TV studio Iliescu headed to the Central Committee building. At the entrance, the following exchange between him and anonymous rioters was caught on tape:

PROTESTER: Film and record everything!

ILIESCU: We are going in the large hall to discuss.

ANOTHER PROTESTER: No! You must talk here. So that we know what is going on. We want to have control.

ILIESCU: We want to form a council.

A VOICE: Yes, but here, my dear.

Around five p.m., Iliescu formed his revolutionary government, the National Salvation Front, consisting of Politburo members, generals, and several dissidents named in absentia. The conference *was* videotaped, but that didn't help: the revolutionary government was of the party and by the party.

Meanwhile, with the departure of the dictator, the fighting got worse. When at night Iliescu went to Ceauşescu's balcony to announce to the gathered crowds that everything was under control, "exchanges of fire were illuminating" the square, a historian writes.

In Bucharest, 162 people had died before Ceauşescu's helicopter took off from the rooftop of the Central Committee building; 942 were killed in the next few days. Fighting was especially severe around the Central Committee headquarters and the television studio; the university library with its precious collection of books and manuscripts was destroyed altogether. Even though "officially" the army had joined the people, the loyalists would not concede. The opposition leader Silviu Brucan says in his memoir that in the television studio people had to stay below window level to escape the sharpshooters' bullets: "most of the time I had to read and write on the carpet. On the way to Studio 4 was a corridor with glass walls where we also had to move on our knees; the temperature there reached freezing after most of the glass was smashed by bullets."

Self-appointed revolutionaries, many of them young people from other parts of the country, encouraged by spontaneous radio and television broadcasts, filled the center of Bucharest. Barricades were built randomly without any obvious strategic purpose; arbitrary checkpoints were erected; stores were looted; patriotic rallies were held; government offices were plundered; Securitate officers or people who were denounced as Securitate officers were lynched. There were rumors of an impending crackdown.

The fighters of the revolution were a motley bunch, but the people who shot at them were even more varied. Called "terrorists" and believed to have full access to the system of tunnels and bunkers under Bucharest, they loomed over the city as a mythical threat: Securitate and army officers, elite security squads, for sure, but also people reported as Palestinian, Syrian, Libyan, and Iranian assassins, as Ceauşescu had been doing business with all those nations. Adding to the paranoia, the residents of coastal towns had spotted Libyan warships in the Black Sea, supposedly bringing reinforcements. In reality, the mysterious force was a random assembly of desperate loyalists willing to perish together with the regime or, maybe, still hoping for Ceauşescu's return.

The helicopter carried Nicolae and Elena Ceauşescu, Ceauşescu's brother-in-law and his prime minister, and two officers of the presidential security detail. Ten minutes after taking off, it landed at a suburban residence. While Elena packed, Nicolae made phone calls. At 1:15 they were airborne again. The two henchmen had left, and the Ceauşescus were flying with just the two bodyguards. They were heading northwest. The couple's exact plans that day are unknown, but since 1985 a Boeing 707 had been parked at an inconspicuous airport always ready to take them into exile—most likely, to Libya. It is still not clear why the helicopter landed on the outskirts of the town of Tîrgoviste, a seemingly random choice. The field where the chopper touched down sat near a road. There the fugitives stopped a car driven by a local doctor, but their journey with him didn't last long, as the car ran out of gas. They stopped another one and drove to the Center for Plant Protection in Tîrgoviste, a model enterprise they had visited before. Again, it is impossible to tell what had led them there. Both bodyguards dispatched to find help disappeared, and the couple was left alone. There two police cars descended on them. Having spent a few hours in the reeds at the edge of a lake waiting out riots in nearby settlements, the police finally took the Ceauşescus to an army barracks. It was the evening of December 22.

The news from Romania was becoming apocalyptic. On December 23, Radio Budapest reported seventy thousand to eighty thousand dead and three hundred thousand wounded. On December 24, the American ambassador to the USSR, Jack Matlock, asked to see Soviet Deputy Foreign Minister Ivan Aboimov.

Jack Matlock was one of the finest career diplomats the U.S. foreign service had. A powerhouse in Gorbachev's Moscow, now he made a most interesting inquiry. Having discussed the humanitarian crisis in Romania, Matlock made an explicit condominium statement. According to Aboimov:

> Then Matlock touched on the issue that, apparently, he wanted to raise from the very beginning of the conversation. The Administration, he said, is very interested in knowing if the possibility of military assistance by the Soviet Union to the Romanian National Salvation Front is totally out of question. Matlock suggested the following option: what would the Soviet Union do if an appropriate appeal came from the Front? Simultaneously, the Ambassador hinted at the idea, apparently on instructions from Washington. He let us know that under the present circumstances the military involvement of the Soviet

Union in Romanian affairs might not be regarded in the context of "the Brezhnev doctrine."

To this sounding out by the American I gave the entirely clear and unequivocal answer, presenting our principled position. I declared that we did not visualize, even theoretically, such a scenario. We stand against any interference in the domestic affairs of other states and we intend to pursue this line firmly and without deviation. Thus, the American side may consider that "the Brezhnev doctrine" is now theirs as our gift.

Developing this thesis further, as a clarification, I drew the interlocutor's attention to the fact that it was on the basis of these considerations that the Soviet Union was and still is against convening the Security Council (SC) to consider the situation in Romania.

The American, however, immediately inquired what would be the Soviet reaction if the National Salvation Front itself appeals to convene the SC.

I said that we are still not ready to contemplate such a hypothetical possibility.

In 1989, even the best Russia experts like Matlock grossly overestimated Soviet power in Eastern Europe and the empire's will to enforce it. To Moscow elites, the very notion of sending troops abroad for whatever cause now sounded fantastic. On the day Matlock visited Aboimov, the Soviet parliament, the Congress of People's Deputies, closed its stormy twelve-day session. The storm had started on the first day, when the leading dissident, Andrei Sakharov, demanded abolishing the constitutional guarantee of Communist Party rule—the infamous Article 6 of the constitution. A foreign correspondent reported from Moscow:

In a quavering voice, Sakharov urged the more than 2,000 parliamentarians to change the agenda of the meeting and discuss deleting articles from the constitution that stand in the way of urgently needed economic reforms. Disapproving murmurs rumbled through the hall. Was Sakharov trying to derail the proceedings? Why was he wasting time with such matters? An impatient Gorbachev finally cut Sakharov off in mid-sentence: "I have the impression that you don't know how to realize your suggestions — and we don't either."

But Sakharov was not quite finished. He handed Gorbachev a handful of cables supporting the abolition of Article 6, which grants the Communist Party a monopoly on power.

"You come see me," snapped Gorbachev. "I'll give you three files with thousands of such cables . . ."

"I have 60,000 of them," countered Sakharov.

"Let's not put pressure on each other by manipulating public opinion," said Gorbachev, waving his hand. "There's no need." Dismissed, Sakharov slowly walked off the stage.

Two days later, on December 14, Sakharov died of a heart attack. His death at the age of sixty-eight, now blamed on Gorbachev's mean remarks during the last public exchange, energized the opposition. Sakharov's funeral turned into a revolutionary vigil. At the Congress, the opposition insisted on taking a vote on Article 6. It lost 839 to 1,138, but the relatively narrow margin made Gorbachev furious.

On the evening of December 24, the National Salvation Front leaders decided to put the Ceauşescus on trial immediately. Violence in Bucharest was mounting, and Tîrgoviste, where the Ceauşescus were confined, was not safe, the NSF said. But that was more of a pretext. The NSF was made up of second-tier party functionaries, and its leaders didn't want any unnecessary revelations from their former puppeteer, were a proper and public trial to be scheduled.

The couple remained strong and imperious. Elena pronounced the food "inedible"; Nicolae demanded "reports" about the situation from his captors. "My fate was decided in Malta," he kept pronouncing gravely.

On Christmas Day, military commanders in Tîrgoviste received a communication ordering them to be ready for a group of helicopters. The lead helicopter, the communication continued, would be carrying a lady's yellow scarf. The choppers were bringing the tribunal and a firing squad.

The couple was sentenced to death in fifty-five minutes. At the wall, they held hands. When a soldier bumped into Elena, the defiant woman shouted, "You keep away from me, you motherfucker." The firing squad took aim. Nicolae began humming the "Internationale."

Moscow's plotting in Romania did look fantastic, but neither in December 1989 nor later was anyone able to declare with certainty the nature of the bloody civil war in Romania—spontaneous revolution or planned coup. It is clear, though, that the National Salvation Front led by Ion Iliescu was not even remotely democratic; in January and June of 1990, confronted with student unrest in Bucharest, Iliescu would do exactly what Ceauşescu had done before—summon "patriotic" workers armed with clubs to disperse the rebels. In 2008, the massacres were still under investigation, as the case was a difficult one for the Romanian courts: by that time, Iliescu, the man who "stole" the revolution, had served three terms as president of Romania.

Epilogue

They pulled the old marshal out of the grave just a few days after the funeral. In September, the nights were already long and the cemetery was deserted, except for the packs of lanky mongrels.

The marshal had ended up at the unprotected burial site due to a chain of unfortunate choices, one ultimately leading to another and culminating, first, in his Kremlin office, where he killed himself, and then at this undistinguished cemetery, his grave cracked open, the clothes peeled off his sixty-eight-year-old body.

Half a century before, he aspired to be a writer, but when Stalin asked the best and the brightest to join the army, he went to military school enthusiastically. When war began, he was eighteen and by luck happened to be in the 4 percent of the 1941 eighteen-year-old warriors who lived to see 1945. Later, instead of resigning from the army and starting to write, he stayed, the choice chaining him to the Soviet military behemoth.

When the unwise men of the Kremlin sent troops into Afghanistan, Sergei Akhromeyev, already a four-star general, registered his strong disapproval, pronouncing the war unwinnable, but obediently doing his superiors' bidding, he followed another lost generation to Kabul.

His earnest attempt to defeat the Afghan insurgency failed but the effort brought him the rank of marshal and the position of head of the General Staff.

When the same unwise men of the Kremlin voted Mikhail Sergeyevich Gorbachev into power, the new leader announced that the army had to be rejuvenated and suggested that Akhromeyev be replaced. He became Gorbachev's advisor on strategic matters.

The months at Gorbachev's side proved maddening: domestic revolts, economic nosedive, the loss of Eastern Europe, the weakening of the union. When on the morning of August 19, 1991, he heard a radio broadcast announcing that a junta including all the key cabinet ministers had replaced Gorbachev, who was vacationing in the village of Foros in the Crimea, he rejoiced. On first-name terms with many of the plotters, he shared their basic assumption: as soon as you agree to meet the opposition at a round table, you might as well start packing up your office; this was the lesson learned from the revolutions in Eastern Europe. A second lesson, learned in the same part of the world, was equally disheartening: reformers swearing to stay on your side if you allow them just a little freedom will eventually proclaim your ship sinking and abandon it. On December 4, 1989, the reformist leaders of Eastern Europe dutifully attended a Warsaw Pact summit in Moscow; only nineteen months later, on July 1, 1991, the bloc was officially dissolved.

Akhromeyev's friends struck at the eleventh hour: on the next day, August 20, Gorbachev was scheduled to sign a revised Union Treaty with soviet socialist republics such as Ukraine and Kazakhstan, and the hawks correctly judged that this would effectively mean the death of the union state.

The village of Foros had no jobs before the party resort opened on the coast. Thick, short groves—dwarf oak, thorn, blackberry, pine—carpeted the slopes, home to birds, foxes, and small pythons; on the beach, large pebbles made sunbathing torturous, and jellyfish bobbed along the coastline. Foros was definitely not a popular destination. The party leaders felt safe there.

That's where the Gorbachevs had decided to build. The resulting residence turned out quite un-Soviet, as it was brazenly visible from the sea, and now the guides aboard the tour boats shuttling between

Sevastopol and Yalta made caustic comments at Mikhail Sergeyevich and Raisa's expense, to the mirthless laughs of passengers.

Gorbachev departed for Foros on August 4, a few days after a summit with Bush in Moscow. On the eve of his departure, sitting down on the arm of a chair and chatting with a trusted aide, Gorbachev acknowledged the fact that he felt spent: "The harvest, transportation, debts, communications, no money, the market falling apart . . . Oh Tolya," he said, addressing the aide by a nickname, "everything has become so petty, vulgar, provincial. You look at it and think, to hell with it all! But whom would I leave it to? I am so tired."

If Gorbachev described the state of affairs as petty and vulgar, foreign leaders were more likely to use terms like *failure of trust*. Former allies from the Eastern bloc had found themselves abandoned. Markus Wolf, chief of East German intelligence for thirty years, now persecuted in Germany, wrote: "I retained a shred of hope that Gorbachev, as a friend of Helmut Kohl's, would plead for clemency on our behalf . . . I addressed a letter to him, but received no answer." Margaret Thatcher, formerly a fan, now felt indignant that Gorbachev had yielded to Chancellor Kohl's pressure, agreeing that "the unity of the German nation must be decided by the Germans themselves" and that "the reunited Germany should be part of NATO." The leaders of Poland complained that Gorbachev had washed his hands of German reunification without first arranging a "proper treaty to settle Germany's border." Later, in her memoirs, Thatcher acidly described the Gorbachev-Kohl quid pro quo: "the West German Chancellor agreed to provide what must have seemed to the Soviets a huge sum, though they could in fact have extracted much more, to cover the costs of providing for the Soviet troops who would be withdrawn from East Germany."

Spending two uneventful weeks on the Crimean coast, Gorbachev intended to fly out on the nineteenth for the signing of the Union Treaty the day after, but in the early morning he, his family, and his aides were put under house arrest. All lines of communication were cut, including control over the "nuclear briefcase"—now, presumably, transferred to the minister of defense, Marshal Dmitri Yazov.

According to Gorbachev's interpreter, less than three weeks earlier, sitting next to Gorbachev in the backseat of the limo, Bush suddenly asked: "What do you think about Yazov, Mikhail? Do you trust him?"

"I do," Gorbachev replied. "He is a reasonable man. It is not easy to keep the military under control in such turbulent times, and he is helping me do it. He is respected by the officers. He is solid."

Now, in the backyard of the residence, facing the cliffs, Gorbachev, in shorts and a sweater, cursed the plotters as "agents of suicide" and "scoundrels." The detainees had a shortwave radio, so from the broadcasts of Radio Free Europe, the BBC, and the Voice of America they knew what was unfolding in Moscow: the downtown occupied by troops, Yeltsin besieged in his residence, hundreds of thousands of Muscovites forming a living ring around it, angry rallies all over the city; leaflets, revolutionary graffiti, barricades.

On the twentieth, in a changing room on the beach, Gorbachev dictated the text of his statement condemning the junta and darkly hinting at the possibility of some kind of unpleasant future for him personally. In the evening, his son-in-law filmed him reading it. About eighteen hours later, a task force dispatched to the Crimea by a victorious Yeltsin rescued them all.

The Russian revolution peaked on the morning of August 19, when Muscovites started assembling at the Russian government residence, ironically nicknamed the White House. Just a few hundred were there to witness the historic moment when Yeltsin climbed a tank to pronounce his determination to fight, but by nighttime at least one hundred thousand people surrounded the residence in a protective human ring. For the next two nights the ring kept swelling, and the junta, its troops spread over downtown Moscow, realized that it was just not possible to kill that many people—and surrendered.

On the morning of August 19, many upper-echelon leaders were envious of Marshal Sergei Akhromeyev's situation. That day, the marshal was conveniently far from Moscow—in the city of Sochi on the Black Sea, vacationing with his family—and that gave him a chance to wait and see. Instead, that morning he bought a ticket to Moscow on a commercial jet. The ticket would cost him his life.

When in three days the junta capitulated, he could have easily repented and resigned like so many others—for example, Foreign Minister Bessmertnykh. Over those three fateful days in the Kremlin, the marshal hadn't done anything criminal or, for that matter, meaningful at all. But he spent the next forty-eight hours writing farewell notes, including one to the Kremlin canteen apologizing for owing it money (50 rubles, or $1.56; the payment was enclosed). His last note, addressed to no one in particular, said: "Very bad in making suicide tools. The first attempt at 9:40 p.m. didn't work—the rope broke. Gathering my strength to try it again."

Adding the note to the five others already lying on his desk, he reattached the rope to a window handle with duct tape, sat down on the floor, and started to pull.

Had he died of a heart attack or cancer, he would have been buried in a heavily patrolled nomenklatura location, where no intruder would have dared approach his grave, let alone dig his body up, throw it on the ground, and strip it all the way down to the underwear. The identities of the perpetrators of the desecration remained unknown, but in all likelihood they were silly young men or tipsy bums hoping to salvage the marshal's medal collection from his corpse. The set *was* precious, as it included not just the medals the marshal got for fighting the Germans, expensive in blood but cheap in metal, but also the awards he accumulated in the years of peace mostly for just being there. The Golden Star of the Hero of the Soviet Union alone would have fetched a handsome price; its historic value aside, even as a plain scrap of metal the star, twenty-one grams of pure gold, would have fetched at least $250. Meanwhile, in the fall of 1991, bread in Moscow stores was sold out by 10 a.m., inflation ran at 4 percent a week, and the official poverty level was set at sixteen dollars per month per person. But, of course, there were no medals on the corpse, so the only spoils the men got was the marshal's uniform.

When the news of the suicide and then violation of the corpse reached the White House, both President Bush and the man closest to him, National Security Advisor Brent Scowcroft, were upset. "I felt a deep sense of sadness," the president admitted. "He was an honorable and honest professional soldier, who had, as he had once told Brent, witnessed the destruction of everything he valued and worked for all his life." The person to write an obituary in *Time* was Akhromeyev's counterpart, Admiral William J. Crowe, the former chairman of the Joint Chiefs of Staff. The piece opened with a heartfelt phrase: "Marshal of the Soviet Union Sergei Fyodorovich Akhromeyev was my friend. His death last week by his own hand was a tragedy that mirrors the convulsions racking the Soviet Union. He was a communist, a patriot and a soldier, and my guess is that he would have listed his affiliations in that order . . . He was a man of honor, integrity and intelligence. He was devoted to Marxist-Leninist ideals, taking great pride that he owned little more than the clothes on his back."

As the phrase of the day had it, on August 21, 1991, Gorbachev returned to a different country. When people say that you have returned to a different partner, friend, family, or country, this means that you no longer really belong. The coup, staged to save the Soviet Union and the Communist Party, had instead annihilated both. What followed, culminating in the formal dissolution of the Soviet Union in December, was emotional but anticlimactic. Yeltsin took over Russia, and the republics seceded from the union in all but name. Dual power was not an option, the USSR and Gorbachev just redundant. When in December Yeltsin and the then presidents of Ukraine and Belarus, their names fast forgotten by history, assembled in a lounge on the hunting grounds of the tsars, Belovezh, and pronounced the USSR dead, the first person they called was not Gorbachev but Bush.

The events leading to 1989 and the dramas of the revolutionary year are extraordinary, but so is the bigger picture behind them. There is nothing in the story to support the conventional image of the good masses throwing off Moscow. Rebellion was a domestic matter. Eastern Europeans were, naturally, very happy to see the Soviets go, but they were fighting not the empire, as in 1989 it was at its nadir, but their own rulers. What happened in Eastern Europe was a clash of classes revealed as civil war in Poland and Romania, nonviolent revolution in Czechoslovakia, and peaceful transfer of power in Hungary and Bulgaria.

A lot remains to be said about the world leaders involved in the unraveling of the Eastern bloc. George H. W. Bush, on whose watch the 1989 change happened, didn't do much to encourage or help it—except for the brief intercession in the East German refugee crisis in September. President Ronald Reagan was the Western leader deservedly credited for inspiring revolution in Eastern Europe, if not exactly bringing the cold war to an end. As for Mikhail Gorbachev, throughout his political career, he has been the husband of all wives and the wife of all husbands. There has hardly been a popular concept (Stalin's greatness; law and order; socialism with a human face) that Gorbachev at some point wouldn't embrace, to drop instantly when the wind changed. He never had a cause and treated his peers and associates in the same weather-vane fashion, and that's why at the end of his life he found himself alone. Pope John Paul II found a brilliant term for him—a providential man: a tool of history unaware of its place and role. Naturally, he should be given credit for launching perestroika and glasnost, but as those were an honest attempt on his part to strengthen communism in the Soviet Union, the revolutionary change that followed was an exemplary case of unintended consequences. It would be absurd to credit the inventors of fireworks in ancient China with ICBMs or cruise missiles.

No person had done more for the 1989 revolutions than the pope, who called 1989 an "annus mirabilis." John Paul II was a miracle himself. His unexpected election as pope awakened Poland, and he worked consistently and tirelessly to cultivate that awakening and make sure that it bore fruit. The role Marian adoration played in the transformation of Poland cannot be emphasized strongly enough, supplying modern history with an example of a truly revolutionary theology.

But the eventual fruits of the 1989–91 revolutions were bittersweet. Every gardener knows that if some plants take care of themselves, others are difficult to grow. When an acorn lands in a backyard, before the owner knows it, he has got a new tree   granted, about three inches tall in its first spring, but if he doesn't pull it out, people living on the street fifty years later will love the beautiful old oak, or hate it, depending on the direction in which the tree casts its shadow. That's how the free market takes root and grows.

With the fall of communism, no one had to teach Poles or Russians the basics of a market economy. Following its number-one rule ("Grab!"), entrepreneurs devoured collective or, rather, state-owned property in the process known as "privatization." The things to "privatize" or, rather, loot, were astounding in variety: oil tankers; steel mills; diamond mines; gold depositories; oil fields; woods; car factories; newsstand kiosks; blueberry farms; aircraft; toilets; hospitals; parking lots; cows; skating rinks; wheat fields; wastelands; emeralds; nickel; newspapers; water; airwaves.

The looting came as a surprise to the international mass media, though some Eastern European thinkers had started worrying about it ten years before it came. Recall that in 1980, confronted by a spontaneous pro–free market movement in Poland, the primate of Poland, Stefan Cardinal Wyszyński, warned its leader, Lech Wałesa: "It's not a question of wanting to change the leaders, it's they who must change. We must make sure—and I make this comparison quite deliberately—that one gang of robbers doesn't steal the keys of the state treasury from another similar gang."

No one listened, and Eastern Europe found itself in the maelstrom of unbridled capitalism—again. Ironically, on the fiftieth anniversary of the 1956 revolution in Hungary, Budapest saw the worst violence since then, the people protesting against a gang of robbers that *had* stolen the keys of the state treasury from another similar gang. Someone had leaked to the Hungarian media a tape on which Prime Minister Ferenc Gyurcsány was caught saying, "We lied in the morning, we lied in the evening"—referring to his misrepresentations of the state of the economy in the election campaign. Gyurcsány was a millionaire *and* a former Hungarian Young Communist Organization official, who had made his fortune during the daring privatization of the 1990s.

During the October 2006 riots in Budapest, 150 protesters were injured—by far more casualties than during the velvet revolution of 1989. A university student told the *New York Times* correspondent, "We should learn from the spirit of '56. We should finish off what began in 1956, because in 1989 there wasn't really a complete change."

What the young man likely had in mind was a humane social contract, which makes rights to life and liberty unalienable, and pursuit of (material) happiness possible. A contract of such a kind needs to be served carefully and maintained diligently, as it goes against the individualistic streak in human nature. Like millions of other Eastern Europeans, by 2006 the young man must have realized that free elections do not necessarily lead to more freedom and that the free market can impoverish a nation as effectively as central planning. Ironically, democracy involves just as much social engineering as its alternative—communism—which earlier generations of critical thinkers had tried and failed to establish.

Notes

Introduction

3   "A 65-year-old railwayman". Reuters, June 2, 2007.

4   "Berlin streets were in constant uproar": Taylor, p. 28.

4   the communists got over 25 percent of the popular vote: *Anchor Atlas*, 2, p. 246.

4   a civil war that claimed at least fifty thousand lives: United Nations Special Committee on the Balkans, p. 1.

6   "The stories of pain": Anguelov, p. 7.

7   "annus mirabilis": Dziwisz, *A Life with Karol*, p. 179.

7   six hundred thousand moved to Britain alone: Reuters, April 25, 2007.

Chapter 1. War Brings License

11   "The extant furniture, china, cutlery, and decorations": Weigel, p. 28.

11   "a deeply religious and patriotic upbringing": Michnik, *Letters from Freedom*, p. 260.

11   "Our neighbors had avoided it": Walesa, *A Way of Hope*, p. 14.

12   They all lost fathers to World War II: Ibid., p. 26; Weigel, p. 68.

12   "They [the German soldiers] smiled from afar": Nemirovsky, p. 219.

13   "Of the houses, all that remained were brick chimneys": Spasowski, p. 60.

13   Nazi Germany and the Soviet Union dismembered Poland: Lukowski and Zawadzki, p. 229; Prazmowska, *A History of Poland*, p. 179.

13 Hitler's viceroy in Poland, Hans Frank: Spasowski, p. 272.

13 Wojtyla fled Kraków in September 1939: Weigel, pp. 29, 32, 68.

14 wearing "their very best": Boyd, p. 15.

14 "a chapel on the N.E. side": Baedeker, p. 8.

14 "Inside the church," she wrote, "when the large bronze gates": Boyd, p. 33.

14 The losers proposed a different explanation: *Voennyi entsiklopedichesky slovar*, p. 246.

14 one of them was Joseph Stalin: Conquest, p. 87.

15 *Si Deus Nobiscum Quis Contra Nos*: Weigel, p. 51.

15 the clandestine Rhapsodic Theater: Ibid., pp. 64–65.

15 "A Drama from the Old Testament": Wojtyla, *The Collected Plays*, p. 25.

15 God had made a bet with Satan about Job's "integrity": Job 1:6–12.

15 "I cry to you, O God": Job 30:20.

15 "Where were you when I laid the foundations": Job 38:4–34.

16 "I take back everything I said": Job 42:6.

16 "unafraid of ridicule and seemingly able": Weigel, p. 57.

17 "How well I know the spring that brims and flows": Brenan, p. 165 (poem translated by Lynda Nicholson).

17 Archbishop Adam Stefan Sapieha ran an underground seminary: Weigel, pp. 29–69.

17 a "short man of iron will": Ibid., p. 52.

17 When Hans Frank invited himself to dinner: Ibid., p. 73.

17 "The Red Army soldiers seemed strange": Spasowski, p. 223.

18 "As Gregor Samsa awoke one morning from uneasy dreams": Kafka, *Complete Stories*, p. 89.

18 "The bourgeoisie, wherever it has got the upper hand": Marx, pp. 9–10.

19 "In the course of that very first day": Kafka, *Complete Stories*, pp. 89–110.

19 "he nerved himself to the great effort": Ibid., p. 112.

19 In Bulgaria, Communist fighters arranged a very special funeral: Crampton, p. 145.

19 "One strength of the Communist system": Einstein, p. 199.

19 "The history of early Christianity": Marx and Engels, p. 168.

19 "If I wanted to give you an idea of the early Christian communities": Ibid., p. 170.

20 "Religion is the sigh of the oppressed creature": Marx, p. 263.

20 "a gaiety of the soul": Lane, p. 20.

20 "a bar of music, composed extemporaneously": Ibid., p. 26.

20 "Ragged, half-starved peasants": Strong, p. 181.

21 a church that owned about a million acres of land: Weigel, p. 52.

21 "In 1935 there were 0.7 motor cars": Boyd, p. 9.

21   there could be no political accord in a society like that: Lukowski and Zawadzki, pp. 214–19; Prazmowska, *A History of Poland*, pp. 169–70.

21   "The sky was dark with millionaires": Crisp, p. 1.

22   Here is a description of a childhood in a left-leaning family: Spasowski, pp. 15–31.

22   five thousand Polish Communists were shot: McDermott and Agnew, p. 147.

23   "Poland is part of Europe": John Paul II, *Memory*, p. 91.

24   "The dense crowd waited tensely": Spasowski, p. 27.

24   A woman started working for the Gestapo: Strong, pp. 63–64.

24   a man helped the Germans to round up slave labor: Ibid., pp. 62–63.

24   a girl, unhappy about her father's second marriage: Ibid., p. 63.

25   One Polish historian cites the year as the beginning of a civil war in Poland: Prazmowska, *Civil War in Poland*, p. x.

25   The biggest force, the Armia Krajowa: Lukowski and Zawadzki, pp. 181–82; Prazmowska, *Civil War in Poland*, p. 65.

25   Stalin ordered executions of twenty-one thousand Polish officers: Lukowski and Zawadzki, pp. 227, 237; Prazmowska, *A History of Poland*, p. 178.

26   "with a view to establishing an independent Polish administration": Lukowski and Zawadzki, p. 241.

26   The Soviet commander watched Warsaw burn: Rokossovsky, p. 353.

26   Stalin's generals and later revisionist scholarship suggested: Ibid.; Roberts, p. 206.

26   "most perturbed over the robbery, rape and murder": Lane, p. 161.

26   "Do you see what a complicated thing is man's soul": Stalin quoted in Roberts, p. 264.

27   a radical land reform, distributing among the rural poor: Lukowski and Zawadzki, pp. 238, 241–42.

27   "To make sure that any resistance would be summarily crushed": Weigel, p. 17.

27   "taciturn and expressionless," giving the "impression of granite strength": Lane, p. 149.

28   Teaching his son German: Weigel, p. 30.

28   When years later Weigel asked the pope: Ibid., p.28.

28   "The two sets of Poles have arrived": Soames, p. 506.

29   "destroyed the city methodically": Lane, pp. 20 21.

29   "What had once been one of the liveliest capitals of Europe". Strong, p. 24.

29   the government nationalized all industrial enterprises employing more than fifty workers: Lukowski and Zawadzki, p. 251.

29   "These last days of war were the easiest time for the transfer": Strong, p. 195.

29   "thirty-seven rooms in a big park": Ibid., p. 181.

29　"Two thirds of the land in prewar Poland": Ibid., p. 182.

29　"The smallest 'estate,' a farm of only one hundred and fifty acres": Ibid., p. 194.

30　As late as March 1946, the antigovernment forces: "Doneseniye S.N. Kruglova I.V. Stalinu, V.M. Molotovu, L.P. Beriya, G.M. Malenkovu o deyatelnosti anti-pravitelstvennogo podpolya v Polshe i borbe s nim polskikh organov obshchest-vennoi bezopasnosti" (Report of S. N. Kruglov to I. V. Stalin, V. M. Molotov, L. P. Beria, G. M. Malenkov on the Antigovernment Underground in Poland and Polish Security Forces' Fight on It), April 23, 1946, in *Vostochnaya Evropa*, pp. 425–27.

30　five million Ukrainians lived in Poland as an oppressed minority: Prazmowska, *Civil War in Poland*, pp. 184, 185; Prazmowska, *A History of Poland*, p. 190.

30　both groups expected reimbursement: Prazmowska, *A History of Poland*, p. 179. See also: "Zapis besedy I.V. Stalina s B. Berutom i E. Osubka-Moravskim po vo-prosam ekonomicheskogo i politicheskogo stroitelstva dvukh stran" (Minutes of I. V. Stalin's Meeting with B. Bierut and E. Osóbka-Morawski on Economic and Political Issues), May 24, 1946, in *Vostochnaya Evropa*, p. 463.

31　Compared to 1939, the Poland of 1945 was 20 percent smaller: Lukowski and Zawadzki, p. 250.

31　"In areas inhabited by a Ukrainian community": Prazmowska, *Civil War in Po-land*, p. 127.

31　"exploited the army's action to plunder Ukrainian villages": Ibid.

31　"Pillaging and rape . . . inevitably accompanied the army's actions": Ibid., p. 180.

31　"One of the difficulties encountered by the Poles at this stage": Ibid.

31　Polish authorities kept about fifty thousand German prisoners of war: Prazmowska, *A History of Poland*, p. 183.

32　"Although no organizational collaboration was established": Ibid.

32　"Reports that some Jews in eastern Poland": Lukowski and Zawadzki, p. 232.

32　the Holocaust survivors—about two hundred thousand: Prazmowska, *Civil War in Poland*, pp. 171–73.

32　"Among the workers, the view that Jews enjoyed a high standard of living": Ibid., pp. 170–71.

32　"drained Christian children of blood": Ibid., p. 170.

32　The first postwar pogrom: Lane, pp. 246–48.

32　"Although it was most difficult for a Polish Gentile": Ibid., p. 252.

33　"From Stettin in the Baltic to Trieste in the Adriatic": quoted in Van Doren and McHenry, p. 510.

34　In May 1946, the leftist leaders of the coalition government visited Stalin: "Zapis besedy I.V. Stalina s B. Berutom i E. Osubka-Moravskim po voprosam ekonomicheskogo i politicheskogo stroitelstva dvukh stran" (Minutes of I. V.

Stalin's Meeting with B. Bierut and E. Osóbka-Morawski on Economic and Political Issues), May 24, 1946, in *Vostochnaya Evropa*, pp. 457–60.

34   "Even in bourgeois countries": "Zapis besedy I.V. Stalina s liderami PPS E. Osubka-Moravskim, St. Shvalbe, Yu. Tsirankevichem o roli PPS v politicheskom razvitii Polshi" (Minutes of I. V. Stalin's Meeting with the Leaders of the PPS E. Osóbka-Morawski, St. Shvalbe, and Yu. Tsirankevich on the PPS's Role in the Development of Poland), August 19, 1946, in *Vostochnaya Evropa*, p. 512.

34   Ambassador Lane rightfully noticed: Lane, p. 278.

35   the nation, according to Western observers, was calm and apathetic: Ibid., p. 286.

35   described by modern-day Polish historians as just "fragmentary studies": Lukowski and Zawadzki, p. 253.

35   Jerzy Lukowski and Hubert Zawadzki write: Ibid., p. 252.

36   "Religion is the self-consciousness and self-esteem": Marx, p. 301.

38   Visiting Paris, Wojtyla stayed: Weigel, pp. 82–87.

38   "Distance, budgets, and Karol's responsibilities": Ibid., p. 84.

38   "The Lord allowed the experience of such an evil": John Paul II, *Memory*, p. 46.

Chapter 2. Communism Rises

42   "Its triumphal showcase was": Lukowski and Zawadzki, pp. 256–57.

42   "In admission to secondary schools": Prazmowska, *A History of Poland*, pp. 195–96.

43   "*Together* with an immense expansion": Lenin, *State and Revolution*, p. 73.

43   "is an organ": Ibid., p. 9.

44   "His face changed color": Markov, p. 9.

44   "It was my task to expose": Snyder, p. 289.

45   When during the war Churchill flew into Moscow: Soames, p. 506.

45   straight out of Kafka: Kafka, *The Trial*, pp. 3, 145, 231.

45   "The party secretary ordered my mother": László Kolozsy interviewed in Körösi, p. 30.

45   Soviet advisors descended on Warsaw and Budapest: Andrew and Mitrokhin, p. 247.

45   Bulgaria, for example, hosted a hundred prison camps: Todorov and Zaretsky, pp. 39–41; Markov, p. 88.

46   "somebody at the party committee": László Tihanyi interviewed in Körösi, p. 80.

46   "We were literally kicked out of the flat": Ildikó Mecséri in ibid., p. 75.

46   "the confiscation of assets": György Fenyöfalvi in ibid., p. 29.

46   The security force grew to two hundred thousand: Lukowski and Zawadzki, p. 255.

46   "stood and watched while Warsaw fought": Spasowski, p. 291.

47   75 percent of Polish generals: Lukowski and Zawadzki, p. 256.

47   Anne Applebaum notes: Applebaum, p. 457.

47   "In the Penal Colony": Kafka, *Complete Stories*, pp. 141–67.

48   "When Stalin died there were": Khrushchev, *The Glasnost Tapes*, p. 40.

48   "Khrushchev's speech denouncing Stalin was the bravest": Taubman, p. 274.

48   "After Bierut's death there were": Ibid., pp. 43–44.

49   "weakness for toys and ingenious Western gadgets": Spasowski, p. 345.

49   "We teach that it is proper": *Time*, May 20, 1957.

50   Khrushchev came to visit: Taubman, pp. 293–94.

50   "the most remarkable prelate": *Time*, May 20, 1957.

51   "Life was better, and food more plentiful": Korda, p. 80.

51   "In April 1955, Nagy was removed": Ibid., p. 87.

52   "of anti-Rákosi communists and intellectuals": Ibid., p. 90.

52   In July 1956, he forced Rákosi to resign: Gough, p. 74.

52   "By the early evening a mass of people": Korda, pp. 94–95.

53   "Gero's speech was harsh, threatening, and unconciliatory": Ibid., pp. 95–96.

53   At least four thousand Hungarians: Ibid., p. 97.

53   "Tank crews like open country": Ibid., p. 98.

54   On October 28, the Kremlin ordered: Taubman, p. 296.

54   "The streets [of Budapest] were littered with broken glass": Korda, pp. 130–31.

54   "shot at point-blank range": Ibid., p. 129.

54   "This was, of course, to deny the reality": Ibid., p. 145.

55   After painful deliberation, Khrushchev reversed course: Taubman, pp. 296–99.

55   "a full-scale return to capitalism": Korda, p. 150.

55   "an antitotalitarian socialist": Michnik, *The Church*, p. 247.

56   "Yesterday's Party member becomes": Ibid., p. 198.

57   *Travels with Herodotus*: Kapuściński, pp. 8–14.

58   "spent a long time at the Budapest farmers' market": Gorbachev, *Zhizn i reformy*, 2, p. 323.

58   "fashions à la Warsaw Pact": Kapuściński, p. 12.

58   Flowers, waving, clapping, cheering: Nixon, p. 213.

58   "Your American houses are built": www.teachingamericanhistory.org/library/index.asp?document=176.

59   Nicolae and Elena Ceauşescu ordered fresh orchids: Behr, p. 227.

59   Nicolae shot thousands of animals: Ibid., pp. 228–29.

59   "the world record for antler trophies": Markov, pp. 247, 249.

59   Even the ascetic Erich Honecker: Pryce-Jones, p. 273.

60   a severance package for a "failed" chief executive: *The New York Times*, January 7, 2007.

60   "I know that I can die at any moment": Chazov, p. 31.

60   When one of the most powerful men in Bulgaria: Markov, p. 206.

60   "People who could leave the country": Wolf, p. 99.

61   more than 10 percent: Curtis, p. 56.

61   11.6 million: Staar, pp. 54–195.

61   in the poet Anna Akhmatova's words: Akhmatova, p. 325.

62   "[Relatives] began to withdraw from us": József Andi interviewed in Körösi, p. 77.

62   "some forgotten poets": Havel, *Disturbing the Peace*, p. 32.

62   "the very idea of sprawling comfortably": Kapuściński, p. 19.

62   "There were people in the Village": Broyard, p. 31.

63   "the rock'n'roll underground": Stoppard, pp. xvi–xvii.

65   "a deal: in return for their good behavior": Williams, p. 146.

66   On January 16, 1969: Ibid., p. 190.

66   a celebration that turned into a countrywide anti-Soviet manifestation: Ibid., pp. 198–99.

66   Moscow threatened to send more troops: Ibid., p. 200.

66   "All over the country, orchestrated demonstrations": Lukowski and Zawadzki, p. 266.

66   in December, the government announced price increases: Falk, p. 27.

67   "In the new system": Walesa, *A Way of Hope*, p. 31.

67   "Drinking on the job": Ibid., p. 55.

67   the December 14, 1970, events: Ibid., p. 61.

68   "mud onto the slits": Ibid.

68   "One worker then stepped out of the crowd": Ibid., p. 70.

68   "like a film by Eisenstein": Ibid., p. 59.

68   "provoked beyond endurance": Falk, p. 28.

69   "The seventies were bland, boring": Havel, *Disturbing the Peace*, pp. 119–20.

69   "Everything is connected in a chain": Voltaire, p. 7.

69   "we must cultivate our garden": Ibid., p. 100.

69   "into a kind of internal exile": Havel, *Disturbing the Peace*, p. 120.

69   the USSR quickly became a major exporter: Staar, p. 311.

69   A popular Bulgarian joke: Markov, p. 109.

70   Marquis de Custine, 1839: De Custine, p. 43.

70   "Among flags we preferred the Union Jack": Brodsky, p. 20.

70   "New York impressed me": Trotsky, *My Life*, p. 270.

71   "It could be a set": Brodsky, p. 5.

72 "He flavored his goat stews with": Clarke, p. 25.

72 "skeletons clutching rusted revolvers": Ibid., p. 22.

72 "I decided I could have met": Ibid., p. 37.

72 To paraphrase Oriana Fallaci: Fallaci, p. 185.

73 "people were saying that Poland": Spasowski, pp. 524–25.

73 "There was no question that the Soviets": Ibid., p. 525.

73 "What drew Nixon there": Kissinger, p. 1265.

73 crowds giving Nixon an enthusiastic welcome: Spasowski, p. 507.

74 Fidel Castro descended on Poland: Ibid., pp. 509–12.

75 Gierek announced a sharp price increase: Falk, pp. 34–35.

75 "for the first time intellectuals, students, and farmers": Gian Franco Sviderco-schi in Dziwisz, *A Life with Karol*, pp. 48–49.

Chapter 3. The Pope Arms 150 Divisions

76 "I approach you saying, not 'Come' ": John Paul II, *Memory*, p. 155.

77 "The Lord allowed the experience": Ibid., p. 46.

77 "The harm done by fascism": Ibid., p 49.

77 "This will happen if we learn": Ibid., p. 8.

77 "was reduced to an element within": Ibid., p. 10.

78 "halted the Mongol invasion": Ibid., p. 138.

78 enumerating writers "of genius": Ibid., p. 61.

78 "deep bond between the spiritual and the material": Ibid.

78 "My train doesn't leave for Kraków": Weigel, p. 147.

78 "The chapel was where he would carry on": Dziwisz, *A Life with Karol*, p. 11.

79 "The Virgin Mary, Queen of Poland": *Time*, June 27, 1983.

79 "To Jesus through Mary": Weigel, p. 78.

79 an eighteenth-century French theologian: Ibid., p. 57.

79 "to hear the Mother's 'heartbeat' ": Dziwisz, *A Life with Karol*, p. 12.

79 "He is a poet": Weigel, p. 186.

80 "The entire archbishop's residence": Dziwisz, *A Life with Karol*, pp. 42–43.

80 calling them his "guardian angels": Ibid., p. 43.

80 "At night, the seminarians would bravely": Ibid., p. 46.

81 15 percent of Polish priests: *The New York Times*, January 7, 2007.

81 the Vatican diplomat Agostino Casaroli: Weigel, p. 231.

81 "This is Poland. Only there is this possible": Ibid., p. 219.

81 Wojtyla visited Polish communities: Ibid., pp. 222–26.

81 particularly Franz Cardinal König: Dziwisz, *A Life with Karol*, pp. 16–17.

81 "We extend our hands to you": Ibid., pp. 21–23.

82 the Year of Three Popes: Ibid., p. 56.

82 "The whole world, the whole Church": Ibid., p. 59.

82   a copy of a Marxist philosophical journal: Greeley, p. 210.

82   "had gotten him worried": Dziwisz, *A Life with Karol*, p. 59.

82   König asked Wyszyński: Weigel, p. 253.

83   The conclave opened on October 14: Dziwisz, *A Life with Karol*, pp. 60–61; Greeley, p. 196; Weigel, p. 253.

83   On the square outside St. Peter's: Greeley, p. 223.

83   Italian (which was still pretty bad): Dziwisz et al., *Let Me Go to the Father's House*, p. 54.

84   Andropov allegedly called the KGB station: Weigel, p. 279.

84   "The greatest feat of the People's Republic of Poland": Dziwisz, *A Life with Karol*, p. 70.

84   In Washington, the Polish ambassador: Spasowski, p. 597.

84   "was married and lost his wife": Greeley, p. 201.

84   "taking Jewish families out of the ghettos": Blazynski, p. 49; Greeley, p. 200. The wording is almost identical in both.

85   "a large capital M": Weigel, p. 265.

85   "The relationship between the two men": Ibid., p. 277.

85   "friend and confidant": Dziwisz et al., *Let Me Go to the Father's House*, p. viii.

85   The Rome Tourist Council: Weigel, p. 332.

85   The government sent him a congratulatory telegram: Ibid., p. 269.

85   He met with the exiled Josyf Cardinal Slipyj: Ibid., p. 280.

85   Receiving the Soviet foreign minister, Andrei Gromyko: Ibid., p. 299.

86   "brought with me from Poland": John Paul II, *Memory*, p. 5.

86   "attack on man's very dignity": Weigel, p. 288.

86   "I would like to help": Ibid., p. 300.

86   "Tell the Pope—he's a wise man": Ibid., p. 301.

86   On the eve of the papal visit: Spasowski, p. 604.

86   Three million people: Weigel, p. 291.

86   Wojtyla had fixed his eyes on them: Ibid., p. 322.

87   "political earthquake": Dziwisz, *A Life with Karol*, p. 115.

87   "practically shouted the prayer to the Holy Spirit": Ibid., pp. 116–17.

87   "As soon as the Pope started speaking": Gian Franco Svidercoschi, ibid., p. xi.

87   "like a big Irish labor boss": Nixon, p. 619.

87   "You don't know what life is like": Burlatsky, p. 223.

88   "Morons . . ." he mumbled: Sukhodrev, p. 329.

88   the Nixon-Brezhnev summit: Ibid., pp. 303–10.

88   "Not my fault!": Ibid., p. 345.

88   "To my surprise, we found ourselves": Carter, p. 261.

88   He was ambassador to Hungary: Medvedev, p. 25.

88   Talking to the people he trusted: Ibid., p. 155.

88   Andropov met with popular poets: Ibid., pp. 89–93.

89 Between 1976 and 1980, the KGB: Ibid., p. 120.

89 Andropov was anti-Stalin: Ibid., pp. 129–30.

89 He was definitely lenient toward the two: Ibid., pp. 136, 147–48; Arbatov, p. 267.

89 One of the KGB chairman's unlikely protégés: Medvedev, pp. 135, 328.

89 "He's Polish, he's Slavic, he's us": Vysotsky, "Vpechatlenie ot lektzii o mezhdunarodnom polozhenii": Vysotsky, 1, p. 224.

90 The Politburo meeting on March 17, 1979: Politburo minutes, March 17, 1979, Cold War International History Project (CWIHP), www.wilsoncenter.org/index.cfm?fuseaction-topics.publications&topic_id=1409&imageField.x=23&imageField.y=11.

90 "Now I shall go far and far into the North": Kipling, *Kim*, p. 359.

92 "The attention of the Afghan leadership": Ponomarev, CC CPSU to Erich Honecker, October 13, 1978, CWIHP.

92 a characteristically independent mind, granted it: CC CPSU Concerning the Appeal to the Czechoslovak Communist Party About B. Karmal, November 9, 1978, CWIHP.

92 "participate in antigovernment activity": Decree of the CC CPSU Secretariat Concerning an Appeal to the Czechoslovak Communist Party About K. Babrak, November 15, 1978, CWIHP.

92 The Politburo meeting on March 17, 1979: Politburo minutes, March 17, 1979, CWIHP.

94 "Take up the White Man's burden": Kipling, *Poems*, p. 96.

94 "The Burrow": Kafka, *Complete Stories*, pp. 325, 326, 343, 352.

94 The Politburo meetings on March 18–22: Transcript of the CC CPSU Politburo Session on Afghanistan, March 17–19, 22, 1979, CWIHP.

96 the party line on Afghanistan: Gromyko-Andropov-Ustinov-Ponomarev Report to CC CPSU on Situation in Afghanistan, June 28, 1979, CWIHP.

96 Andropov sent a personal letter to Brezhnev: Personal memorandum, Andropov to Brezhnev, December 1, 1979, CWIHP.

98 The Politburo meeting on December 10: CC CPSU Politburo Session, December 10, 1979, CWIHP.

98 Andropov . . . stayed up all night: Medvedev, pp. 228–29.

98 "When you're wounded and left on Afghanistan's plains": Kipling, *War Stories and Poems*, p. 56.

99 "I could not dig: I dared not rob": Kipling, *Poems*, p. 226.

Chapter 4. The Working Class Strikes

103 "deeming it too dreadful": Walesa, *A Way of Hope*, p. 14.

103 the opening of Tolstoy's *Hadji Murad*: Tolstoy, p. 550.

103   refused to provide showers for the workers: Walesa, *A Way of Hope*, pp. 43–44.

103   he forced the doors with a wrench: Ibid., p. 65.

104   Because of the sun: Camus, p. 103.

104   Anna Walentynowicz: Weigel, p. 400; Walesa, *A Way of Hope*, p. 118.

104   "We began to draw up a plan of action": Ibid., p. 102.

104   he would become the "ringleader": Ibid., p. 118.

104   93 percent of the eggs: Staar, p. 170.

105   "In an ironic sense Karl Marx was right": quoted in Lawler and Schaefer, p. 383.

105   Father Jankowski blessed Wałesa: Walesa, *A Way of Hope*, p. 323; Weigel, p. 400.

105   "Walesa speaks with the voice of the dead": *The Book of Lech*, p. 184.

106   he had *not* brought down communism "single-handedly": John Paul II, *Memory*, p. 165.

106   "workers who are striving": Weigel, p. 401.

106   what the pope was waiting for: Ibid.

107   "Maybe the moment has come!": Dziwisz, *A Life with Karol*, p. 125.

107   "regarding the news which has come from Poland": Weigel, p. 401.

107   "aid the nation in its struggle": Ibid.

107   the primate declared that Polish workers: Ibid., p. 402.

107   "The strike movement is operating on a countrywide scale": Memorandum to the CC CPSU Politburo from the Suslov Commission, August 28, 1980, CWIHP.

108   a souvenir pen with a picture of the pope: Weigel, p. 323.

109   "History has taught us": Staar, p. 176.

109   "Are all the children yours?": *The Book of Lech*, p. 96.

109   the government gave him a new apartment: Ibid., p. 97.

109   "spokesman for the Catholics in Poland": Ibid., pp. 98, 153, 157.

109   "What I feel for Lech Wałesa": Ibid., p. 186.

110   "No, this is improbable": Ibid., p. 184.

110   "I am an ordinary worm": Ibid., p. 102.

110   "And then something happened": Ibid., pp. 102–103.

110   "Faith is something very private to me": Ibid., pp. 104–105.

110   " 'dictatorship' of the street": Trotsky, pp. 57–58.

111   "It's not a question": *The Book of Lech*, p. 144.

112   Warsaw Pact troops had been standing: Weigel, p. 405.

112   President Carter shared his concerns: Lukowski and Zawadzki, p. 274.

112   The pope wrote a letter to Brezhnev: Ibid., pp. 406–407.

112   Wałesa's January 1981 visit to Rome: Walesa, *A Way of Hope*, pp. 165–66.

113   Wałesa in Japan: Ibid., pp. 167–68.

113   "I was overcome": Ibid., p. 168.

113   "reacted promptly, strengthening the measures": Ibid., p. 169.

113   "Man, how could you do this?": Ibid.

113   May 13 attack: Dziwisz, *A Life with Karol*, pp. 130–34.

113   "motherly hand which guided the bullet's path": Dziwisz et al., *Let Me Go to the Father's House*, p. 113.

114   Mehmet Ali Ağca: Weigel, pp. 423–24.

114   "Ali Ağca was a perfect killer": Dziwisz, *A Life with Karol*, pp. 139–40.

114   Brezhnev sent the pope a dry message: Weigel, p. 424.

114   "Of course you live better": *The Book of Lech*, p. 92.

114   American businessmen on their way to Poland: Walesa, *A Way of Hope*, pp. 169–71.

115   "Lech the Fireman": Ibid., p. 174.

115   "middleman between Solidarity and the government": Ibid., p. 178.

115   "Not since the tumultuous days of last August": *Time*, February 9, 1981.

115   "All that was known": Walesa, *A Way of Hope*, p. 180.

115   "faultless," "lively" Polish: Ibid.

116   one million Communist Party members: Staar, p. 160.

116   one week after his inauguration, strikes ended: Walesa, *A Way of Hope*, pp. 181–82.

116   "I admire people": Ibid., p. 183.

117   "current of understanding": Ibid., p.184.

117   More meetings would follow: Ibid., p. 185.

117   "Let's talk before any fires spread": *Time*, March 23, 1981.

117   "We don't want to overthrow the Communist Party": *Time*, April 6, 1981.

117   imminent declaration of martial law: Ibid., p. 186.

117   On March 4, in Moscow: Medvedev, pp. 240–41.

117   Polish generals sent a letter: Ibid., p. 242.

118   on April 4, Andropov and Ustinov: Ibid., p. 243.

118   Wyszyński died of cancer: Weigel, pp. 415, 903.

118   Józef Glemp: Ibid., pp. 416–17.

118   The Polish Party Extraordinary Congress: Lukowski and Zawadzki, p. 275; Medvedev, p. 244.

118   Erich Honecker of East Germany to Brezhnev: Transcript of the Meeting Between Comrade L. I. Brezhnev and Comrade E. Honecker at the Crimea, August 3, 1981, CWIHP.

119   55 percent of the vote: Weigel, p. 418.

119   *Laborem Exercens*: Ibid., p. 420.

120   "Tears rolled down his cheeks": *Time*, November 16, 1981.

120   the "Big Three": Walesa, *A Way of Hope*, pp. 196–97.

120   The Politburo meeting on December 10: Transcript of the CC CPSU Politburo meeting, December 10, 1981, CWIHP.

121   Moscow's loans to Poland in 1980–81: Staar, p. 177.

122 "the Poles themselves must resolve": The Anoshkin Notebook on the Polish Crisis, December 1981, CWIHP.

123 "All communications by telephone and telex have been cut": Walesa, *A Way of Hope*, p. 206.

Chapter 5. The Revolution Winters

124 Operation X: Pryce-Jones, p. 196; Weigel, p. 433.

124 Communists did start leaving the Party ranks: Staar, p. 156.

124 the "longest vacation" of his life: Walesa, *A Way of Hope*, p. 229.

125 Wałesa's internment: Ibid., pp. 218, 228, 230.

125 to "General Wojciech Jaruzelski": Ibid., pp. 238–39.

125 Andropov in power: Burlatsky, p. 266; Chazov, pp. 171–94; Medvedev, p. 308.

126 the Soviets "were more dedicated": Reagan, p. 266.

127 "brave shipyard workers": Ibid., p. 302.

127 Reagan "assumed that there could be changes": Matlock, pp. 590–91.

127 "We can't let this revolution against Communism fail": Reagan, p. 304.

127 the United States was imposing sanctions: Ibid., pp. 304–306.

127 "wanted to defect immediately": Ibid., p. 303.

127 "stiff and as cold as a Siberian winter": Ibid., p. 575.

128 "I also tried to send out a signal": Ibid., p. 552.

128 "When the Russians wouldn't agree": Ibid., p. 551.

128 "The great dynamic success of capitalism": Ibid., p. 267.

128 "What if free people could live": Ibid., pp. 574–75.

128 "We knew from the intercepted communications": Ibid., pp. 582–83.

129 *The Day After*: Ibid., p. 585.

129 "In several ways, the sequence of events": Ibid., p. 586.

129 Wałesa set up opposition headquarters: Walesa, *A Way of Hope*, pp. 254–55.

129 "he must lead": *Time*, March 28, 1983.

129 "On my first day back": Walesa, *A Way of Hope*, p. 265.

129 "The winter is yours": *Time*, March 28, 1983.

130 the "de facto Primate of Poland": Weigel, p. 417.

130 Glemp followed the Wyszyński model: Falk, p. 54.

130 John Paul was very angry with Glemp: Weigel, p. 417.

130 Jerzy Popieluszko: Walesa, *A Way of Hope*, pp. 278–79; Weigel, p. 460.

130 "he made known his intention": Dziwisz, *A Life with Karol*, p. 151.

130 "What does he want?": Weigel, pp. 462–63.

131 "Truth be told, John Paul II": Dziwisz, *A Life with Karol*, pp. 135–36.

131 "I know I was aiming right": Ibid., p. 137.

131 "a Marian celebration": Ibid., p. 152.

132 "In the private interview": Ibid., pp. 151–54.

132 "The important thing at that point": Ibid., p. 155.

132 "One curious thing struck me": Walesa, *A Way of Hope*, p. 278.

133 Father Jerzy Popieluszko disappeared: Weigel, pp. 479–80.

133 "In the second Secret, she said": Dziwisz, *A Life with Karol*, p. 180.

133 "identifying several items" on his plate: Reagan, p. 369.

134 "During that beautiful spring": Ibid., pp. 368–72.

134 "How am I supposed": Ibid., p. 611.

135 There were long walks in Kislovodsk: Medvedev, pp. 327–31.

135 "self-confident" and "easygoing": *The Washington Post*, December 23, 1984.

135 "Natty Gorbachevs Take London": *The Washington Post*, December 20, 1984.

135 "[Raisa] was dressed in a smart western style outfit": Thatcher, p. 459.

136 "the new Gucci comrades": *The Washington Post*, December 20, 1984.

136 "she chose earrings, costing several hundred pounds": Archie Brown, e-mail of April 8, 2004, in www.cdi.org/russia/johnson/8156-1.cfm.

136 "no 'Star Wars' antimissile defense system would be deployed": *The Washington Post*, December 23, 1984.

137 "Noble as Gorbachev's aims were": Moskoff, p. 91.

137 "Jam tomorrow and, meanwhile, no vodka today": Thatcher, p. 470.

137 "I absolutely reject": Gorbachev, *Memoirs*, p. 189.

137 nine thousand deaths over the next twenty years: According to the World Health Organization, quoted in Reuters, November 19, 2007.

137 "literally demolished a group of Soviet journalists": Palazchenko, p. 123.

138 Reagan on Gorbachev: Reagan, pp. 635, 641.

138 Kádár and Hungary: Burant, pp. 55, 83, 152; Pryce-Jones, p. 219.

139 "Most dissidents faced only sporadic repression": Burant, p. 105.

139 the "bloc's showplace of liberalism": Staar, p. 144.

139 John Paul II and Hungary: Weigel, p. 372.

140 "gain a clearer picture from Mr Kádár of the situation in the USSR": Thatcher, p. 455.

140 "As he put it," Thatcher remembered: Ibid., p. 456.

140 Kádár and Radio Free Europe: Puddington, pp. 140, 256–57, 264.

140 Ceauşescu and Romania: Behr, pp. 158, 160, 163, 229; Goldman, p. 271; Pryce-Jones, p. 337; Puddington, pp. 240–41; Rady, pp. 42, 46–47.

141 Zhivkov and Bulgaria: Markov, pp. 219, 221; Pundeff, pp. 103–105.

142 "the first clarion call for democratization in 1968": Williams, p. 48.

142 "Husák was initially hostile to the Soviets": Ibid., p. 49.

142 Honecker's hometown: Taylor, p. 93.

143 "We set in train": Wolf, p. 313.

143 The USSR's economic growth: Moskoff, p. 9.

143 The decrease of oil prices: Ibid., p. 17.

143 Moscow was "steadily reducing" the amount of oil: Wolf, p. 319.

144 Kolbin: Matlock, pp. 161–62.

145 "We will have to rely on ourselves:" Wolf, p. 319.

145 Gorbachev was hostile to most of the Eastern European leaders: Chernyaev, p. 62.

145 Gorbachev in Bucharest: Gorbachev, *Zhizn i reformy*, 2, pp. 393–400; Rady, pp. 65, 68; Shevardnadze, p. 117.

145 the Warsaw Pact's huge bureaucratic machine: Federal Institute for Soviet and International Studies, pp. 358–60.

146 he "had known nothing about it personally": Reagan, p. 639.

146 That was one of the Soviet leader's habitual lies: In his memoirs, Valery Chazov, minister of health of the USSR and Central Committee member, explicitly says that all Soviet leaders "were constantly informed on developments in Afghanistan": Chazov, p. 151.

146 about one hundred thousand lives: An approximation, as different sources put Afghan 1979–89 casualties anywhere between one million and two million people: *Toronto Star*, May 6, 1991; *USA Today*, April 17, 1992.

146 The Politburo meeting on November 13, 1986: CC CPSU Politburo Meeting Minutes, November 13, 1986, CWIHP.

148 seven hundred thousand a day on average: Moskoff, p. 39.

148 "The hoarding of goods": Ibid., p. 43.

149 "We never touched on the artistic side of the writer's work": Ligachev, p. 99.

152 a "providential man": Weigel, p. 605.

152 Reagan in Berlin: Reagan, pp. 681, 683.

152 Mathias Rust: Matlock, p. 135.

153 "The Soviet state has a new leader": Michnik, *Letters from Prison*, p. 92.

153 "All the changes taking place": Michnik, *Letters from Freedom*, p. 96.

153 "wants to defend the system": Ibid., p. 97.

153 "One privately owned café": Walesa, *The Struggle*, p. 125.

153 Havel on Gorbachev: Havel, *Open Letters*, pp. 351–54.

154 Havel's writings: Falk, pp. 200, 215; Urban, p. 112.

154 His open letter to the Party leader: Havel, *Open Letters*, pp. 53, 54, 74.

154 "From the end of 1987": Urban, p. 114.

154 "From now on, whatever happened in Eastern Europe": Ibid.

154 "suddenly, the streets of Prague": Ibid., p. 113.

155 "As I was pondering this problem": Gaddis, "On Starting All Over Again," p. 28.

155 "John Paul II wasn't expecting it": Dziwisz, *A Life with Karol*, p. 179.

155 "those internees who desist from activities": Michnik: *Letters from Prison*, p. 3.

155 "few strokes of the pen": Ibid.

155 an offer to leave the country: Ibid., p. 16.

155 "This is an undeclared war": Ibid., p. 25.

156 this was about appearances: Ibid., pp. 81–82.

156 Realizing that the leaders of the dissolved KOR: Labedz, p. 81.

156 Rosa Luxemburg, Jacobinism, Karl Jaspers, Hegel: Michnik, *Letters from Prison*, pp. 298–329.

156 "a kind of barometer": Walesa, *The Struggle*, p. 59.

156 Cohn-Bendit: Michnik, *Letters from Freedom*, p. 29.

156 Elton John: Walesa, *The Struggle*, pp. 66–67.

156 "What if some strange turn of events": Michnik, *Letters from Freedom*, p. 99.

156 "a process of social detotalitarianization": Michnik, *Letters from Prison*, p. 5.

157 Wałesa in 1986: Walesa, *The Struggle*, pp. 108–109.

157 "young peasant girl": Walesa, Ibid., pp. 110–22; Weigel, pp. 543–48.

158 Poland in 1988: Walesa, *The Struggle*, pp. 137–72; Weigel, pp. 585–86.

158 New Year's Eve: Walesa, *The Struggle*, p. 173.

158 the Soviet Politburo decided to start pulling out: Anatoly Chernyaev's Notes from the Politburo Session, January 21, 1989, CWIHP.

Chapter 6. The "Polish Disease" Spreads

164 "historic step": Walesa, *The Struggle*, p. 174.

164 "Why was it twenty-eight feet wide?": Ibid.

164 "The Round Table completed its mission": Ibid., p. 180.

164 "Today I wish to thank You": Ibid., p. 189.

164 "the thirty-five percent democracy": Ibid., p. 200.

165 "We came here to thank you": Ibid., p. 190.

165 On April 20, the pope received Wałesa: Ibid., p. 191.

165 the Congress of People's Deputies: Sakharov, pp. 96–97.

165 On June 4, Poland went to the polls: Walesa, *The Struggle*, p. 205.

166 America's "resources had shrunk": Scowcroft in Bush and Scowcroft, pp. 113–14.

166 Egypt received $968 million: http://qesdb.cdie.org/gbk/index.html.

166 "sparsely attended by the citizens of Warsaw": Scowcroft in Bush and Scowcroft, p. 116.

166 Nixon's 1972 triumphal ride: Ibid., p. 117.

166 "Jaruzelski opened his heart": Bush in Bush and Scowcroft, p. 117.

167 "Solidarity was demanding that farmers get": Ibid., pp. 117–18.

167 Jaruzelski was "very special": Ibid., p. 123.

167 "some forty Communist, Solidarity, and Catholic leaders": Ibid., p. 119.

167 "a bit uncertain and unrealistic": Ibid., p. 121.

167 "When perestroika began": Baker, p. 63.

168 Hungary under Kádár: Burant, pp. 83, 100, 133; Körösi, p. 66; Staar, pp. 137–38.

168 "drunks, children with bad school reports": István Horváth quoted in Pryce-Jones, p. 231.

168 Hungarian dissidents were either spoiled nomenklatura children: Ibid., p. 230.

168 "had to go to the Soviet leadership": Gorbachev, *Memoirs*, p. 485.

169 $18 billion in foreign debt: Burant, p. xxix.

169 The group created a basic stock market: Goldman, p. 187; Burant, pp. 126–28.

169 New political groups: Burant, p. 106.

169 distributed across 170 bases: Pryce-Jones, p. 219.

169 but their withdrawal was already under way: Memorandum of Conversation between President Mikhail Gorbachev, President Rezsö Nyers, and General Secretary of the Hungarian Socialist Workers' Party (HSWP) Karoly Grosz, Moscow, July 1, 1989, CWIHP.

170 Talking to Németh on March 3: Record of Conversation between President M. S. Gorbachev and Miklos Nemeth, Member of the CC HSWP Politburo, Chairman of the Council of Ministers of the People's Republic of Hungary, March 3, 1989, CWIHP.

170 "Where the hell do we find counterrevolutionary ideas": Minutes of the Meeting of the CC HSWP Political Committee, January 31, 1989, CWIHP.

170 The Hungarian secret police worked hard: Hungarian Secret Police Memorandum, "Ensuring the Security of Preparations for the Burial of Imre Nagy and His Associates," May, 1989, CWIHP.

171 "with his passing Hungarian political life has lost one of its greatest figures": Gough, p. 256.

171 expressing his respect for the good Communist: Ibid.

171 "The people were drenched": Scowcroft in Bush and Scowcroft, p. 124.

171 "difference in mood between Poland and Hungary": Ibid., p. 123.

171 "could manage the hard transition": Ibid., p. 126.

172 modest U.S. financial aid: Bush in Bush and Scowcroft, pp. 124–26.

172 Bush didn't particularly care for Grósz: Ibid., p. 125.

172 "A generation waited to honor": Ibid.

172 the KGB chairman, Vladimir Kryuchkov: KGB Chief Kryuchkov's Report, June 16, 1989, CWIHP.

172 "I was struck by the contrast": Scowcroft in Bush and Scowcroft, p. 126.

173 "like a Soviet May Day parade": Ibid., p. 128.

173 The G7 quickly dismissed: Ibid.

173 "Although it was not specifically a request": Bush in Bush and Scowcroft, p. 129.

174 "there was some press grousing": Scowcroft in Bush and Scowcroft, p. 129.

174 On July 16: Ibid.

174 On January 18, 1989: Anatoly Chernyaev's Notes from the Politburo Session, January 21, 1989, CWIHP.

175 Jack Matlock, now U.S. ambassador to Moscow: Matlock, pp. 187–89.

176 Bush penned a letter to Gorbachev: Bush, pp. 433–34; Bush in Bush and Scowcroft, p. 132.

177 On July 22: Tolz, pp. 390, 395, 398, 401.

177 fifty million pairs of pantyhose: Moskoff, p. 61.

177 "The frustration of the whole population": Ibid., pp. 63–64.

177 "a foolproof way to ensure absolute secrecy": Scowcroft in Bush and Scowcroft, p. 132.

177 "honorable and honest professional soldier": Bush in Bush and Scowcroft, p. 537.

177 Deeply disliking Shevardnadze, Akhromeyev gladly kept him in the dark: Baker, p. 169.

178 "Gorbachev's anxiety grew": Matlock, p. 197.

178 "Tell the president": Ibid., pp. 198–99.

178 Bush suggested a shipboard meeting in Malta: Baker, p. 169.

178 "The most vital secrets": Matlock, p. 199.

178 "Our marching orders are clear": quoted in Jones, p. 486.

178 "The question came up": Bush, p. 440.

179 "The President and I": Scowcroft in Bush and Scowcroft, p. 142.

179 "I wanted to see Yeltsin": Bush in Bush and Scowcroft, p. 142.

179 "large, physically intimidating man": Baker, p. 142.

179 Running half an hour late, on September 12: Scowcroft in Bush and Scowcroft, p. 143.

180 Rice took this personally: Baker, p. 142.

180 Yeltsin "left a bad impression": Matlock, p. 251.

180 "caused difficulties" by "exaggerated pretensions": Memorandum from Foreign Minister Peter Mladenov to the Politburo of the Central Committee of the Bulgarian Communist Party, July 12, 1989, CWIHP.

180 In Moscow, President Nyers: Memorandum of Conversation Between President Mikhail Gorbachev, President Rezsö Nyers, and General Secretary of the Hungarian Socialist Workers' Party (HSWP) Károly Grósz, Moscow, July 1, 1989, CWIHP.

181 Nyers promised Gorbachev "democratic socialism": Minutes of the Meeting of the Hungarian Socialist Workers' Party [HSWP] CC Political Executive Committee, July 24, 1989, CWIHP.

181 Representatives of the opposition met with the Soviet ambassador: Record of Conversation Between Representatives of the Opposition Roundtable and Boris Stukalin, Soviet Ambassador in Budapest, August 18, 1989, CWIHP.

181 a "very imperfect Russian mechanism": István Horváth quoted in Pryce-Jones, pp. 231–32.

182 Honecker, by the way, had praised the Tiananmen massacre: Taylor, p. 402.

182 "At the beginning of that summer": István Horváth quoted in Pryce-Jones, pp. 231–32.

182 "By the end of the summer": Baker, p. 160.

182 "Poland and Hungary were then the only two countries": Kálmán Kulcsár quoted in Pryce-Jones, pp. 224–25.

183 Rezsö Nyers offers more evidence: Nyers quoted in Pryce-Jones, p. 228.

183 Meanwhile, Radio Free Europe: Paddington, p. 302.

183 "posed an exquisite dilemma": Scowcroft in Bush and Scowcroft, p. 145.

183 "The East German population": Baker, p. 161.

183 "Our reaction was one of guarded optimism": Scowcroft in Bush and Scowcroft, p. 146.

183 "without any further ado": quoted in Taylor, p. 406.

183 "They walked with fixed intent": Urban, p. 115.

184 Honecker, meanwhile, was in a hospital: Taylor, p. 404.

184 "What can I do for you?": Baker, p. 160.

184 "With America acting as broker": Taylor, p. 406.

184 All in all, twelve thousand East Germans: Ibid., p. 407.

Chapter 7. The Wall Opens Up; the Magic Theater Raises the Curtain

185 The ninety-six miles of this barrier: Taylor, pp. 162, 365–66.

186 he had approached the United States: Ibid., pp. 75–76.

187 the workers of East Berlin took to the streets on June 16, 1953: Ostermann, pp. 106, 115

187 "the Soviets favored, when possible": Harrison, pp. 47–48.

187 "ideological issues are decided by the stomach": Khrushchev, *The Glasnost Tapes*, p. 165.

187 "I never got out of the car": Khrushchev, *The Last Testament*, p. 506.

188 The Wall stopped many but not everyone: Taylor, p. 442.

188 In 1972, the two Germanies signed: Ibid., p. 368.

188 the release of 33,755 political prisoners: *The New York Times*, August 23, 2008; Wolf, p. 120.

189 "where they had everything": Putin, p. 70.

189 twenty-six pounds in five years: Ibid.

189 "potatoes with a heavy sauce": Stern, p. 323.

189 "The abrupt collapse of that structure and the system it symbolized": Gaddis, *We Now Know*, p. 115.

189 "Honecker jutted out his obstinate jaw": Wolf, p. 323.

190 "tossed them out of the train windows": Taylor, p. 407.

190 Christian Führer: Pryce-Jones, p. 244.

190 "They are fools and dreamers": Wolf, p. 323.

192 "Has your population enough food": Honecker quoted in Taylor, p. 409.

192 at least two thousand Berliners: Tolz, p. 537.

192 Gorbachev left, arrests were made: Pryce-Jones, p. 241.

192 Honecker felt free to apply a Tiananmen-style solution: Ibid., pp. 242–46.

192 "He lost his vision": Memorandum of Conversation Between Egon Krenz, Secretary General of the Socialist Unity Party (SED), and Mikhail S. Gorbachev, Secretary General of the Communist Party of the Soviet Union (CPSU), November 1, 1989, CWIHP.

193 Schabowski went on air at 6:53 p.m.: Taylor, pp. 422–24.

193 "At five past seven": Ibid., p. 425.

194 "Zhivkov reported on the work of the committee": Dimitrov, p. 408.

194 105 people were shot: Pryce-Jones, p. 296.

194 the assassination attempt on the pope's life: See Henze, *The Plot to Kill the Pope*.

194 the leading Bulgarian dissident, Georgi Markov: Markov, pp. ix–xiii.

194 "More Catholic than the Pope": Ibid., p. 197.

194 "Comrades, the most dangerous ideological sabotage": Ibid.

194 42 percent had a telephone: Staar, p. 49.

195 three hundred industrial projects: Ibid., p. 52.

195 in 1989 alone approximately forty-five thousand: Ibid., p. 52.

195 the authorities forced nine hundred thousand ethnic Turks: Ibid., p. 50.

195 "Men were called up in the army": Anguelov, p. 136.

196 "would go from house to house": Ibid., p. 137.

196 One hundred Turks were killed: Staar, p. 50.

196 Circumcision and the washing of the dead were banned: Crampton, p. 205.

196 The propaganda machine went out of its way to justify the genocide: Pundeff, p. 107.

196 "We want our real names": *Destroying Ethnic Identity*, pp. 8–9.

196 Zhivkov went on TV: Crampton, p. 210.

196 344,000 Bulgarian Turks had moved: Ibid.

196 "unerring instinct told him": Markov, p. 235.

197 60 percent of the population: Ibid., p. xii.

197 Voice of America broadcast just 10.5 hours in Bulgarian: Heil, p. 460.

197 "lagging well behind" other countries of Eastern Europe: Bush and Scowcroft, p. 38.

197 a free trade union, Podkrepa: *Destroying*, p. 42.

197 the Club for the Support of Perestroika: Pryce-Jones, pp. 300–304.

197 President François Mitterand visited Bulgaria: Ibid., pp. 301–303; *Destroying Ethnic Identity*, p. 44.

197 Much more popular was the environmentalist movement: Curtis, pp. 69, 140.

197 But, cautiously, the environmentalists focused: Pundeff, p. 108.

198 9.2 percent inflation in 1988: Moskoff, p. 17.

198 meetings with the likes of Hafez al-Assad: Minutes of Conversation Between Todor Zhivkov and Hafez al-Assad, Damascus, April 22, 1980, CWIHP.

198 Zhivkov "kept trying to instruct Gorbachev": Chernyaev, p. 62.

199 Moscow subsidized Bulgaria's foreign debt: Curtis, p. 162.

199 "We were each sitting": Mladenov quoted in Pryce-Jones, p. 309.

199 Mladenov had a "final talk": Ibid., p. 310.

200 "I have come to the conclusion": Letter from Foreign Minister Peter Mladenov to the CC BCP, October 24, 1989, CWIHP.

200 another conspirator, Lukanov, went to Moscow: Lukanov quoted in Pryce-Jones, p. 307; Gorbachev, *Zhizn i reformy*, 2., p. 372; Pundeff, p. 108.

201 On October 26, they put a table: Pryce-Jones, pp. 297, 302.

201 "They were hit a couple of times": Ibid., p. 302.

201 "nervous crowds had started demolishing the Berlin Wall": Anguelov, p. 4.

201 the party plenum: Lukanov quoted in Pryce-Jones, p. 308; Mladenov quoted in Pryce-Jones, pp. 310–11.

202 "What happened in Berlin last week was a combination": *Time*, November 20, 1989.

202 November 18 rally: Anguelov, pp. 5–6.

203 what happened on November 17 in Prague: Wheaton and Kavan, pp. 40–41, 47, 50; Ash, p. 80; Pryce-Jones, pp. 316–17.

203 Martin Smid: Urban, pp. 116–17; Radio Praha, at www.radio.cz.

204 In the early 1950s, Gorbachev and Mlynář: Gorbachev and Mlynar, p. 2.

204 "an absolute majority of Czech theaters": Urban, p. 118.

205 formed a group called Civic Forum: Ibid.

205 Havel was at his country retreat: Keane, p. 340; Urban, p. 119; Kriseova, p. 245.

205 a theater called the Magic Lantern: Urban, pp. 119–20.

205 Incredibly excited, Ash exclaimed: Ash, pp. 78–79.

205 "Please let in and out": Ibid., p. 79.

205 "Short, with light hair": Ibid., p. 117.

206 "slips away off stage": Ibid., p. 108.

206 He said he missed his two cats: Ibid., p. 98.

206 November 21–26: Urban, pp. 120; Ash, pp. 80, 95, 98, 101, 107, 115.

207 "The Big Lie": *Time*, November 13, 1989.

207 "reunification of Germany into a giant": *Time*, November 20, 1989.

Chapter 8. Gorbachev Stumbles, Ceauşescu Falls

208 "We love the Germans so much": Quoted in Palazchenko, pp. 158–59.

209 Secretary of State Baker promised: Baker, p. 167.

209 on November 22, Bush sent Gorbachev another letter: Bush, p. 444.

209 According to Baker . . . "he had never experienced": Baker, p. 169.

209 He managed to "squeeze in some time": Bush in Bush and Scowcroft, p. 162.

209 The first session: Bush and Scowcroft, pp. 161–67; Gorbachev, *Zhizn i reformy*, 2, pp. 142–45; Palazchenko, p. 155; Bush, p. 445; Matlock, p. 271.

210 The evening session had to be cancelled: Bush and Scowcroft, p. 168.

211 Bush, nevertheless, was in high spirits: Ibid.

211 Radio communications with Washington: Scowcroft in Bush and Scowcroft, p. 169.

211 leaders of the opposition, led by Yeltsin: Tolz, pp. 655–57.

211 "to learn the lessons of East Germany": *Time*, December 25, 1989.

211 Admiral Vladimir Chernavin: Palazchenko, p. 154.

211 "so we went back": Bush in Bush and Scowcroft, p. 169.

211 the Soviets spread a rumor: Palazchenko, p. 154.

211 the second day of negotiations: Bush and Scowcroft, pp. 169–72; Baker, pp. 170–71; Matlock, pp. 271–74.

212 "Western values": Baker, p. 171; Gorbachev, *Zhizn i reformy*, 2, p. 148; Matlock, p. 273.

212 Gorbachev had to face another summit: Gorbachev, *Zhizn i reformy*, 2, pp. 402–403.

213 Gorbachev had always strongly disliked "the Romanian Führer": Chernyaev, p. 62; Gorbachev, *Zhizn i reformy*, 2, pp. 390–93.

213 he liked what he saw: Gorbachev, *Zhizn i reformy*, 2, p. 404.

213 Gorbachev and Ceauşescu conversation: Minutes of the Meeting Between Nicolae Ceausescu and Mikhail S. Gorbachev, Moscow, December 4, 1989, CWIHP. At the meeting were also present comrades Constantin Dascalescu, Prime Minister of the Government of the Socialist Republic of Romania, and Nikolai I. Ryzhkov, President of the Council of Ministers of the USSR.

214 Gorbachev believed that it wouldn't have needed all that Soviet oil: Gorbachev, *Zhizn i reformy*, 2, p. 399.

214 "Only about ten million tons": ten million tons of oil roughly equals 200,000 barrels per day. In 2007, that would have made Romania number 40 among the world's oil producers.

215 Ceauşescu was indeed a megalomaniac: Rady, pp. 67–68; Siani-Davies, p. 13.

215 thousands of abandoned dogs: Benderson, p. 150.

215 In 1981, the dictator was forced to introduce rationing: Siani-Davies, pp. 9, 11; Rady, pp. 64–65, 78–79.

216 Worried by declining birthrates: Goldman, pp. 272–73.

216 the infamous secret police: Ibid., p. 270; Siani-Davies, p. 12; Rady, p. 56; Puddington, pp. 240–41.

216 László Tökés: Siani-Davies, pp. 56–58; Rady, pp. 85–89.

217 December 15: Siani-Davies, pp. 58–59.

217 December 16: Ibid., pp. 60–61.

217 December 17: Ibid., pp. 62–68; Rady, p. 93.

218 Ceauşescu focused his attention on the Timişoara crisis: somewhat conflicting reports in Siani-Davies, pp. 63–68; Pryce-Jones, p. 341; Rady, pp. 93–94; Behr, pp. 247–48.

218 "fortified by troops along its whole length": Record of Conversation with the Ambassador of the SFRY [Socialist Federal Republic of Yugoslavia] in the USSR, Milan Veres, December 22, 1989, CWIHP.

218 the Romanian embassy in Moscow: Telegram from the Romanian Embassy in Moscow to the Ministry of Foreign Affairs (Bucharest), December 18, 1989, CWIHP.

218 Ceauşescu left for Tehran: Pryce-Jones, p. 342; Siani-Davies, pp. 68–70; Ratesh, p. 31.

219 December 19: Siani-Davies, p. 71.

219 December 20: Rady, p. 96.

219 workers armed with clubs: Siani-Davies, pp. 75–77.

219 Riots began to spread to other towns: Pryce-Jones, p. 343.

219 "many Romanians would later testify": Ratesh, p. 35.

220 East Germany, Poland, and Hungary: Ibid., p. 37.

220 Ceauşescu summoned the Soviet chargé d'affaires: Memorandum of Conversation with the Ambassador of the SRR [Socialist Republic of Romania] in the USSR, I. Bucur, December 21, 1989, CWIHP.

220 In his memoirs, Gorbachev admitted: Gorbachev, *Zhizn i reformy*, 2, p. 402.

220 A Romanian Communist Party dissident, Silviu Brucan: Brucan, pp. 150–52.

220 "On the events in Romania in the last few days": Letter from Shevardnadze to Gorbachev, December 20, 1989, CWIHP.

221 Rally on December 21: Siani-Davies, pp. 83–85; Goldman, p. 277; Pryce-Jones, p. 343.

222 The people began building barricades: Siani-Davies, pp. 85–87.

222 "Water cannons and tear gas": Nicolae Dide quoted in Pryce-Jones, p. 349; Ion Caramitru in Pryce-Jones, p. 346; Siani-Davies, p. 87; *Time*, January 1, 1990.

223 On the morning of December 22: Siani-Davies, p. 88.

223 the army "almost immediately went over": Pryce-Jones, p. 344.

223 Today the majority of historians agree: Rady, p. 103.

223 Some units fraternized: Siani-Davies, p. 93; Octavian Andronic quoted in Pryce-Jones, p. 348.

223   Ceauşescu tried to address them from his balcony: Octavian Andronic quoted in Pryce-Jones, p. 348; Ratesh, p. 43.

223   On the rooftop was a waiting helicopter: Siani-Davies, p. 94; Pryce-Jones, p. 344.

223   Television broadcast them live: Ion Caramitru in Pryce-Jones, pp. 346–48.

223   Ion Iliescu: Pryce-Jones, pp. 337–38.

223   calls Iliescu "self-appointed": Gilberg, p. 292.

224   Iliescu implied that he knew Gorbachev: Rady, p. 124.

224   Now, on air at 2:30, Iliescu informed the audience: Ratesh, pp. 48–49.

224   Exchange in front of the Central Committee building: Ibid., p. 53.

224   Iliescu formed his revolutionary government: Siani-Davies, p. 116; Rady, p. 108.

224   "exchanges of fire were illuminating" the square: Ratesh, p. 57.

224   In Bucharest, 162 people had died: Siani-Davies, pp. 97–99.

225   "most of the time I had to read and write": Brucan, p. 173.

225   Barricades were built randomly: Siani-Davies, pp. 117–25.

225   Called "terrorists" and believed to have full access: Ratesh, p. 67; Siani-Davies, pp. 149–65.

225   The Ceauşescus' flight: Siani-Davies, pp. 94–96; Ratesh, pp. 70–72; Behr, pp. 6–16; Brucan, pp. 3–5.

226   The news from Romania was becoming apocalyptic: Siani-Davies, p. 280.

226   On December 24, the American ambassador: Record of Conversation with US Ambassador to the USSR, J. Matlock, December 24, 1989, CWIHP.

227   "In a quavering voice, Sakharov urged": *Time*, December 25, 1989.

228   The couple remained strong and imperious: Brucan, pp. 5–6; Behr, pp. 16–19.

228   At the wall, they held hands: Brucan, p. 6; Behr, pp. 21–27; Siani-Davies, pp. 136–41.

Epilogue

231   They pulled the old marshal out of the grave: *Krasnaya Zvezda*, April 30, 2003.

233   "The harvest, transportation, debts": Chernyaev, p. 369.

233   "I retained a shred of hope that Gorbachev": Wolf, p. 327.

233   Margaret Thatcher, formerly a fan, now felt indignant: Thatcher, p. 798.

233   The leaders of Poland complained: Ibid., p. 799.

233   "the West German Chancellor agreed to provide": Chernyaev, p. 798.

233   he, his family, and his aides were put under house arrest: Ibid., pp. 372–77.

233   "What do you think about Yazov": Palazchenko, pp. 305–306.

235   Akhromeyev's suicide: Stepankov and Lisov, pp. 236–44; for more documents on the events in Moscow on August 19–21 see *Putsch*.

235   Price of gold in 1991: goldprice.org/30-year-gold-price-history.html.

235   "I felt a deep sense of sadness": Bush in Bush and Scowcroft, p. 537.

235   "Marshal of the Soviet Union": *Time*, September 11, 1991.

236   Gorbachev returned to a different country: Palazchenko, p. 315. For a description of Gorbachev's last 120 days in the Kremlin see Grachev, *Dalshe bez menya.*

238   "It's not a question": Walesa, *A Way of Hope*, p. 144.

238   Riots in Hungary: *The New York Times*, October 24, 2006.

Bibliography

Reference Works

The Anchor Atlas of World History, vols. 1 and 2. New York: Doubleday, 1978.

Baedeker, Karl. *Russia with Teheran, Port Arthur, and Peking: Handbook for Travellers*. Leipzig: Karl Baedeker, 1914.

The Cultural Guide to Jewish Europe. San Francisco: Seuil Chronicle, 2004.

Frank, Leonard Roy. *Freedom: Quotes and Passages from the World's Greatest Freethinkers*. New York: Random House, 2003.

Lawler, Peter Augustine, and Robert Martin Schaefer. *American Political Rhetoric*. New York: Rowman and Littlefield, 2005.

Snyder, Louis L. *Encyclopedia of the Third Reich*. New York: McGraw-Hill, 1976.

Tolz, Vera. *The USSR in 1989: A Record of Events*. Boulder, Colo.: Westview Press, 1990.

Van Doren, Charles, and Robert McHenry. *Webster's Guide to American History*. Springfield, Mass.: G. and C. Merriam, 1971.

Voennyi entsiklopedichesky slovar. Moscow: Bolshaya Rossiiskaya Entsiklopediya, 2002.

Primary Sources

Anguelov, Zlatko. *Communism and the Remorse of an Innocent Victimizer*. College Station: Texas A&M University Press, 2002.

Arbatov, Georgi. *The System: An Insider's Life in Soviet Politics*. New York: Times Books, 1992.

Ash, Timothy Garton. *The Magic Lantern*. New York: Vintage, 1993.

Baker, James A., III. *The Politics of Diplomacy: Revolution, War and Peace, 1989–1992*. New York: G. P. Putnam's Sons, 1995.

Book of Lech Walesa, The. Introduced by Neal Ascherson. New York: Simon and Schuster, 1982.

Boyd, Louise A. *Polish Countrysides*. New York: American Geographic Society, 1937.

Broyard, Anatole. *Kafka Was the Rage*. New York: Vintage, 1997.

Brucan, Silviu. *The Wasted Generation: Memoirs of the Romanian Journey from Capitalism to Socialism and Back*. Boulder, Colo.: Westview Press, 1993.

Burlatsky, Fedor. *Khrushchev and the First Russian Spring*. New York: Scribner, 1988.

Burr, William, ed. *The Kissinger Transcripts: The Top Secret Talks with Beijing and Moscow*. New York: New Press, 1998.

Bush, George. *All the Best: My Life in Letters and Other Writings*. New York: Scribner, 1999.

Bush, George, and Brent Scowcroft. *A World Transformed*. New York: Knopf, 1998.

Carter, Jimmy. *Keeping Faith: Memoirs of a President*. New York: Bantam Books, 1982.

Chazov, Evgeni. *Zdorovye i vlast*. Moscow: Novosti, 1992.

Chernyaev, Anatoly S. *My Six Years with Gorbachev*. University Park: Pennsylvania State University Press, 2000.

Crisp, Quentin. *The Naked Civil Servant*. New York: New American Library, 1977.

De Cuistine, Marquis. *Empire of the Czar: A Journey Through Eternal Russia*. New York: Anchor Books, 1989.

Destroying Ethnic Identity: The Expulsion of the Bulgarian Turks. A Helsinki Watch Report, October 1989. Washington, D.C.: Human Rights Watch, 1989.

Dimitrov, Georgy. *The Diary of Georgy Dimitrov, 1933–1949*, ed. Ivo Banac. New Haven: Yale University Press, 2003.

Dziwisz, Stanislaw. *A Life with Karol: My Forty-Year Friendship with the Man Who Became Pope*. New York: Doubleday, 2008.

Dziwisz, Stanislaw, Czeslaw Drazek, SJ, Renato Buzzonetti, and Angelo Comastri. *Let Me Go to the Father's House: John Paul II's Strength in Weakness*. Boston: Pauline Press, 2006.

Einstein, Albert. *Out of My Later Years*. New York: Citadel Press, 1995.

Fallaci, Oriana. *The Force of Reason*. New York: Rizzoli, 2006.

Furtado, Charles F., Jr., and Andrea Chandler, eds. *Perestroika in the Soviet Republics: Documents on the National Question*. Boulder, Colo.: Westview Press, 1992.

Gorbachev, Mikhail. *Memoirs*. New York: Doubleday, 1995.

———. *Zhizn i reformy*, vols. 1 and 2. Moscow: Novosti, 1995.

Gorbachev, Mikhail, and Zdenek Mlynar. *Conversations with Gorbachev: On Perestroika, the Prague Spring, and the Crossroads of Socialism*. New York: Columbia University Press, 2002.

Grachev, Andrey. *Dalshe bez menya . . . Uhod prezidenta*. Moscow: Progress, 1994.

Greeley, Andrew M. *The Making of the Popes 1978: The Politics of Intrigue in the Vatican*. Kansas City: Andrews and McMeel, 1979.

Havel, Vaclav. *Disturbing the Peace: A Conversation with Karel Hvizdala*. New York: Vintage, 1991.

———. *Open Letters: Selected Writings, 1965–1990*. New York: Knopf, 1991.

———. *The Power of the Powerless: Citizens Against the State in Central-Eastern Europe*. Armonk, N.Y.: M. E. Sharpe, 1985.

John Paul II. *Memory and Identity: Conversation at the Dawn of a Millennium*. New York: Rizzoli, 2005.

Kapuściński, Ryszard. *Travels with Herodotus*. New York: Knopf, 2004.

Komintern i ideya mirovoi revoliutsii. Dokumenty. Moscow: Nauka, 1998.

Khrushchev, Nikita. *Khrushchev Remembers: The Glasnost Tapes*. Boston: Little, Brown and Company, 1990.

———. *Khrushchev Remembers: The Last Testament*. Boston: Little, Brown and Company, 1974.

Kissinger, Henry. *White House Years*. Boston: Little, Brown and Company, 1979.

Korda, Michael. *Journey to a Revolution: A Personal Memoir and History of the Hungarian Revolution of 1956*. New York: HarperCollins, 2006.

Körösi, Zsuzsanna, and Adrienne Molnár. *Carrying a Secret in my Heart . . . Children of the Victims of the Reprisals After the Hungarian Revolution in 1956: An Oral History*. Budapest: Central European University Press, 2003.

Labedz, Leopold, ed. *Poland Under Jaruzelski: A Comprehensive Sourcebook on Poland During and After Martial Law*. New York: Scribner, 1984.

Lane, Arthur Bliss. *I Saw Poland Betrayed: An American Ambassador Reports to the American People*. New York: Bobbs-Merrill, 1948.

Lenin, V. I. *State and Revolution*. New York: International Publishers, 1943.

Ligachev, Yegor. *Inside Gorbachev's Kremlin: The Memoirs of Yegor Ligachev*. New York: Pantheon Books, 1993.

Lopinski, Maciej, Marcin Moskit, and Mariusz Wilk. *Konspira: Solidarity Underground*. Berkeley: University of California Press, 1990.

Markov, Georgi. *The Truth That Killed*. London: Weidenfeld and Nicolson, 1983.

Marx, Karl. *A Reader*. Cambridge: Cambridge University Press, 1986.

Marx, Karl, and Friedrich Engels. *Basic Writings on Politics and Philosophy*. New York: Anchor Books, 1989.

Matlock, Jack F., Jr. *Autopsy of an Empire: The American Ambassador's Account of the Collapse of the Soviet Union*. New York: Random House, 1995.

Michnik, Adam. *The Church and the Left*. Chicago: University of Chicago Press, 1993.

———. *Letters from Freedom: Post-Cold War Realities and Perspectives*. Berkeley: University of California Press, 1998.

———. *Letters from Prison and Other Essays*. Berkeley: University of California Press, 1985.

Nixon, Richard. *The Memoirs of Richard Nixon*. New York: Grosset and Dunlap, 1978.

Ostermann, Christian F., ed. *Uprising in East Germany, 1953: The Cold War, the German Question, and the First Major Upheaval Behind the Iron Curtain*. Budapest: Central European University Press, 2001.

Palazchenko, Pavel. *My Years with Gorbachev and Shevardnadze: The Memoir of a Soviet Interpreter*. University Park: Pennsylvania State University Press, 1997.

Pryce-Jones, David. *The Strange Death of the Soviet Empire*. New York: Henry Holt, 1995.

Putin, Vladimir. *First Person*. New York: Public Affairs, 2000.

Putsch. Khronika trevozhnykh dney. Moscow: Progress, 1991.

Reagan, Ronald. *An American Life*. New York: Simon and Schuster, 1990.

Rokossovsky, Konstantin. *Soldatsky dolg*. Moscow: Olma-Press, 2002.

Sakharov, Andrei. *Moscow and Beyond, 1986 to 1989*. New York: Knopf, 1991.

Shevardnadze, Eduard. *The Future Belongs to Freedom*. New York: Free Press, 1991.

Soames, Mary, ed. *Winston and Clementine: The Personal Letters of the Churchills*. Boston: Houghton Mifflin, 1999.

Spasowski, Romuald. *The Liberation of One*. New York: Harcourt Brace Jovanovich, 1986.

Stern, Fritz. *Five Germanys I Have Known*. New York: Farrar, Straus and Giroux, 2006.

Stepankov, V., and E. Lisov. *Kremlevsky zagovor*. Moscow: Ogonyok, 1992.

Strong, Anna Louise. *I Saw the New Poland*. Boston: Little, Brown and Company, 1946.

Sukhodrev, V. M. *Yazyk moi—drug moi. Ot Khrushcheva do Gorbacheva*. Moscow: AST, 1999.

Thatcher, Margaret. *The Downing Street Years*. New York: HarperCollins, 1993.

Todorov, Tzvetan, and Robert Zaretsky, eds. *Voices from the Gulag: Life and Death in Communist Bulgaria*. University Park: Pennsylvania State University Press, 1999.

Trotsky, Leon. *My Life: An Attempt at an Autobiography*. Atlanta, Ga.: Pathfinder Press, 1970.

———. *The Permanent Revolution* and *Results and Prospects*. New York: Merit Publishers, 1969.

Urban, Jan. "Czechoslovakia: The Power and Politics of Humiliation," in *Spring in Winter: The 1989 Revolutions*, ed. Gwyn Prins. Manchester, U.K.: Manchester University Press, 1990.

Walesa, Lech. *The Struggle and the Triumph: An Autobiography*. New York: Arcade Publishing, 1992.

———. *A Way of Hope*. New York: Henry Holt, 1987.

Wolf, Markus. *Man Without a Face: The Autobiography of Communism's Greatest Spymaster*. New York: Random House, 1997.

Vostochnaya Evropa v dokumentakh rossiiskikh arkhivov, 1944–1953, vols. 1 and 2. Novosibirsk: Sibirsky Khronograf, 1997.

Fiction and Poetry

Akhmatova, Anna. *Selected Poems*. Highgreen, Northumberland, U.K.: Bloodaxe Books, 1989.

Benderson, Bruce. *The Romanian: Story of an Obsession*. New York: Penguin, 2006.

Brodsky, Joseph. *On Grief and Reason*. New York: Farrar, Straus and Giroux, 1995.

Camus, Albert. *The Stranger*. New York: Vintage, 1989.

Havel, Vaclav. *The Garden Party and Other Plays*. New York: Grove Press, 1993.

Kafka, Franz. *The Complete Stories*. New York: Schocken Books, 1971.

——. *The Trial*. New York: Schocken Books, 1998.

Kipling, Rudyard. *Kim*. London: Macmillan, 1908.

——. *Poems*. New York: Knopf, 2007.

——. *War Stories and Poems*. New York: Oxford University Press, 1999.

Nemirovsky, Irene. *Suite Française*. New York: Vintage, 2007.

Stoppard, Tom. *Rock'n'Roll*. New York: Grove Press, 2007.

Tolstoy, Leo. *Great Short Works of Leo Tolstoy*. New York: Perennial, 2004.

Voltaire. *Candide and Other Stories*. New York: Oxford University Press, 1990.

Vysotsky, Vladimir. *Sobranie stikhov i pesen*, 3 vols. ed. Alexander Sumerkin. New York: Russica Publishers, 1988.

Wojtyla, Karol. *The Collected Plays and Writings on Theater*. Berkeley: University of California Press, 1987.

Secondary Sources

Andrew, Christopher, and Vasili Mitrokhin. *The Sword and the Shield: The Mitrokhin Archive and the Secret History of the KGB*. New York: Basic Books, 1999.

Applebaum, Anne. *Gulag: A History*. New York: Doubleday, 2003.

Behr, Edward. *Kiss the Hand You Cannot Bite: The Rise and Fall of the Ceausescus*. New York: Villard Books, 1991.

Beschloss, Michael R., and Strobe Talbott. *At the Highest Levels: The Inside Story of the End of the Cold War*. Boston: Little, Brown and Company, 1993.

Blazynski, George. *Pope John Paul II*. London: Sphere Books, 1979.

Brenan, Gerald. *St. John of the Cross: His Life and Poetry*. Cambridge: Cambridge University Press, 1973.

Burant, Stephen R., ed. *Hungary: A Country Study*. Washington, D.C.: Library of Congress, 1990.

Clarke, Thurston. *Searching for Paradise: A Grand Tour of the World's Unspoiled Islands*. New York: Ballantine, 2002.

Conquest, Robert. *Stalin: Breaker of Nations*. New York: Penguin, 1991.

Crampton, R. J. *A Concise History of Bulgaria*. Cambridge: Cambridge University Press, 2005.

Cruise, Edwina. "A Moscow Journal." *The Christian Science Monitor,* November 22, 1991.

Curtis, Glenn E., ed. *Bulgaria. A Country Study.* Washington, D.C.: Library of Congress, 1993.

Falk, Barbara J. *The Dilemmas of Dissidence in East-Central Europe: Citizen Intellectuals and Philosopher Kings.* Budapest: Central European University Press, 2003.

Federal Institute for Soviet International Studies, ed. *The Soviet Union, 1988-1989: Perestroika in Crisis?* Boulder, Colo.: Westview Press, 1990.

Gaddis, John Lewis. "On Starting All Over Again: A Naïve Approach to the Study of the Cold War," in *Reviewing the Cold War: Approaches, Interpretations, Theory,* ed. Odd Arne Westad. London: Frank Cass, 2000.

———. *We Now Know: Rethinking Cold War History.* Oxford: Clarendon Press, 1997.

Gilberg, Trond. "The Multiple Legacies of History: Romania in the Year 1990," in *The Columbia History of Eastern Europe in the Twentieth Century,* ed. Joseph Held. New York: Columbia University Press, 1992.

Goldman, Minton F. *Revolution and Change in Central and Eastern Europe: Political, Economic, and Social Challenges.* Armonk, N.Y.: M. E. Sharpe, 1997.

Gough, Roger. *A Good Communist: János Kádár, Communism and Hungary.* London: I. B. Tauris, 2006.

Harrison, Hope M. *Driving the Soviets up the Wall: Soviet-East German Relations, 1953–1961.* Princeton, N.J.: Princeton University Press, 2003.

Heil, Alan L., Jr. *Voice of America: A History.* New York: Columbia University Press, 2003.

Henze, Paul B. *The Plot to Kill the Pope.* New York: Scribner, 1983.

Jones, Howard. *Crucible of Power: A History of U.S. Foreign Relations Since 1897.* New York: Rowman and Littlefield, 2001.

Keane, John. *Vaclav Havel: A Political Tragedy in Six Acts.* New York: Basic Books, 2000.

Kriseova, Eda. *Vaclav Havel: The Authorized Biography.* New York: St. Martin's Press, 1993.

Lukowski, Jerzy, and Hubert Zawadzki. *A Concise History of Poland.* Cambridge: Cambridge University Press, 2001.

McDermott, Kevin, and Jeremy Agnew. *The Comintern: A History of International Communism from Lenin to Stalin.* New York: St. Martin's Press, 1997.

Medvedev, Roi. *Neizvestny Andropov. Politicheskaya biografiya Yuriya Andropova.* Moscow: Prava cheloveka, 1999.

Miller, Marshall Lee. *Bulgaria During the Second World War.* Stanford, Calif.: Stanford University Press, 1975.

Moskoff, William. *Hard Times: Impoverishment and Protest in the Perestroika Years. The Soviet Union 1985–1991.* London: M. E. Sharpe, 1993.

Prazmowska, Anita J. *A History of Poland.* London: Palgrave, 2004.

———. *Civil War in Poland, 1942-1948.* New York: Palgrave, 2004.

Puddington, Arch. *Broadcasting Freedom: The Cold War Triumph of Radio Free Europe and Radio Liberty.* Lexington: University Press of Kentucky, 2000.

Pundeff, Marin. "Bulgaria," in *The Columbia History of Eastern Europe in the Twentieth Century,* ed. Joseph Held. New York: Columbia University Press, 1992.

Rady, Martyn. *Romania in Turmoil: A Contemporary History.* London: I. B. Tauris, 1992.

Ratesh, Nestor. *Romania: The Entangled Revolution.* New York: Praeger, 1991.

Rev, Istvan. *Retroactive Justice: Prehistory of Post-Communism.* Stanford, Calif.: Stanford University Press, 2005.

Roberts, Geoffrey. *Stalin's Wars: From World War to Cold War, 1939–1953.* New Haven: Yale University Press, 2006.

Siani-Davies, Peter. *The Romanian Revolution of December 1989.* Ithaca, N.Y.: Cornell University Press, 2005.

Staar, Richard F. *Communist Regimes in Eastern Europe.* Stanford, Calif.: Hoover Institution Press, 1988.

Taubman, William. *Khrushchev: The Man and His Era.* New York: W. W. Norton, 2003.

Taylor, Frederick. *The Berlin Wall: A World Divided, 1961–1989.* New York: HarperCollins, 2006.

United Nations Special Committee on the Balkans, 1947–1952. *International Intervention in the Greek Civil War.* New York: Praeger, 1990.

Volkogonov, Dmitri. *Autopsy for an Empire: The Seven Leaders Who Built the Soviet Regime.* New York: Free Press, 1998.

Weigel, George. *Witness to Hope: The Biography of Pope John Paul II.* New York: Cliff Street Books, 1999.

Wheaton, Bernard, and Zdenek Kavan. *The Velvet Revolution: Czechoslovakia, 1988–1991.* Boulder, Colo.: Westview Press, 1992.

Williams, Kieran. *The Prague Spring and Its Aftermath: Czechoslovak Politics, 1968–1970.* Cambridge: Cambridge University Press, 1997.

Acknowledgments

As this book doesn't pretend to be a comprehensive history of 1989, but rather a more essayistic exercise, in writing it I relied on other authors' research and feel very much indebted to each and every one of them. In quoting from their work, I tried keeping their voices untainted, and if I erred, then I did so inadvertently.

No book dealing with the cold war is possible without the use of the Cold War International History Project archival collection, now graciously posted online.

My agent, Susan Rabiner, as always, sharpened the book proposal's argument and trimmed its narrative, and introduced me to Eric Chinski of Farrar, Straus and Giroux. Eric patiently guided me through three drafts of the manuscript. I cannot imagine a better editor or publisher.

I'd like to thank Eugenie Cha, Susan Goldfarb, and John McGhee for making the final draft readable. Thanks to them, the manuscript is now fit to print.

Writing this book was a roller coaster, and for the toughest years, the past two, my partner, S.S.C., has been my lifeline. Sometimes "Go back to work" sounds better than "I love you, too."

Mama Elza, I know I can always count on you to blame my follies on someone or something else.

Almost inconceivably, my children, Anna and Anton, seem to have retained their childhood awe of the Dad-is-working situation. It meant a lot to me that over the past three summers, they prefaced all their requests with "If you are not too busy."

Professor Edwina Cruise—you *do* have the biggest heart in the world.

Tanya Babyonysheva—we know what the Red Atlantis was about.

Thanks to Joan Cocks, for revolutionary spirit.

To Stephen Jones, for disgusting British humor.

To Don O'Shea, for making exceptions.

To Lyonya Serebriakov, for his friendship.

To Sasha Zotikov, for being my Moscow anchor.

Index